PORN AGAIN

a memoir

JOSH SABARRA

J|B|S

Porn Again: A Memoir

For further information about the author, please visit http://www.joshsabarra.com. Inquiries about this book and author appearances can be addressed to information@breakingnewspr.com. While the author has made every effort to provide accurate contact information at the time of publication, he assumes no responsibility for errors or for changes that occur after publication.

ISBN: 978-0-9907546-1-9 (Trade Paperback)
ISBN: 978-0-9907546-0-2 (eBook)
LCCN: 2014915396

For my parents, Howard and Deborah, and my sister, Nancy.
It feels good to belong.

CONTENTS

PORN AGAIN

a memoir

BROADWAY BOUND

Jacob was an adorable nerd of a fuck buddy who introduced me to extraterrestrial sex.

Apparently, life forms in other galaxies have particularly large appendages as well as orifices that are uniquely accommodating. Before Jacob dragged me to the gay comic book convention, I had no idea about the ins and outs of interplanetary sexual activity. I could, however, sense what a cute backside he had and what a nicely proportioned package he was carrying in his jeans, which made me considerably more tolerant of his Trekkie tendencies.

A blue-eyed blonde with an appealingly athletic physique, Jacob met me for our first date at a small café on Robertson Boulevard in the heart of West Hollywood. Over salads, we covered the requisite details – parents, siblings, dating histories – and I was pleasantly surprised by how easily our conversation flowed. He was a good Christian from the Midwest, which definitely accounted for some cultural differences, but, all in all, our mutual interests called for a second date. This time a late night dinner, Round Two was as pleasant and casual as our initial meeting and confirmed my physical attraction to Jacob's boyish good looks. It also revealed a particularly quirky personality trait: he spoke in cartoon character voices throughout the evening.

"How about another date?" Jacob said, as I got into my Porsche Cayenne to head home.

"Sure," I smiled. "Dinner later in the week?"

"Boing! Yes!"

At that point, the cartoon exclamations were endearing, and I already had a hard-on for Jacob. I wanted to climb into bed with him as soon as possible. He was fairly tightlipped – and not in a provocative way – when the subject of sex came up during our second date, but we were able to determine that we would definitely be compatible when it came to our roles in the bedroom.

"Why don't you come to my house on Thursday night, and we can walk to one of the restaurants in my neighborhood," I suggested, knowing that we would have a bed to fall into after we ate.

"Sounds perfect."

By the time Thursday rolled around, I was definitely hungry for some pasta at Cucina Bene, and my appetite for Jacob hadn't waned either. After a bowl of spaghetti and some chicken parmigiana, it was understood that dessert would be served in my bedroom.

Jacob and I walked the two short blocks to my house,

holding hands and politely discussing what was about to take place.

"Just so you know," Jacob said, in almost a whisper, "I can't really have 'big boy' sex."

I am usually fast on the uptake, but this one eluded me. "'Big boy' sex?"

"You know, intercourse."

"Really?" I questioned, my penis going almost completely soft as the words left my lips. "Why is that?"

"I have some fissures 'back there,' and it makes sex too uncomfortable. I always liked being the bottom, so it has been a problem."

My father is a urologist – who, at 70, still has a thriving medical practice – so I am very familiar with the mechanics of coitus and the body parts necessary for a satisfying roll in the sheets. Conversations about fissures, erections and ejaculation were just as likely to take place at my family dinner table as they were at my dad's office.

"I can see where anal tears might be a problem if you're a bottom," I sympathized, half ready to call it a night and fall into bed with *People* magazine instead of a rectally challenged farm boy.

"I make do with a pair of hands," Jacob said, like he was resigned to a limited sexual repertoire for the rest of his days. "They do the trick. Plus, I don't have such a high sex drive anyway. Ruh-roh, right?"

I could have snuggled up in the disappointment and fallen asleep on the spot, but I had been anticipating sex with Jacob so much that I decided to take what I could get for the evening – even if it was a simple hand job exchange. Never mind that he was talking like Scooby-Doo.

I pulled a large, four-foot long container from under my bed, giving Jacob his pick of the various sex toys, chains and cuffs that I had collected over the years. Everything was neatly organized and labeled in individual compartments; he had his choice of stainless steel, glass, rubber or latex.

"Wowzers! You have everything. I think the glass toy and some rope might work – that dildo looks smooth and probably wouldn't hurt 'back there' too much."

Jacob crawled onto the bed, lying on his back with his eyes closed. He looked like a five year-old, bracing to get a shot at the doctor's office, as I tied his wrists together. It was clear that I was going to have to direct the action.

I straddled Jacob's midsection, and, as I leaned in to kiss him, he winced.

"Are you uncomfortable?" I asked. "I feel like you might not be into this."

"I am totally into it," Jacob replied, "It's just that it has been a little while since I was in bed with someone."

We kissed gently for a few minutes before I removed his short-sleeved Polo shirt. I licked his chest, working my mouth down to the band of his artfully distressed jeans. I noticed that the front section of his pants was stretched to the seams, indicating a level of enjoyment that seemed absent only moments prior.

As I unbuckled his leather belt and unfastened his five-button fly, I saw that Jacob was wearing a sexy, red jock strap. Clearly, he had made a deliberate choice of under-pants – and, oddly, one that provided easy access to the area of his body that he was most tentative about inviting to the party.

We used our mouths, our hands and the glass toy over the

course of the next hour, all of which culminated in creamy, white success. To my surprise, the proceedings turned out to be much more satisfying than I expected, and Jacob seemed to have had the time of his life.

"Leapin' lizards!" he said. "That was crazy good."

Somehow, he had morphed from Scooby-Doo into Little Orphan Annie, but I was too spent to make anything of it. We both fell asleep, lying with our arms around each other until we woke for breakfast the following morning.

"Next weekend," Jacob began, over a plate of scrambled eggs and pancakes at Jerry's Deli, "there's a gay-themed comic book convention in Downtown LA. There are going to be some interesting people and books there. Wanna go?"

I have always been way too grounded to be taken with objects that are of the unidentified flying variety, but I wasn't going to pass up the opportunity to observe and comment on some science fiction fanatics.

"Sure," I said. "Count me in."

"Great! Plan to come for dinner the night before, and you can stay over at my loft. Coolzoids!"

Considering Jacob's interests, I couldn't wait to see his apartment and the décor. I pictured his shelves to be filled with horror and fantasy chazerai – comic books still in plastic preservation wrap and enough space paraphernalia to make William Shatner crap his pants. As it turns out, Jacob's three-story rental apartment was a really interesting living space (despite being on Skid Row), but it did, indeed, display signs of overzealous sci-fi fandom.

"I am so excited about the convention tomorrow," Jacob told me over dinner the night before. "I am hoping I will be able to find some of the figurines that are missing from my collection. And there will probably be some sexy stuff there, since it's all about gay artists."

"Have you always been into this type of thing?" I asked, trying to gauge just how long he had been collecting.

"Basically, since I was little. My mom has a huge doll collection – she responds to all of those offers in magazines like *The National Enquirer* and *Parade*. Then she puts the dolls in plastic display boxes. There's a room in her house dedicated to them."

The divide between us had just gotten wider. You will never meet someone who dislikes cutesy collectibles more than I do. In fact, I have always imagined a fantasy scenario in which I enter a Hallmark store – Ellen's, Theresa's, Lynn's, whosever franchise – with a baseball bat to single handedly destroy every Precious Moment and Snow Baby in sight.

Unfortunately, there was more to Jacob's doll story.

"Every season," he continued, "my mom changes the outfit of each doll. This way, she's dressed for whatever holiday falls during those months. It's really cool. I'll get my mom to text a picture." (She did ultimately send a photo, a creepy snapshot that would have scared Madame Alexander.)

Jacob clearly stood for everything I was against: science fiction, cute collectibles, what had now become annoying character voices and sexual hang-ups. I felt obligated, though, to stay the night and follow through with our plans.

As he undressed to get into bed, Jacob showed off a pair of very sexy purple briefs. They were definitely the kind that were made to be ripped off with my teeth, which made it all the more surprising when he got comfortable under the covers and turned out the lights.

"Goodnight?" I said, in the form of a question.

"Goodnight! I am so full from dinner, plus I am excited for tomorrow. Need to get some rest."

I don't think my groan stayed in my head – in fact, I am fairly certain it escaped my lips.

"Did you want to have sex?" he asked.

"Kinda, yeah. It has been a week, and, well, we're two young guys who are attracted to each other, right? Aren't we supposed to have our hands all over the place?"

"Let's fool around in the morning. Cool?"

Not really "cool," no, I thought, and I went to bed annoyed and frustrated. I slept on my back the whole night, a shift from my traditional stomach-sleep positioning, and I stayed on my side of the mattress. I was hoping that Jacob would feel the cold air from the right.

As I woke the following morning, Jacob was lying on his side, looking at me from his area of the bed. The minute I opened my eyes, his hands traveled to the front of my black Calvins. I was aroused in no time, considering I had been ready for action since 9:00PM the night before. Jacob's lukewarm sex drive never allowed for any bedroom acrobatics, but who would say no to a satisfying hand job to start the day? He had the art of the tug down to a science – and a really soft, pleasantly fragrant hand lotion. Plus, if I was going to spend the entire afternoon walking around a convention floor next to people dressed as storm troopers, I was going to need to be as relaxed as possible.

It took poor Jacob quite a long time to ejaculate, and, as much as I was willing to give back, my hand doesn't run on batteries. Following a particularly long "massage," Jacob told me to give my wrist a break; he sensed that my movements became robotic. He grabbed his stereo remote control and flipped through his stored music. He bypassed the rock, pop, country and jazz selections, landing on the show tunes library. There was a relatively extensive list of choices, and he toggled back and forth between songs from various Broadway musicals – with one finger, mind you. The others never left his penis.

As "Popular," the hit song from *Wicked*, began to play through his speaker system, he took matters into his own hands. I could see his strokes hasten, and he began to sing along. At first, his voice was soft and unsure, but as his heart rate increased, so did his volume and pitch. He had every nuance and inflection of the recording down; this clearly wasn't his debut performance.

No more than eight bars into the jingle, Jacob shot across his stomach like a 17 year-old on prom night, singing into the morning sunlight like he was on stage with Idina Menzel. The puddle probably would have drowned little Kristin Chenoweth, and I had never seen anything quite like it. The only thing gayer than cumming while singing out loud to a Broadway musical soundtrack would be marrying Liza Minnelli herself.

HARD TO BE GOOD

No one seemed to have a last name before I turned five. Miss Liz. Miss Judy. Miss Irene. The cold truth of their identities – the Johnsons, Smiths and Goldbergs that made them real people – was tenderly hidden in the soft, cotton-like security of the pre-school walls at the Jewish Community Center. Greta Nicholson, an icy, German Amazon, eschewed the traditional warmth for the hard sounding "Miss Nicholson," creating a rock-like divide between my sensitivity and her gray-brick stoicism. Looking back, her extreme reaction to catching me with another little boy in the bathroom makes perfect sense.

The heat was stifling on the afternoon of my first sexual encounter. Palm Beach County's signature humidity weighed on my 55-pound body like a wooden bucket of water floating through the atmosphere, and I wanted nothing less than to be climbing the metal play structures on the sparse asphalt court behind the pre-school classrooms. The temperature rose from the ground in a visible shield, a refraction phenomenon that bent the light waves in an effort to remind all of the senses that the outdoor air was, indeed, unbearable.

Recess period was my least favorite. I found shaded sections of the playground and sheltered myself in clouded corners of an otherwise burning blacktop. Too hot for my small palms, the metal monkey bars held no appeal, and the curvy slides would undoubtedly scorch my tiny legs. The other kids – a dozen boys and girls whose parents were all linked socially – busied themselves with no attention to the elements. They scurried from one ladder to the other, lording over their make-believe castles and guarding pretend pirate treasure that they had hidden in plastic chests. I tended to be grounded in reality, leaving fantastical imagination games to everyone else. Little Teddy Smith was similarly inclined.

Teddy and I sat together, "Indian-style," on a small, cool strip of tarmac, staring at our classmates who would inevitably suffer as adults because of their exposure to the sun. I had subconsciously begun a facial care regimen that would keep my smooth skin looking flawless through the years. Under the protection of the small shadows cast by the surrounding buildings, Teddy and I didn't have much to say to each other. Lady Elaine from *Mister Rogers' Neighborhood* and Mr. Green Jeans from *Captain Kangaroo* could account for only so much conversation, and, at five, the decline of Western Civilization wasn't necessarily on the menu of topics. The dearth of talking points – coupled with his interest in superhero action figures – channeled my attention to Teddy's "golden boy" looks. While we didn't connect on any interpersonal level, there was something about him that had me transfixed; I wanted to be around him.

The five year-old equivalent of an Abercrombie & Fitch model, Teddy's silky blond hair and deep sea-green eyes pulled all of my attention. I had no understanding of my attraction to his perfectly high cheekbones and square jaw; I just wished that I looked like he did. My mousy brown bowl cut and round face – even at my young age – seemed so much less attractive.

"I don't like sitting outside," Teddy announced. "It's really hot."

"That's why I stay in the shade," I agreed.

"Maybe we can go inside and play," he said.

I would have followed Teddy anywhere, and while I knew we were supposed to stay in eye sight of the teachers, I was excited about breaking the rules with this pre-school rebel.

"You mean, just walk inside, without anyone knowing?"

"Why not?" he said. "We're just gonna play until everyone comes back from the playground."

We sneaked around the corner from our shaded patch and walked through a side door. The hallway leading to our classroom was paneled with cheap, dark wood on which were bulletin boards lined with colorful letters and crepe paper. Between the displays marking Miss Liz's "Little Sprouts," Miss Irene's "Rainbow Room" and a seasonal presentation announcing the beginning of summer – all hand cut out of construction paper and stapled to the cork bases – was a communal, unisex bathroom with multiple stalls.

Teddy grabbed my hand, which sent an unfamiliar electricity through my chest.

"Come on," he said, "let's find the Superman toys."

My interest in Superman was virtually nonexistent, but I wanted to experience more of Teddy's touch.

"Let's go in the bathroom," I said, not really knowing what I expected to do there.

"Do you have to make?" Teddy asked.

"Yeah. And wouldn't it be funny to stand and pee in the same toilet?" I realized, at that point, that I wanted to see underneath Teddy's clothes.

"That would be pretty silly," he said. He giggled and gave me a naughty grin. Teddy seemed game for anything that was against authority, another part of his appeal. "Let's try it."

We hurried into the first bathroom stall and unbuttoned our shorts. He laughed as he pulled his tiny briefs to his hips, taking his small penis into his right hand. As though he was holding a high-pressure hose, he began to urinate erratically, splashing all over the commode with wild disregard for any sort of aim. My heart was racing as I watched his penis flop around, to the point that I was able to stand with my pants around my knees but couldn't actually make myself go to the bathroom. There was an overwhelming excitement in the pit of my stomach. I had never felt anything like it before; it was a rattling sensation, and I wanted to keep it going.

"You're peeing all over the place," I said.

"I know," Teddy replied, laughing hysterically as he continued to dribble everywhere.

Without any further thought, I reached across the toilet and took the shaft of his penis between my fingers. His stream steadied, but his giddy recklessness disappeared.

"What are you doing?" he asked.

"Trying not to make a mess," I said, still holding his now firm penis.

"It doesn't matter," he said, "they won't know we were in here anyway."

Just as I reluctantly lightened my grip on Teddy's dingle, I felt Fraulein Nicholson's oversized man-hands grab my fragile wrist. My right hand released its grip as Teddy yanked his underwear and Dockers back up to his waist.

"What are you doing?" she screamed in her harsh, German accent. It sounded like she was coughing up a fur ball.

"We just had to go to the bathroom," I stammered, using my one free hand to fasten the zipper and button on my shorts as she dragged me from the bathroom down the industrially carpeted hallway.

"You have to ask a teacher if you want to use the bathroom," she scolded. "And it's one person at time. Why were you touching Teddy?"

I stood in the hallway, silently.

"Why were you touching Teddy?" she said again, hitting a screechingly high octave that I don't think is even possible for a Kraut.

"He was making a mess." He had to have gotten a severe case of road burn from being thrown under that bus.

"I don't care," she continued, holding both of my shoulders and shaking me so strenuously that she'd be drawn and quartered by a child watchdog group had she tried it today. "You don't ever, ever touch someone in their private areas." I think she meant "*his* private areas," but I didn't know enough about the language yet to correct her grammar.

I looked down at my feet, avoiding the stares of the other kids who were returning to the classroom following recess. All of them heard Miss Nicholson's diatribe, and she was hell-bent on making an example out of me. The shame and embarrassment of being verbally flogged in a public square was almost unbearable; it was crushing to feel humiliated about something that seemed so natural. And, it wasn't as though Teddy was entirely innocent; he avoided reprimand only because Miss Nicholson perceived me to be the aggressor. After all, *his* penis was in *my* hand. I may have, in fact, been the more active participant, but he was more than willing to play along. Maybe that explains why, to this day, I am so easily able to convince my partners to be more active, giving me blowjobs rather than the other way around. At least Miss Nicholson scores points for that.

I said nothing about the bathroom brouhaha to my mother when she picked me up in our oversized, beige station wagon, but Miss Nicholson must have called our house that evening; I overheard my parents talking in the kitchen.

"She said that Josh lured Teddy Smith into the bathroom and was fondling him." My mom's voice seemed calm, but my heart started to race. What if my parents reacted the same way Miss Nicholson did that afternoon?

"How did she handle it?" my father asked.

"She told me that she separated them but tried not to turn it into an incident," my mom replied, as she walked out of the kitchen and into my bedroom.

"Josh, did something happen today with Teddy Smith?"

"Nothing really," I said, nervous that I would push my mother to shake or scream at me. She had never given me a reason to think she would behave that way, but neither had Miss Nicholson before that day. "We went to the bathroom at the same time, and Miss Nicholson got angry."

"OK, honey. But Miss Nicholson said that you took

Teddy into the bathroom with you so you could touch him. We don't touch other kids, OK?"

I nodded with understanding.

"You know, next year you will start kindergarten, and it's very important that you follow the rules. You're going to be in a school for big kids," my mother said. It made me nervous to think about the big, bad public school that my older sister was already attending.

The principal at Highland Elementary was named Elizabeth Taylor. There were no White Diamonds or lavender eyes, but the name alone laid a foundation of glamour under my size 5 Stride Rite sneakers. The only thing better would have been a guidance counselor named Cher or a lunch lady from Nutbush, Tennessee, who had changed her name from Anna Mae to Tina. Sadly, Karen Hill, a young kindergarten teacher with a bad pixie cut and a chip on her shoulder, was as pedestrian as her name would imply. She was less than interested in my brand.

My January birthday always fell just after the winter holiday breaks, and, at age six, I couldn't wait to take my favorite gift – a ventriloquist dummy modeled after classic comedian W.C. Fields – to show-and-tell. I loved that doll and wanted to share it with my classmates. While I had a passion for my puppet, I wasn't really interested in Barbie dolls or toys marketed to my sister. In fact, I used to take pleasure in giving her Glamour Gals buzz cuts. She would go to bed, resting easily that she had perfectly styled all of her dolls' tresses. When she'd wake up the following morning, at least one would look like Susan Powter. Stop the insanity, indeed.

Karen, may she rest in peace (OK, she may not have died;

just wishful thinking), told me that I couldn't bring the toy onto the playground because there would be no one to supervise. I approached one of her teacher's aides and asked if she would keep an eye on me. With her blessing, I trotted into the yard with the jewel of my birthday bounty. Karen was none too happy.

"You went behind my back, Josh," she yelled in a voice that far from matched her Susie Homemaker looks. She sounded like a 45-speed record slowed down to a 33 rotation.

"But you told me I needed supervision," I said, on the brink of tears.

"I should have just told you no, without an explanation. My mistake." Bitch.

She presented a reason for which I could not do what I wanted, and I eliminated the brick wall. It had to be evident that I was an executive in the making because that was the first of hundreds of walls that I would bust through during my life. Small-minded Karen would never find her way out of construction paper, Crayola crayons and Elmer's paste, and eventually I would be hobnobbing with the rich and famous. Winning battles doesn't mean winning wars, and I am fairly sure that Karen doesn't have any medals or monuments around her house.

The same could not be said for Karen's "teacher's aides," both of whom couldn't get enough of me. In fact, when I emerged from the dress-up room in heels and a cap pretending to be a flight attendant, they were glued to my every word and motion.

"Thank you for flying Eastern Airlines," I would start. "Please follow along on the safety card in the back of your seat pocket." I was, at even such a young age, stereotypically attracted to the work of stewardesses, and I had memorized every line of the safety demonstrations during family trips to and from New York.

"A portion of our flight takes us over water. Your life jacket is located in a small bag beneath your seat, and please note that your cushion can be used as a floatation device, as well." I am fairly certain that the silver pumps would have been against airline regulations, but they represented the kind of edgy and exciting crew member I wanted to be.

"What about oxygen?" one of the aides would ask, encouraging me to continue my presentation.

"Should there be a change in cabin pressure," I answered, "your oxygen mask will distend from the ceiling. Place the yellow cup over your nose and mouth, and breathe normally. The bag won't inflate, but oxygen will be flowing freely."

The two aides would laugh riotously, impressed, I assumed, by the details of air travel that I had memorized and delivered in such a professional manner. While their delight more likely came from the sight of a six year-old boy in shorts, a military hat and glowing high heels spouting pre-flight rhetoric, I was uninhibited and not yet aware of how gender roles applied to the way I moved through the world.

I was raised on *Free to Be... You and Me*, a book and music collection that charmed a generation of families through the early 1970s and 1980s. The poems, stories and songs were all about being oneself unapologetically. It attempted to shatter gender stereotypes: boys could play with dolls, and girls could be taxi drivers. As early as I heard the album for the first time, I bought into the concept. Unfortunately, "Marlo Thomas and Friends" didn't come with the record as playground back-up support. It was one thing to encourage youngsters to be who they were born to be but facing less enlightened kids, teachers and camp counselors was another hurdle altogether. Marlo – yes, "that girl" with the ahead-of-its-time nose job – stirred the pot but high-tailed it out of sight before the meal was served in the form of teasing, taunts and slurs.

"Do it again," the aides would say, prompting me to ad-lib lines that would have them rolling on the floor. Until, of course, Karen spotted the corner of the room in which I was delivering my award-winning performance.

"Josh, you need to be outside playing with the other kids," she would scold. "Put on the shoes that you *should* be wearing, and get to the sandbox."

With the cross words, our threesome disbanded until sometime over the next day or two when Karen's attention was divided and my airline career could continue. Eventually, my tenure at Eastern came to an abrupt end when Karen called my parents to school for a conference.

"Josh has a complete lack of self-control," she said. "He spends all of his time talking to adults and not interacting with the other children."

"He has always been a little more mature than kids his own age," my mother replied. Having been a teacher herself – not to mention Highland's PTA president – she had some credibility and a whole lot of leverage. "I don't really see it as a lack of self-control. He simply has specific needs; is it possible that your style isn't capable of meeting them?"

"I have to disagree," Karen said. "He can't control himself, and I am going to have to make that clear on his progress report."

"He's in kindergarten," my father jumped in. "I hardly think your assessment will follow him far."

With a grimace, Karen ended the meeting, realizing that she was getting nowhere with Dr. and Mrs. Sabarra. It was bold for a young teacher to be so contentious with two adults who were particularly active in the school's administration and even bolder to be so openly disdainful of me throughout the remainder of the school year. Fortunately for Karen, I never let on to my parents that she was such a terror. I didn't tell them that she would glare at me non-stop, offering silent disapproval of my every move. I knew I was different – that my interests and activity choices were not those shared by other boys my age – and Karen made clear that there was something wrong with that.

Imagine the *Silkwood* meltdown she would have had if she knew what was going on while she wasn't watching. During the 30-minute teacher break each day, the aides would allow two children at a time to go into the "reading fort," an enclosed cardboard structure filled with stacks of books. Completely out of view of every adult, it was five minutes of unsupervised time to look at each other's "privates." Almost all of the kindergarteners engaged in this exploration, and I was always thrilled to have a peek at the forbidden. Plus, I hadn't seen a naked penis since the incident with Teddy Smith. There was no rhyme or reason to how the students were paired, so, when I was sent into the fort with a little boy, I couldn't wait until he pulled his underwear down. When I was partnered with a girl, needless to say, I actually got some reading done.

"Do you wanna see my pee-pee," I remember one female classmate saying, as I sat in the fort with a dog-eared copy of

Caps for Sale in my lap. I didn't, but I knew even then to be polite.

"Yes," I said, as she pulled her Wonder Woman Underoos down from her waist.

"Do you want to touch it?" she asked.

"They might catch us," I whispered, knowing full well that none of the aides ever looked in. "We could get in trouble."

By the time the full conversation ended, our five minutes were up, and it was time to let the next pair of students into the fort.

On the days that I was sent inside to read with a boy, the proceedings were altogether different; I became the initiator. Especially when it was Max, a blue-eyed all-American who had captured my attention.

"What kind of underwear do you have on," I asked Max, not terribly dissimilar to the types of sexting conversations I would have 30 years later.

"I think they're just white," he said, pulling his pants to his knees to show me his briefs.

"Those are nice; can I see inside them?" Without a word, he yanked them down. His circumcised penis was sticking straight forward, which I didn't understand at the time.

"Mine does that sometimes, too," I said. "Like right now."

"Can I see?" Max asked.

As I unhooked my belt – it was fastened with a magnet – I felt my heart rate increase as a sense of excitement fell over me. I removed my underpants at the same time Max reached over to touch the tip of my penis. The sensation was overwhelming. Without asking, I reached out and lightly stroked his small erection.

"It feels tingly," he said.

"Mine does, too." I didn't know what any of it meant. But I liked it.

With only one minute left on the reading fort time clock, Max and I pulled our underwear and pants up, tucking in our shirts and buckling or tying anything that could indicate an activity other than reading. Thank goodness it was even harder for cardboard to talk than drywall.

My trysts with Max and some of the other kids in that 5'x5' corrugated construction were the extent of my interaction with peers. I just wasn't as interested in them when their clothes were on. I wanted to talk about movies and music that appealed to me, like *Fame* and *Coal Miner's Daughter*, and I needed adults for those conversations. Unlike the other boys, I couldn't care less about Hot Wheels or G.I. Joe, but Irene Cara's latest single – which my parents would play on a cassette tape at home – was a hot topic.

I was particularly careful to avoid being caught "playing doctor" by teachers after the pre-school debacle, and, likewise, often took my curiosity out of the classroom. Whenever possible, I would examine my handful of friends after school hours. Jordan Wenner was one of my best customers.

Jordan's parents were divorced, and his mother – an obese, bipolar marshmallow – had a bulldog mug with a personality to match. My mother used to describe her as having a "sweet face," which, to this day, she still says about all fat people. There was nothing sweet about Jordan's mother's face – other than the Hostess Cupcakes she stuffed into it. Because of her imbalanced mental state, she would frequently leave Jordan at our house for long stretches of time. My mother cooked dinner while we hung out in the playroom and backyard.

"Do you want to play doctor?" I asked Jordan while arranging Smurf figurines on the cold, tiled floor of the play area.

"That would be fun," he said, walking right into the en suite bathroom without having to be directed. He had obviously been examined before. His pants were around his ankles before I could even unzip mine. I immediately reached towards his already hard penis.

"So, do you know how people have sex?" he asked.

I didn't. I had heard the word, but applied to gender and not human behavior. I shook my head no.

"A man puts his penis in a woman's vagina and moves it around." He took a step closer to me so that the tips of our penises were touching. He laughed at the sensation and then turned around quickly so that the head of my penis was touching one cheek of his backside. He turned his head, and looked at me behind him.

"This is not having sex because I don't have a vagina," he continued. "This is just looking at each other."

It was clear that, according to Jordan, sex couldn't happen between two boys, but we "looked at each other" every time we were together for the next year or so. One evening, after Jordan's mom had picked him up, I announced to my mother that I knew all about sex.

"You do?" she asked. "What do you know?"

"I know that a man puts his penis in a woman's vagina and moves it around. So I guess two men can't have sex, because there's no vagina. Right? Two men can't have sex?"

"It wouldn't be natural," my mother answered.

Natural. Natural was how my attraction to boys felt. Obviously, there was something extremely nontraditional about it. I had to know more without anyone catching on, and, thankfully, one of our neighbors had a son who was excited to learn the ropes, too.

Michael Goldstein and his sister Julie lived around the block in a modest, one-level home that was never landscaped as nicely as the surrounding properties. Their single mother was newly divorced from her philandering husband, and they came and went on their own with little at-home structure. We all attended the same public school and would often play at their house after being dropped off by the bright yellow school bus at the end of each day.

It was Julie who first suggested that we play doctor, and I obliged, somewhat titillated by the off-limits nature of the activity. She pretended to visit my office (her bedroom) after a lunch appointment at a local restaurant (her kitchen). The nurse (her brother) would show her to the examining table and leave the room after checking her vitals. When she removed her clothes and her underwear, I touched her stomach, looked at her vagina and sent her on her way with a clean bill of health. Her appointments were relatively short, as I never cared for her southern parts. The nurse, however, was another story.

Michael was small-framed with a mop of thick, black hair that made him look like a miniature T-Bird from *Grease*. He was solid and compact, accounted for by the fact that he was three years older than Julie and I. Because he was a number of grade levels beyond us, he never spent time playing in Julie's bedroom and was typically holed up in his own cave down the hall. Painted with dark colors and lined with dioramas of the solar system, his room was claustrophobic and uninviting.

One particularly rainy day in the spring of 1982, Julie

was preoccupied with an afterschool television special. Bored, I left the couch and meandered to Michael's bedroom.

"Do you wanna build a robot?" he asked, putting down his school textbook and pencil.

"Sure," I said, thrilled to escape Nancy McKeon's star turn alongside Patty Duke in *Please Don't Hit Me, Mom.*

Michael opened a box of plastic pieces that, when assembled, became a three-dimensional robot with fully articulated joints. For twenty minutes, we worked side by side to put the toy together, eventually tiring of the do-it-yourself nature of the project.

"What should we do now?" Michael was ready to move on.

"We could always play doctor," I said, hoping he'd be as willing a patient as his sister.

"OK, I haven't had a check-up in a long time." He took off his shirt and lay on the shag carpet that covered the floor of his room. I listened to his heart with my ear, its accelerated beat unmistakable.

"Should I take my pants off?" he asked.

This was easier than I thought.

"Yes," I said. "But leave your underwear on." Even at seven, I had a thing for undies.

I touched his stomach, his knees and his feet, instinctively saving the most exciting part for the finale. I could see the growing bulge in Michael's Fruit of the Looms, and I eventually slid my hand into his underpants to get my first feel of his substantial penis. He still had no pubic hair but was discernibly aroused by the situation.

"Does everything look OK, Doctor?" he asked, half smiling.

"I don't know. I may have to remove your underwear to double check."

"OK, Doctor," he replied.

With Michael's permission, I removed his last remaining article of clothing. His thick, rock-hard penis nearly made my heart stop. In hindsight, it was impressive comparative to many adult dicks I have seen. Or held. Or sucked. But, for a 10 year-old? It was in *Ripley's Believe It or Not* territory.

Being in his room, touching Michael's penis, felt so right to me. I stroked him as though I was a pro, making spiral hand motions up and down his shaft as naturally as a puppy paddles when placed into a pool of water for the first time.

"You may need some medicine to make this go down," I said, having no understanding of the irony in that statement, especially considering what was about to, well, *go down*.

"Maybe it needs some ointment," Michael suggested. "A cream of some kind."

Without missing a beat, I leaned over and put the head of his penis into my mouth.

"How does that feel?" I asked.

"Much better," Michael responded. "I need a little more."

I continued to bob my head up and down, stopping only when I heard Julie walking down the hallway towards her brother's room.

"We better quit," Michael said, throwing his clothes back on in record time. "And don't tell anyone about this, OK?"

"OK," I said, wiping saliva from the corners of my mouth. "But Julie can know, right? We play doctor all the time."

"No," Michael said. "This is different."

As Julie yelled down the hall, looking for me to play in her room, Michael went back to his schoolwork. I, unfortunately, had to give Julie an internal exam before heading home for supper – without letting on that I was already tired from servicing the nurse.

Unbeknownst to me, that was the first and only blowjob I would give for another 24 years. I didn't even know that something sexual had actually occurred. What I did know, however, was that I could never tell anyone about my feelings and physical instincts. Miss Nicholson said so. Karen Hill said so. Michael Goldstein said so.

After that torrentially wet Thursday in April, I didn't touch another penis until I officially lost my virginity at 31. Enough people around me indicated that my hyper-sexual tendencies were not acceptable – who I felt I was inside was not acceptable.

TAKE IT LIKE A MAN

Camp Shalom was a ramshackle excuse for a day camp, a Hebrew hacienda nestled in a grassy patch near West Palm Beach's outer city limits. Run by the county's Jewish Community Center – which is where my parents sent me to preschool – the camp represented everything that was against the nature of a gay, 7 year-old boy. It was dirty, it was overly structured, and it was staffed by some of the most unattractive people in town. Where was the one hunk whom everyone drooled over, glistening with beads of pool water in a pair of tight Speedos? He must have been at a sleepaway camp up north, where they filmed genre comedies like *Meatballs*. Even *Friday the 13th's* Camp Crystal Lake recognized the value of bulging eye candy, regardless of the fact that he would be dismembered by Act 2.

My mother wanted my sister, Nancy, and me to keep

busy over the summers between our elementary school terms, and our neighbor's daughter was a senior counselor at Camp Shalom. Reassured by the Jewish Community Center's brand and its cultural influence – along with the watchful eyes of our neighbor – Mom enrolled us in double sessions.

"You can't just sit home," my mother would say when I'd complain about being shipped off for the day.

"Why not?" I thought. It wasn't exactly as though she was distracted by a job that would preclude her from looking after me. She was a stay-at-home mom, having given up her teaching career once my sister and I were born. The house-keeping was handled by our maid, so there wasn't a pile of laundry or toilets to be cleaned – nothing to divide her attention.

"You should be outside, around other kids," she reasoned. Mom just wanted some down time.

I was uneasy about being around other children because I didn't feel like I fit in. It wasn't about my appearance or a lack of confidence in my ability to communicate with them. And, it wasn't as though I knew yet that my precocious interest in the arts set me apart. At that age, it was simply a fiber of awareness that ran through my body. My skin was a costume that I was wearing to a party that didn't call for dress-up. My exterior told the story of a typical little boy who was cute, clean cut and running toward tomorrow; my insides knew better.

I didn't know how to tell my mother about the unsettled nature of my feelings, nor was I able to understand the anxiety that was attached to them. At times, I felt like I was in a dream, trying to scream out but unable to make a sound. My 7 year-old mind couldn't come up with a way to put words to my feelings, so suggesting an alternative to camp – other than staying home, which was my safety zone – seemed the best way to move forward.

"I want to take tap dancing classes. Can't I learn how to dance instead of going to camp?" I begged my mom for the music and the mirror.

"I don't think that's a great idea," she said. "Other boys wouldn't understand."

What was there to understand about tap dancing? It seemed as simple as "toe-heel-touch" to me. Plus, as part of the *Free to Be…You and Me* generation, the book and song collection crushed all of the gender stereotypes that had briséd through my head. I am sure Marlo Thomas would have frowned on the fact that my mother identified dance as a "girl" activity, but Mom didn't want me to be teased by peers because of my more, well, "artistic" sensibility. She had no problem throwing me in the back of our car to schlep my sister to and from various dance classes – as long as I didn't throw on a pair of tights myself. A recital wasn't in the cards for me; I would just have to survive camp.

For two months, my sister and I would take a yellow school bus from our neighborhood enclave to the rugged terrain of Palm Beach – yes, camp in Palm Beach, FL, as ridiculous as it sounds – for recreational activities that included the typical kiddie fare: drama, arts and crafts, swimming and sports. I used to dread the first day of camp, and I would pray for the last. It was a hell on earth for me.

I was never Mother Nature's biggest fan, particularly when it came to the outdoor elements and any creature that wasn't furry and domesticated. The South Florida heat, the oppressively heavy humidity and the endless parade of insect pests seemed like jungle atmosphere to a pale, Jewish kid who was most comfortable sitting next to a record player in his air-conditioned bedroom. Couple that with my aversion to peer bonding, and you had the Devil's fiery pit burning bright in the wilds of Palm Beach County. Each night, I would have trouble falling asleep, tossing and turning until dawn or running to the security of my parents' bedroom mid-way through the night. I would check the neon clock next to the bed almost hourly, bracing myself for the dreaded display of 7:30AM.

My mom would help dress me in a pair of khaki shorts, a braided belt and, ironically, a "Camp Shalom: Home Away From Home" t-shirt. As we walked to the bus stop, two blocks away, I was sprayed down with a can of Off! bug repellent. It left a greasy film on my face, arms and legs and drowned me in the pungent smell that represented my entire camp experience. On top of that, my fair complexion called for a healthy dollop of Coppertone, piled over the insect spray, to create an armor of chemicals impenetrable to almost everything.

My stomach felt hollow as I climbed up the steep steps of the bus, settling myself next to a window. I counted on the fresh air and the daydreams that lived beyond the rectangular piece of glass at the side of my head. It was easy to imagine where all of the cars that whizzed by the Camp Shalom Express were headed – day jobs, summer vacations, movies and shopping malls. For the 45-minute ride, I pretended to be a passenger in those Hondas and Toyotas that were on their way to everywhere but camp.

I tried as best I could to communicate all of the anxiety that had taken up residency in my midsection. Unfortunately, it didn't seem to get through to my parents until four years later, when my tour of duty would end with the start of my fourth grade year of school. There were miles to travel before then.

My folks couldn't identify with the horror that was, for example, "Crazy Hat Day," a once-per-summer event that required each camper to design and showcase some wild headgear. My father has always been creative with paint and design and didn't hold back when it came to the summer's crowning pageant. In fact, he helped construct a wearable piece of art that won the ribbon for "Most Delicious."

In a tin foil pie pan, my father used Styrofoam and paint to create what looked like a hot fudge sundae – complete with a fuzzy, red cherry on top. He punched holes in the sides and attached a piece of yarn that extended under my chin to hold the faux dessert on my head. Today, I'd probably win *RuPaul's Drag Race* with just the hat and a sassy name like "Haute Fudge," but, in 1982, I was labeled simply "Most Delicious." If only the foam melted like real ice cream and drowned me, the embarrassment would have been easier to handle. Somehow, tap dancing concerned my mother, but this didn't? I would have scratched my head in disbelief if it wasn't buried beneath what looked like a late-night treat from Denny's.

Each summer, Camp Shalom would host a sleepover evening. The campers spent the night in tents under the stars, and the parents got their money's worth in babysitting dollars. I was never one for a slumber party – in fact, I was always the first to call my parents to pick me up before bedtime when invited to stay the night at a friend's house – and, naturally, I wasn't a fan of the creepy crawly elements that somehow seemed more threatening in the later hours.

In spite of my trepidation, my folks pushed me to "join the group" and "rough it" for one very long night.

My brain was swimming in frustration, as though I were a tourist in a foreign country trying to communicate with someone who didn't speak my native language. How did my parents not understand that a sleepover at camp would hotwire my nerves to an almost paralyzing burnout? They had to remember the four or five times that they were called to rescue me from a birthday sleepover just before midnight, no?

There was an intimacy and vulnerability to sleeping, and it was something that I was comfortable doing only in the cocoon of my own home. I loved the idea of being like the other kids, who just flopped down on a sleeping bag and drifted off, but it wasn't in my make-up. I never believed that other houses were as clean or cared for as mine, and I felt too unguarded with my eyes closed in strange surroundings. At my parents' urging, I tried a number of times to overcome my natural inclination, but, on those occasions, my heart would race at frightening speeds. The tightening in my chest represented a state of panic that was unbearable, but I was able to describe it only as "being afraid."

To complicate matters, it wasn't until I was well into my twenties that I even considered eating food prepared by anyone other than a family member or reputable restaurant. These tendencies weren't demonstrated or reinforced by my parents; in fact, they would encourage me to "live a little."

"It's not going to kill you to eat a piece of chicken prepared by someone else," my mom would say. In hindsight, *her* cooking was probably more likely to put me in the ground. Tuna casserole was her signature dish, and there was nothing deadlier in my estimation than a meal topped with cornflake crumble. Or, of course, her chicken and rice, which was known in the family as the "death dish;" she'd whip up a pan whenever she had to deliver food to a grieving neighbor or relative. You know how, when one half of an older couple passes away, they say the other is soon to follow? My mom's chicken and rice was likely responsible for that theory. Out of the womb, I was a little bit of a snob. My parents always disclaimed that part of my personality, but it certainly accounted for my dislike of crunchy toppings on savory foods.

Nevertheless, I was one of the first campers to be signed up for "Shalom Under the Stars." The name of the event sounded so much more glamorous than the large, grassy field would suggest. The campground included an open pavilion that housed various activity rooms along with some wooden tables and benches. A burned out school bus that was converted to an administrative office and a couple of bungalows were the only other structures on the site. Beyond the far end of the camp's property line was an intimidating looking forest that would appear to be home to the animals and monsters of storybook legend. Or, the Ku Klux Klan.

The sleepover evening included a dusk-time "ghost tour" of the camp. The counselors made up stories that were spooky but seemingly harmless while we walked around the outer perimeter of the lot. As we trudged towards the back of the field, we passed the entryway to the forest, which was now draped with a torn piece of a white, cotton sheet.

"They're here," one male counselor whispered.

"Who's here?" asked a female assistant, in mock concern.

"The KKK. A piece of one of their robes must have gotten caught."

I didn't know anything about the KKK at that age, but I could tell from the look on the older kids' faces that it wasn't made up of Peter Pan and his Lost Boys.

"What's the KKK?" a camper asked.

"They're a group of horrible people who dress up in white sheets and kill Jews," one of the counselors replied.

Without looking back, I took off like Flo Jo, running to the main pavilion as fast as my skinny legs could carry me. I stayed awake all night, worried that the KKK members would make their way into Camp Shalom. Even at that age, it made sense to me that the Klan, if they were at all efficient, would come to a Jewish facility to do their dirty work. In my mind, it was a no-brainer: if you drop your line in a fish tank, you are certain to catch something. It was a horrible, thoughtless prank that terrified me and, naturally, added to my anxiety about camp.

A solid case of Obsessive Compulsive Disorder, which has remained manageable as long as I can control particular aspects of a situation, didn't help things either. For as long as I can remember, things have had to be in order for me to feel centered. Whether it was a set of play blocks, puzzle pieces or Lincoln Logs as a child, everything had to be stored or positioned in a modular way. Chaos and clutter – or any disorganization, for that matter – shook my sense of security. Similarly, any surface that wasn't perfectly clean would throw me into an internal spin.

In truth, keeping my toys organized wasn't too big of a problem because I was interested mostly in cleaning supplies and related equipment; the action figures rarely got any attention. My OCD fueled a bizarre interest in Comet and Soft Scrub, not to mention any Hoover, Royal or Electrolux that I could get my hands on. My mother had to crane-lift me out of the grocery store aisle that was stocked with cleansers, as I could spend hours reading the labels to determine which of the latest products would best keep my surroundings clean.

"Josh, honey, the store is about to close," my mother would call out. "Let's get a move on."

I was inert, mesmerized by the selection of pastes, powders and liquids. They were, quite literally, the solutions to my seven year-old problems.

"Josh! Let's go!"

All I could do was look up at the perfectly merchandised shelves. On them were the products that made everything right in the world. Knowing they were even available gave me a sense of calm and the tranquility that came with knowing that dirt and germs couldn't touch me.

"I just need another minute," I remember yelling back, hoping she would lose track of time.

"Now!" she'd reply tersely, not understanding how the cleansers made me feel in control of my environment.

The OCD brought even more good news. My parents never had to bring toys or coloring books along with them to keep me occupied during any appointment or outing. They would just call ahead to make sure that the location had a vacuum cleaner, and we were all set. As soon as I arrived at someone's home or business, I went to work making it clean enough for my comfort – a hamster wheel situation.

In Fort Lauderdale, which seemed like an endless 30-minute drive from our West Palm Beach home, was a children's clothing store that specialized in "husky" formal wear. Apparently, between growth spurts, I was compact and required outfits that were generous with fabric. I knew the word "husky" classified the clothes as different in some way, but I didn't realize at the time that it was the juvenile equivalent to "big and tall." Fortunately, I wasn't yet interested in fashion or plagued by my body type – I just wanted a clean place to sit while I was stuffed in and out of jackets and pants by an overbearing Miami yenta.

"Hi, Judy, it's Debbie Sabarra." I remember my mom making the call early one Saturday morning. "We're on our way down to see you; we need to get Josh a suit for a wedding."

My ears perked up, and then my heart sank as I realized I'd be spending the day trying on "husky wear."

"I know this might sound odd, but do you have a vacuum cleaner in the store?" she asked.

My heart floated back into my chest.

"You do? Fantastic. If you wouldn't mind having it out, it will keep Josh happy while we shop."

It was the first time that I looked forward to arriving at the boutique department store, and it never had more of a sparkle and shine than when I left that afternoon. We, indeed, found a suit without any drama or tantrums. I had a clean place to sit while we shopped, and the janitorial activities kept me distracted from all of the talk about my shape and height.

As a 7 year-old, it was hard to articulate my mindset or the emotions behind my actions. Popular clinical labels of the now were not applied as freely then, and I remember my mother referring to my behavior as "idiosyncratic" and "quirky." For example, I had an aversion to getting even a drop of water on my dry clothes, and I didn't like to linger in a wet bathing suit once out of a pool. The discomfort of dampness against my dry skin was unbearable (and I can't say I have entirely moved past it), especially when water would hit a cuff, sock or fabric that was tight against my body. In the instances during which I would get wet – a spill, rain, a water balloon – I would need to be changed from head to toe. No matter that only one area of my clothing might have been affected. Everything had to be swapped out; my shirt, my pants, my socks and my underwear. I know, it was a little weird; even I was aware that this protocol was somewhat non-traditional. By this age, I already knew there was something different in terms of my sexuality, and I assumed that this "quirkiness" was what it was all about.

Naturally, the camp setting was a mine field of potential water disasters, and my mother tried to accommodate my OCD by sending a complete change of clothes in my camp bag each morning. The drawstring sack held every lifeline I needed to get through a day at Camp Shalom, and my mom sewed a squiggly, yellow strand of ribbon across the upper portion. This way, it could be easily identified among the heap of standard issue bags that were tossed in one area of the main pavilion when kids arrived each morning. I could quickly get my hands on extra bug spray and sunscreen, not to mention the brown bag lunch of peanut butter and jelly that my mother prepared between slices of Pepperidge Farm white. It was one meal she actually made well, but I think it was more about the tasty bread than her culinary expertise.

I had a big problem with the pool locker rooms at Camp Shalom for a couple of reasons. First was that the floor was a pounded pebble cesspool of enough bacteria to wipe out a small country. Even the idea of setting my bare feet against the damp grime on the ground sent an electric current from my head, past my shoulders and right into the pit of my stomach. I worked tirelessly to clean every environment I possibly could, but this slime blanket was a mountain that was impossible to get over. The dirt and the lack of control sent me into panic mode.

Second, my emotional wiring made me gravely uncomfortable changing clothes and being undressed in front of other boys. Those teachers had drilled into my head that everything under my pants was private. I also knew, from my anecdotal research during the school year, that touching my crotch resulted in a pleasant stiffening. Likewise, I was compelled to see other penises; I knew it was forbidden and yet provided such a unique physical sensation.

For the most part, I did what I was told, so I understood that my fascination with exploring other boys' bodies had to be kept secret. My concern was that, in the locker room, kids might notice me staring between their legs, and I was self-conscious about them staring between mine. It had nothing to do with comparisons of penis size or shape – I was and continue to be entirely satisfied with my endowment – but rather the idea that someone might spot my erection while I was surrounded by naked boys. There was a shame attached to my carnal interest, as the feelings were all stemming from a part of my body that had to be covered and whispered about. It was a confusing recipe: one part fear and guilt and two parts undiscovered excitement.

My mother put a call in to the camp director, a witchy looking harridan with long, frizzy grey hair, because of my upset over the locker room floors. Naturally, I didn't let on about the whole penis thing.

"Josh has some 'idiosyncrasies,'" I remember my mother saying into the telephone. "I hope we can come up with a plan to make things comfortable and easy for everyone." My parents were on the board of the Jewish Community Center, so their voices were heard without the need for additional explanation.

It was decided that a counselor would escort me to another area following each afternoon at the pool so I could clean up and change into a dry outfit. The Kindergarten Bungalow, which was essentially a double-wide trailer with a fun name, was my saving grace. (A bungalow, pavilion or nook, by the way, sounds a lot less mobile and 100 times more inviting than a trailer.)

The only positive to the camp experience? The Israeli Scouts program. Each session, the JCC would host an "exchange counselor" from Israel – all of whom turned out to be hot. Yes, they were hairy and had natural scents that bordered on BO, but they had a masculine appeal that I didn't understand at the time. I would listen to their harsh accents, rapt as they told stories about their lives in the Holy Land. They would hand out fabric patches to the campers as rewards for good behavior and achievements, and I collected more than anyone else. If I had been a little older and out of the closet, I have no doubt that the scouts would have had to invent some new patches.

Stereotypically unskilled in absolutely every kind of sport – both organized groups and those of the solo variety – I could usually be found mounting short plays with the drama coach. She and I spent hours writing original material that we would perform for any campers who gathered around our makeshift stage. We created scenery out of poster board and foam core, and our costumes were direct from Camp Shalom's "lost and found" bin.

After lunchtime, when the curtain came down on my

performances, I channeled my energy into designing colorful lanyard key chains and necklaces in the arts and crafts room. I would bound through the front door, thrilled by the carefully organized compartments of glitter, glue and pipe cleaners. The rolls of colored butcher paper and endless yards of weaving material lit up my mind while the waxy smells of Crayola crayons and rubber cement transported me to another world. During those hours, I was appreciated for stitching together a beautiful key chain, necklace or cloth potholder. What I couldn't do, however, was tell which shape ball went along with which sports game. Oval is football? Still not sure. It was no wonder that I was identified as gay for the first time during my inaugural summer at Camp Shalom.

The counselor who oversaw my age group was a gangly, tall drink of water who was, generously speaking, homely. His sister, also not gifted in the looks department, was a fellow camper who had a supermodel attitude and a hand model face. Nevertheless, they ruled the grounds, probably for the last time in their lives. Their marquee star status was a product of the time period, an absence of competition and a safety in their familial tie.

One afternoon, after a long day in the sun, I found myself surrounded by the 40 or so campers who shared my route home. Everyone was dirty and reddened by the Florida sunshine, and the kids were wired by the sugary fruit punch that was pumped into their systems all day. Many of the campers wore their wet bathing suits under their dry clothes; I had to look away from those ragamuffins. I could feel the discomfort just by seeing them. The end-of-day departure was a tumultuous process, but I would find my way to the correct bus without any assistance. If I had my choice, I wouldn't have even gotten out of my seat in the morning; I'd have just stayed put, staring out the window, until 3:00PM. A day on a hot, uncomfortable bus seemed like heaven comparatively.

As I began to board, I noticed that I was two steps behind one of the few male friends I had made during that summer. We were chatting away as we walked up towards the driver, and I put my hands on my pal's shoulders. Simultaneously, I heard my counselor's voice barrel at my ear from the left.

"Are you a homo?" he yelled, spit out as more of a statement than a question.

Everything around me stopped, at least in my head. The commotion among the children, scrambling to find their buses, came to a silent flat-line. I had been publicly identified by this foreign word, which immobilized me. It was as though I had been turned to stone by five syllables, and everyone was staring, grateful to have been spared. I had been singled out, discovered for being different. Was a homo someone who liked to clean everything around him? Or maybe homos don't like sleepovers or eating in other people's homes? Perhaps it had to do with that feeling in my penis when I looked at other boys? Regardless, the humiliation was everything that terrified me about getting on that bus each morning. The lotions and the bug sprays may have steeled me against particular physical threats, but the flimsy shield wasn't strong enough to protect my insides.

I picked up one foot and forced the other to move behind it, making my way onto the bus and sinking into a seat made of quicksand. My sister had already boarded and was sitting with our neighbor at the back, never hearing what had happened outside. For the entire ride home, I played the scene over and over in my head, and I continued to think about it until I fell asleep on my *E.T.* sheets that night.

Just before I closed my eyes, I put it all together. I realized that the counselor's "insult" was in direct response to my hands touching my friend. I started to process what the term "homo" meant in that context. Obviously, it was completely innocent at that age; there was nothing remotely sexual about my physical choice in that instance. Today, I would definitely be copping a feel; in 1982, it was unadulterated friendship uncompromised by sexual feelings that would come, in earnest, five years later.

When I returned to camp the following morning, my counselor continued to make off-handed comments about my being gay. He had also mentioned it to a few other staff members who were all too happy to throw mean comments my way throughout the remainder of the summer. From the torment, I could feel edges of my personality emerge – pieces inside of me that would sharpen my tongue and fine-tune an innate wit that could eventually slice through unworthy opponents in seconds. A wall of defense was rising from the ground, and my internal artillery was being loaded for the coming years of battle.

I endured the taunts and got through the sticky hot days of June and July, but I knew – before I even understood how exactly to make any real sense of this feeling inside – that I had to hide who I was in order to get through life. The counselors made me feel uncomfortable and embarrassed for being me, and I didn't want the people who loved me at home to know and be ashamed of me, as well. I kept it all to myself and decided, from that moment forward, that I would ignore this natural inclination for as long as I possibly could. Who knew that it would be nearly 25 years later before I would have the courage to embrace myself?

CUMMING OF AGE

Brianna Horowitz's "Magic & Mazel?" A bust. Adam Finkelstein's "SuperBowl Simcha?" Nothing to write home about.

Josh's "Night at the Movies" was the premier Palm Beach County Bar Mitzvah in 1988, and there was nothing Brianna and Adam could do about it. After all, my parents had retained the state's top event planner, whose enviable credits at the time included a Miss America Pageant after-party – and that was back when people could possibly name the reigning show doll. I still hold Vanessa Williams and *Penthouse* magazine responsible for stripping the shine off that crown.

For a year leading up to the grand fete, I prepared for my Jewish rite of passage. A ritual transition into manhood, my Bar Mitzvah represented a leap from 12 year-old child to 13 year-old adult. I was terrified by what it all meant.

"What if I don't want a Bar Mitzvah?" I asked my parents.

"You're having one. Your sister had her Bat Mitzvah, and you're having a Bar Mitzvah," my mother said.

Apparently, I was already adult enough to know the fault in that argument. "Just because Nancy had one doesn't mean I have to. We're not the same person."

"It's a tradition, and you're having it," my father chimed in. "It's not up for discussion. All of the Sabarra men have been Bar Mitzvahed. That's it. Case closed."

Fuck a duck, I thought. For nearly five years, my parents had been sending me to Sunday School at our local synagogue – and I didn't speak a word of Hebrew before, during or after. With that many classes, I would think that even Marlee Matlin could command the Israeli Army; unfortunately, Rabbi Lipschitz wasn't exactly Anne Sullivan.

Temple Beth Midrash boasted a congregation of mostly seniors; only a handful of members were young enough to urinate without assistance, let alone have children who weren't yet teenagers. Our Sunday morning class was made up of the seven kids whose parents comprised "The Next Generation Committee" of the synagogue. Needless to say, mine was the last graduating class of the Temple's Sunday School.

A tall, German man with more hair on his ears than his head, Rabbi Lipschitz spoke with an accent as thick as potter's clay. I could understand only a couple of words in each of his sentences, and my classmates had similar difficulty translating his speech into English. Each student was the son or daughter of one of the community's affluent professionals, mostly doctors whose patient rosters dipped heavily into the temple's membership. We didn't attend services frequently, but when we did, my father was always cornered by a patient with a urologic concern. I knew which members of the Sisterhood Club were leaking and which gentlemen in the Men's Club were sitting on prostates the size of navel oranges.

The rabbi's articulation problems coupled with the collective sense of entitlement among the doctors' kids created what I called *The Lord of the Chais*. It was anarchy, without a doubt. Two of the girls never looked up from their notepads and glitter pens, even when the rabbi threatened to confiscate their writing tools. The boys were busy laughing at Rabbi Lipschitz's dialect; nothing started a giggle wave faster than the word "growth" pronounced as "groat."

For three hours every Sunday, it was as though *The Breakfast Club* convened around a rectangular card table in the back office of the synagogue. We had the loners, the misfits and the brains, but, sadly, the beauties and the jocks were at His Holy Spirit Church two blocks away. What we also didn't have was enough Hebrew education to find a bathroom in Jerusalem; forget reciting a section of the Torah. Likewise, the idea of having to read Hebrew in front of 200 people in order to complete the Bar Mitzvah service threw my high anxiety into overdrive. As dead set as my parents were on my being Bar Mitzvahed, they didn't seem to acknowledge the educational component.

I had Bar Mitzvah night terrors, almost like the dreams in which you show up to school naked. The Jewish version had guilt attached. I was in front of the entire temple, including my friends and invited guests, but unable to utter a word. I explained to the crowd that it was my fault for not learning Hebrew and that they could have all of the Bar Mitzvah gifts back.

"You realize that I don't speak a word of Hebrew, correct?" I warned my parents multiple times following these recurring nightmares.

"So, what happens in Sunday School?" my mom asked.

"Nothing."

"Well, something has to be happening during those three hours. I'm sure you're getting more than you realize," she said.

"I think it's going to be a problem," I continued.

"You start working one-on-one with Rabbi Lipschitz in a couple of weeks. It'll be fine."

I didn't know anyone who learned an entire language in a matter of months. Sure, there was nothing to mastering the tunes and chanting tones, but reading the Hebrew lyrics and prayers was going to be a huge issue.

"You'll just have to do it," my mother continued. "Invitations go out shortly, and you don't want to embarrass yourself."

No, I didn't. I didn't want to embarrass myself by not being able to read Hebrew or by having to sing in front of my parents' friends – particularly when I felt overweight and knew that there was speculation about my sexuality. And, it wasn't as though I had to be at the microphone for a few short moments. The good Lord was kind enough to grant me the longest Haftorah portion in the course of the year, the story of Devorah the Prophet.

As soon as Rabbi Lipschitz began meeting with me privately, he realized that he had his work cut out for him. Within a concentrated period, I was going to have to be able to read from the Hebrew Scriptures, and it wasn't as though Bar Mitzvah lessons were available at Rosetta Stone kiosks in shopping malls.

"Oh boy," the rabbi said, almost surprised by how little I knew. "Let me think."

After five minutes, I saw him scribble some notes on a piece of lined, loose-leaf paper. He pushed it in front of me.

"Read this," he told me.

The paper had what looked like two sentences written at the top.

"Bar-uch ah-tah," I began.

The rabbi smiled. "That'll do it."

He sent me home that week and presented me with a collated set of papers and an audiocassette the following session. On the pages, he had written out my entire Torah portion phonetically, and the tape contained a vocal demonstration of how the words were to be delivered. He realized that the whole "learning Hebrew" thing was a lost cause – never mind that it was an important part of becoming a Bar Mitzvah – and came up with a corner-cutting alternative that was fool-proof. All I had to do was chant the words convincingly, and no one would know better. And they didn't.

It was by no fault of my own that I hadn't learned Hebrew at Sunday School; a coherent lesson was never offered. I certainly wasn't any less capable than the children of my parents' friends who learned the language in earnest at neighboring synagogues. Nevertheless, I felt like a fraud. I knew that my Bar Mitzvah was somewhat of a charade, a theatrical performance that represented what I was supposed to be doing socially and culturally – but not what was in my head and my heart. I had become accustomed to dealing with that emotion, and I swallowed it with some carrot cake. The spiced sweetness made it all better.

Each week, during the months before my Bar Mitzvah, my

mother would drive me to Temple Beth Midrash for rehearsal with Rabbi Lipschitz. With my cheat-sheet in front of me, I knocked it out of the park in almost every run-through. I called it "Kiddush Karaoke," but instead of singing a power ballad from Ann and Nancy Wilson of Heart, I belted out a dated, Hebrew "story song" as though I was Barbra at Madison Square Garden. I could carry a tune, but I wasn't going to be competing in the "male vocalist" category on *Star Search* either; Barbra's record deal was safe.

Sometimes, before the rabbi arrived, I would sneak into the sanctuary and stand on the front platform while my mother sat in the back row. She would pay bills and update her calendar – never looking up – while I gripped the microphone stand. I closed my eyes tightly and then opened them again, imagining before me an adoring audience. They were clapping and screaming to an almost deafening frenzy, until I began to open my mouth. The throngs hushed, waiting for my first words. I was wearing a sequined one-piece – think Diana Ross in Central Park, minus the wind, the rain and the whole winter storm – and my dazzling persona was everything the crowd wanted.

I tilted my head backward, glancing up at the ceiling, then to both sides of the auditorium. My well-timed banter – a couple of quick jokes and a set-up of my forthcoming song – held everyone's attention. This wasn't a simple cabaret act; it was *big*. I mean, Liza big. Maybe even Judy.

With the gay gene came my affinity for a dramatic lyric. I sang my heart out: seeds that, in the winter, became "The Rose" and "Memories" that lit the corners of my mind were all on the set list, and I lost myself in the fantasy until the rabbi came through the door. The fans in my head were inevitably disappointed when he arrived. None of them wanted to hear the Hebrew words that were being whispered to me by Rabbi Cyrano; they loved my vocal stylings, song choices and glittering personality. (I think that's how Paula Abdul would have judged my performances, had she been there at the time. We didn't become friends until years later.)

"Josh, let's get to work," my mom would say, as though she didn't see or hear anything until the rabbi entered the room. With her words, the stage lights dimmed and my full orchestra faded into the background.

"The Rabbi just got here," I pointed out. "It's not like I was wasting his time."

"I know, but there's not a minute to play around. We're at the home stretch."

"You heard her," the rabbi added. "We'll start at the top."

I had more of a connection to the Bette Midler and Barbra Streisand songs than I did those with religious significance, and at least I could actually understand the lyrics without an interpreter. Was it lost on everyone that this Bar Mitzvah was a sham? I was simply spitting out sounds that were meaningless to me and yet, somehow, becoming a man at the same time. What it looked like from the outside was its value apparently; not what was beneath the colorful, candy shell.

Four weeks before the main event, my presentation was entirely polished. I could sing the Torah portion without even glancing at the rabbi's phonetic guidebook, and my closing remarks and thank-yous were tweaked to hit every comedic note. I was all ready to go through the motions until my father sat me down for a conversation that would upheave everything.

"I want to give you something," he told me, just after dinner one evening. "It's very important." His tone suggested a gravity that I hadn't heard from him previously.

"This ring," he said, taking a gold piece of jewelry from the box in his right hand, "has been handed down to all of the men in our family at their Bar Mitzvahs."

"But it says 'JS' on it," I pointed out. "Those are *my* initials."

"Correct," my dad said. "The first letter has been changed for each man at his Bar Mitzvah. It had my initials until a few weeks ago."

"Is this for me to wear at the service?" I asked.

"Yes, but more important," he said, "it's for you to pass down to *your* son when he's 13. He will get the family name *and* the ring."

Son? My stomach hollowed out, and I just about threw up the cranberry chicken my mother had attempted to cook that night.

"What if I have a girl?" was the fastest response I could spit out.

My father smiled and rubbed my shoulder, almost as if to reassure me that it was silly to think that way; of course I'd have a boy.

I excused myself from the dinner table and walked casually into my room, under the pretense of having homework assignments to complete. With the door closed, I flopped onto the bed, face down. Shooting pains were jolting through my skull, like ice picks being jammed into one ear until their sharp points poked through the other.

I still didn't know everything there was to know about sexuality, but I was certain that I wasn't attracted to girls.

And, girls had babies. If I wasn't with a girl, I wouldn't be able to have children, not to mention a son. If I didn't have a son, I wouldn't be able to carry on the family name – or pass the heirloom ring to its next rightful owner. At that time, men and women had children; alternative families weren't a conversational topic, and the pressure felt consuming.

With my temples pounding and my face stuffed into a pillow, I tried to make sense of my thoughts. The pace and sound of my heartbeat wouldn't give me a minute to collect myself. It was as though I was trapped in a small room with no windows, no doors and a limited air supply. My breathing became heavy, thankfully muffled by the bedding. The full-on panic attack didn't allow for tears; it left me with no energy. I lied still, hoping it would pass. That thought was the last thing I remembered until I woke up the next morning. The sound of my mother's voice and a buzzing alarm clock jarred me awake simultaneously.

"You must have been really tired," my mom said, as she put her hand on the back of my neck. I hadn't even changed positions during the night. "You fell asleep in your clothes, with all of the lights on."

"What time is it?" I asked, groggy and disoriented.

"Time to get ready for school. And, you have Bar Mitzvah practice after I pick you up today."

Everything flooded back to me: the ring, the family name, the son I'd never have. I pulled myself from the bed and into the bathtub, hopeful that the warm, calming water would take away the weight on my shoulders. I went to school without anyone knowing the emotional upset that was jabbing me like tiny pin pricks as I walked through my day. I kept thinking it all over, ignoring math, science and

English lessons. Would this be the point – this Jewish shift in life stages – that my family would become as ashamed of me as the camp counselors and my classmates? The only thing that comforted me was the idea that there wasn't going to be an immediate reveal. I wouldn't be expected to be having children for at least a decade, and, along the lines of the Bar Mitzvah itself, could continue the pantomime until the last possible moment. That thinking was a superficial balm for the mental aches that continued to stew in my head.

For days, I was plagued by the ring and the responsibilities that came with it. My mother had displayed the shiny piece of precious metal in its box on my bedroom dresser, creating a constant reminder of the expectations I would inevitably fail to meet. Mom and Dad, of course, believed that they had gifted me with a priceless family treasure; they had no under-standing of the private anguish it stirred.

Aside from the unspoken understanding that I would wear the ring throughout my Bar Mitzvah weekend, neither the piece of jewelry nor its significance came up again. Seating arrangements and place card printing became last minute details that overshadowed any worries and sentiments, and my whole family got caught up in the more festive aspects of the event. The ring still loomed in the back of my mind, but, as weeks passed, my focus shifted to the big show.

The official Friday night and Saturday morning services went along seamlessly; my flawless presentation was cheered with applause, accolades and commendations from the syna-gogue's Board of Directors. I made sure not to glance at the fingers on my right hand; I didn't want my performance to be thrown by the gleaming, gold monogram that had already been earmarked for my first-born son.

"That was some service," the temple president remarked. "You must have had extra practice."

"I worked really hard," I said. "Thank you so much." Imagine if he had heard my rendition of "Liza with a 'Z'" during afternoon rehearsal only two days before. He would have been blown away by how effortlessly I channeled Ms. Minnelli.

My parents sponsored a lunch spread immediately following the Saturday morning service, enough to feed both our invited guests and the regular temple members who were in attendance. Those from the "GP" – or "general population," as I liked to call them – were always fun to observe during special events. I watched them leave catered meals with assorted baked goods, pieces of rugalach and pound cake, stuffed into cocktail napkins inside their oversized purses. Sandwiches and cold cuts traveled well, too; it was almost as though Coach structured their bags with hidden pockets, specifically for the older Jew on-the-run.

■ ■ ■

My mother had packed suitcases and laid out all of our evening clothes in preparation for the Saturday night gala. As soon as we returned from the synagogue that afternoon, we drove to The Royce Hotel, where the catering department had provided us with a complimentary suite. We arrived at 4:00PM to meet the photographer, who was set up to take portrait photographs of me, my family and special guests prior to the start of the party.

I showered and changed into my tuxedo pants, shirt and studs.

"Where's my bow tie and cummerbund?" I asked.

"I have them in the suitcase," my mom said. "I think you're going to love them."

My dad, who always paid attention to artistic details, liked the idea of wearing colors that complemented my mother and sister's dresses. He ordered our bow ties and cummerbunds accordingly.

When my mother handed me a black garment bag, I ripped it open, excited to see what my dad had chosen. The youth sizes were all adjustable, so I wasn't with him when the order was placed.

"What's wrong?" my mom asked, surprised by my adverse reaction.

"It's iridescent pink," I said.

"Right. My dress is black with sparkling pink highlights. It matches."

I had seen my mother's dress before that afternoon but mistakenly assumed that my father would have gone for a patterned black, monochromatic look.

"I don't want to be walking around all night in this glowing pink," I said, on the brink of tears. The last thing I needed was word getting around about my pink, glittery outfit.

"There isn't much of a choice at this point, honey," my mother said, trying to calm me down. "It'll look great when we are all standing together."

What were we, a traveling show business family? The short, Jewish version of the Partridges or the Osmonds?

There were no options. I was stuck in an outfit that even Liberace would want to tone down. I took a deep breath, finished dressing, and smiled for two hours of photographs with every overly made-up, overly hair sprayed and overly overbearing relative that we could cram into our room. I couldn't wait to get downstairs for the cocktail hour, away from the cheek-pinching madness happening around me.

Two open bars and a royal spread of hors d'oeuvres lined the wide hallway leading to the grand ballroom, where the live band was warming up with a song list I had provided months earlier. I vetoed the traditional "New York, New York" and "Sunrise, Sunset" for some Whitney and Madonna, as any closeted 13 year-old would do. And, before mingling with arriving guests, I ran into the main dining area to see how the party planner had transformed a traditional hotel banquet hall into a well-dressed soundstage. The room looked like a Hollywood fantasy, similar to the parties I dreamed about at night. There was a glow on everything, and I felt comfortable in the warm colored lights that were strategically placed to showcase the décor.

25 round tables were draped in white satin cloths spotted with black velvet stars. In the center sat film cans holding up movie cameras, director's chairs and movie reels bursting through sparkling streamers. The band area was bookended by two, 10-foot Oscar statues, and the walls were lined with original, mounted movie posters, hand selected by yours truly: *Funny Girl, Pretty in Pink, Top Gun* and *Moonstruck*, among them. I didn't even realize that I was broadcasting my sexuality – I just knew what movies and music I enjoyed.

A few teachers who had taken a particular liking to me were the only representatives of my school life. I was bullied rather than embraced by my classmates, so the peers in attendance were the children of my parents' friends in the local Jewish community. In hindsight, there was an upside to that bit of loneliness: I wasn't faced with the overtly sexual hijinks that became Bar Mitzvah lore, such as the "RainBlow Job."

Word had it that teen girls wore different shades of lipstick, taking turns in the bathroom with the man of the hour. By the time the last lass left the men's lounge, there was a 13 year-old penis with a rainbow of concentric circles around its shaft. Gag reflexes must not develop until after puberty because the widely known "Jewish girls don't give blowjobs" stereotype didn't come from nowhere. And, thankfully, gay, Jewish men were never saddled by the same rumor – what would we do on a first date?

The "RainBlow" phenomenon didn't rear its, um, head for me, thankfully; it would have been an awkward scenario. A flip through my Bar Mitzvah photo album, to this day, would have me hard pressed to choose anyone – man or woman, boy or girl – from whom I would want to receive oral sex.

The requisite candle lighting ceremony – during which relatives and close friends were called to the dance floor for an "honor" – was replaced by an awards presentation. A short poem about each person preceded their walks to the center of the room. There, they received a chocolate Oscar statuette, a kiss and a photo with the Bar Mitzvah boy.

"Relatives came from far and near,
They came from coast to coast.
They traveled with Bar Mitzvah cheer,
To join this special toast.

Aunt Lorraine flew from Queens, N-Y,
To share in all the fun.
She's typically afraid to fly,
So her presence means a ton!"

I don't think T.S. Eliot would have had to worry about sharing shelf space with my father, the wordsmith who crafted 13 similar poems. Equally as touching and fraught with meaning, the remaining 12 stayed trapped on an aging VHS tape that collected dust in the family garage for years.

The night came to an end with a last song – something about the moon and New York City – and we said goodbye to close friends who lingered until even the balloons lost their perk. For weeks after, guests called my parents to congratulate them again and to rave about the classy party. The milestone, the transition from boy to man in the eyes of the Jewish people, seemed lost in the confetti and the music. The party became the centerpiece of the weekend, not the ceremony it was intended to celebrate. It was fine with me, considering that I hadn't really learned to read from the Torah to begin with and didn't want to face the fallout from acknowledging the man I would someday become. It all fit together on the surface.

When I finally collapsed into a chair in the middle of The Royce Hotel ballroom, I removed the gold ring and placed it in my coat pocket. My parents ran around, giving cash tips to the wait staff and the bartenders who had worked throughout the evening, and I stared blankly while the clean-up crew threw sparkly flower arrangements and movie-themed props into oversized trash bins. Within 30 minutes, the Hollywood wonderland was nothing but standard-issue hotel carpeting and moveable, felt walls being rearranged for the next morning's brunch. The show was spectacular, but there was nothing of interest underneath. Did it matter, I thought, as long as the outward presentation was enough to grab people's attention? Was the heart and soul below the surface really *that* important? Maybe a distracting razzle-dazzle act was my path; perhaps I was the human embodiment of what had just occurred.

I went through the motions, delivered the songs and the speeches and wore the pink tuxedo accessories. I said my thank-yous, I opened the gifts, and I cashed the checks. As the last trash can was wheeled out of the ballroom and the industrial vacuums sucked every remnant of the night's festivities into a compressed bag, I realized the one thing I hadn't accomplished. I hadn't become a man.

WHERE THE BOYS AREN'T

Straight males, in my experience, were missing a thread of emotional DNA that allowed for the nurturing sensitivity that made me feel safe. I was an outsider with guys and couldn't relate on any level. I was a talker who needed to express every thought that came to mind and was understood best by those who were wired in a complementary way. Women.

My most fulfilling and secure relationships have always been with the fairer sex. I never once had an itch to experiment with them sexually – not even a test kiss –but our emotional connections were the stuff of dream marriages. If only lady bits caused even the tiniest stir in my designer denim, I would have been on an entirely different romantic trajectory. In fact, I often think I would be happy in a marriage to a woman (with permission to have sex with men a few times per week, of course). Other than on a sexual level, I, to this day, have only surface relationships with men – gay or otherwise. They always seem to have that secret knock or handshake that I am not privy to; they offer a fist bump when I lean in for the awkward hug.

Interacting with men left me feeling as if I were on a different planet, trying to be understood through broken attempts at speaking the alien language. I was a foreigner among my own kind, and I felt isolated because my feelings and interests were not embraced. That discomfort became increasingly unnerving as I aged from a youngster into an adolescent and then into an adult, and I avoided conversations with boys and men at all costs. At six and seven, it was less hurtful and more confusing – as though I was using all of my energy to make myself understood to people who couldn't even hear me. By the teenage years, those people were outwardly dismissive and disdainful, marking me as someone who was undeserving of the human support and courtesies that my peers seemed to generate easily.

Particularly difficult was when my parents would thrust me, against my protest, into organized team sport activities that were coached and populated by males. Walking onto those playing fields paralyzed me, and Little League Baseball left a wound that was impossible to erase from my memory.

The coach was a gruff man's man, the kind of father who would conceivably beat his child for not hitting a home run. Imagine his anger when I stood on the various bases in an almost catatonic state, unable to move because of my magnified sense of not belonging. On the afternoon that he hurled a regulation baseball at my right eye, his festering temper was in high gear.

"Look alive, Josh," he screamed from behind the dugout fence. "We're gonna lose if you aren't guarding third."

I stood there, silent. I was in a daze, thinking about how many minutes were left of this experiment in terror.

"Do you hear me, Josh?" he followed.

I did, in fact, hear him, but I wasn't listening. In my mind, I was sitting in a movie theater, enjoying the air conditioned, flickering light of someone else's drama.

"You're going to ruin this team," he yelled, making so many facial contortions that he resembled Don Knotts. "You're doing nothing for us."

As I looked up to meet his sun-weathered eyes, I saw nine inches of circumference hurtling towards my face. The speed and weight of the ball combined to create an excruciating impact that left my face and right eye disfigured for weeks.

"You see what happens when you don't pay attention," the coach scoffed. "You get hit in the damn face."

The shiner was no accident; the coach threw the ball in an attempt to push me out of my inertia. He was frustrated, and instead of relating to me in a language that I could understand, he launched a physical attack. I didn't want to be there in the first place, so it all felt even more violating.

"The coach didn't mean for that to happen," my mother said, rushing to my side in an attempt to console me. The tears were stinging the broken skin around my eye and cheek. "You just weren't looking, honey," she continued. Apparently, her needlepoint project kept her so busy in the bleachers that she hadn't observed the proceedings. She was as disinterested in the game as I was.

"It'll be fine by next week, and you'll jump right back in," my mom continued. Was she kidding? This was the school year equivalent of Camp Shalom, and my mother was clueless to my unease. Her lack of sensitivity to my anxiety was particularly alarming, considering that her own panic disorder prevented her from even driving a car farther than two miles away from our home.

The coach, whose scorn manifested itself in such a violent turn, instilled a debilitating fear in me. I began to avoid men as much as possible, almost flinching like an abused animal when I was forced to cross paths with them. It was hard enough to walk around knowing that they thought I was "different," but the idea of being physically hurt because of it secured a constant weight on my small shoulders.

Just like baseball, soccer and, after that, tennis, my parents enrolled me in activities that they felt were "what the other kids were doing." Likewise, Boy Scouts was on the plan. The Jewish Edition, as I liked to call it, consisted of Mallomars (Nabisco's answer to s'mores) and a glass of milk in a neighbor's garage; there was no tent pitching, knot tying or knife sharpening in Troop 1102. I don't think the boys in our Palm Beach chapter had any interest in being there beyond the snacks, and I had no female companionship other than the den mother. I felt like Anne Hathaway in the movie version of *Les Misérables* – in extreme close-up but with more to eat and better hair.

We played board games and assembled puzzles for an hour or two each week and never actually earned achievement badges. We did, however, sign up for the Boy Scouts county-wide Halloween party and were all expected to come up with noteworthy costumes. One parent had the idea for our troop to go as Girl Scouts – a gaggle of Caramel deLites (otherwise known as Samoas), if you will – which was executed despite groans from the other boys. That was the only time I didn't complain about attending an organized function.

Women provided a soothing balm for the open wounds inflicted by people who just couldn't wrap their heads around my sensibility. They nourished my four core emotional needs: they offered permission to be my unadulterated self; they modeled a measured edginess that acknowledged the risk-taker I wanted to be; they served as kindred spirits who were also wading through inner turmoil; and, most important, they taught my heart to beat love freely, in and out, in two directions. In return, I was their "gay best friend" long before it was a hip, cultural must-have. I became an innocent, pure voice in their lives who provided a virgin ear and a soft tongue that were still untarnished by the realities of existing in the world as an adult. These female influences may have been represented by the most unlikely faces, but their collective and permanent impact was nothing short of extraordinary.

Della Jackson, my second grade teacher, ultimately set the course for my ongoing friendships and connections to women. A no-nonsense black lady who was basically a *Real Housewife of Atlanta* – just ahead of her time and living in a less glamorous South Florida suburb – Della had a warm heart balanced by a finger-snapping attitude that spoke to my inner diva. Her dark hair was rounded into tight curls that framed a welcoming face, always accented by a colorful neck scarf or sash. What she also had was an accepting, non-judgmental approach that enveloped me like a warm security blanket – even when I would burst into songs from *Annie* in a hooded sweatshirt wrapped around my head like a wig.

"We are going to take a work break," she'd say, focusing the class's attention on my turn as Miss Hannigan. As I sang, moving between desks carefully as not to disturb my make-shift up-do, Della clapped, rallying the other students to join the performance. She wasn't making fun of me; she wasn't judging me. She was letting me be myself. One afternoon, she pulled out a tape recorder to capture my show-stopping rendition of "Little Girls."

"I am recording this one," she said, "and I'm keeping it forever."

"Forever?" I asked.

"Forever," Della repeated. "You're going to be something someday, and I will take this tape out so I can prove that I knew you when."

As much as Karen Hill had pushed me away in kindergarten, Della welcomed me into her life with open arms. She gave me a license to be whoever I wanted to be, so much so that we developed a friendship outside of school.

"Would you like to go to the movies this weekend?" she asked, just as I was leaving school one afternoon. "Your mom and dad said it would be OK."

"Can we see *E.T.*?" I had already seen it five times by that point in 1982, but I was obsessed with the film and every single related toy that was on the market. In fact, not only my bed sheets, but my bath towels and pajamas had E.T. on them.

"You got it," Della said. "We will go on Saturday afternoon."

My parents dropped me off at the AMC Cross County 8 movie complex, where Della and I ate a quick bite before the film started. We talked and laughed – the way most friends who are 35 years apart in age often do – and then watched the story of a lonely boy whose only friend was the ultimate outsider, a space creature from another universe.

Over ice cream cones after the movie, Della told me

about her husband who, in addition to his full time job during the week, managed a North Florida amusement park on weekends. I could sense a loneliness that haunted her; it was similar to the hollow nagging that I felt most of the time.

"At least you have your son at home," I reasoned, "someone to keep you busy."

"That's true," she said. "And, I have you."

I smiled. She made me feel like I had value. After all, she could have chosen any of the other kids in our classroom with whom to spend personal time. She had singled me out.

"You will always have me," I said, throwing my arms around her in a joyful hug.

"You're going to grow up and leave a mark on the world; you won't remember me," she laughed.

"Of course, I will," I reassured. Instinctively, I sensed that she needed the security as much as I needed her support. We filled a void in each other.

"I am going to hold you to it, Josh. Don't forget that."

As it would turn out – surprisingly, considering her sensitive nature – Della had a taste for horror films, and I somehow convinced my parents to allow me to see *Christine*. One Sunday, we planned to watch a matinee screening of Mel Brooks' *To Be or Not To Be*, but Stephen King's story about a possessed automobile seemed more to Della's liking.

"Should we call your parents to see if they'll let you go to *Christine*?" she asked. This was a true rite of passage: my first R-rated film.

"Yes!" I replied enthusiastically, heading to the bank of pay phones at the movie theater's entrance. With little hesitation, my folks signed-off on the plan, and my love for scary movies was born.

As we left the movie theater that day – we'd both seen enough human bodies crushed by a demonic car – Della turned to me with an earnest look on her face.

"I want you to listen to me," she said, with a serious tone. "You are very special."

"What do you mean?" I asked, not understanding where she was going with the conversation.

"There's no one else like you in the world, Josh Sabarra," she said, walking me to a wooden bench where we would sit for a few moments waiting for my parents to pick me up. She sat facing me, holding my hands in her palms. "You are a gift. I don't ever want you to change who you are."

"I won't," I promised, still not sure what she was trying to say.

"People don't always appreciate who we are until we get older, but we just have to keep doing our thing."

"Like what?" I asked.

"Keep singing songs in class. Keep wearing a sweatshirt on your head. Do what makes you feel good," she said.

Della had observed my relationships with other students and teachers, and she didn't want me to fall under their influences. She saw something positive in my differences and encouraged them. Knowing that she was in my corner helped me to sing a little bit louder, even at moments when I thought that being silent just might be easier.

Unfortunately, Della had to spend *some* time with her husband and son, and I had to find a buddy to fill in the gaps. Lucky for me, our next-door neighbors had an adult daughter who loved a good slasher flick.

Sandra would babysit for me and my sister whenever my parents had a function to attend, and, during those evenings, we bonded over homemade nachos and bad 80s television like *T.J. Hooker* and *Cover-Up*. Cute boys in action were Sandra's thing – and not just on TV. From time to time, she would have a boyfriend visit after I had fallen asleep and before my parents returned home. And, on the nights I was restless, I would peek into the media room where Sandra was enjoying some gentleman company right on our yellow, vinyl sofa. Jordan Wenner had already taught me what sex was all about, so I was fairly certain of what I was seeing. I don't think the poor couch, however, knew what hit it. Sandra was far from a looker, and the men she attracted were challenged in the beauty department, as well. She had a round, flat freckled face and thick thighs that she crammed into the same pair of cut-off denim shorts every single day, and her hair was dyed a striking red – one of those hues that doesn't occur in nature. That said, she was a hell of a lot of fun, and we behaved like partners in crime.

"We need to straighten up before your parents get home," Sandra told me one evening. "I think they're bringing their friends back here for dessert and coffee."

"OK, I will stand on one side of the kitchen table, and you can slide everything to me. I will put it all away." Sliding things across the table made it more of a game and saved time.

"Get ready to catch this," Sandra said, as she began to push an Entenmann's frosted yellow cake towards me. Before I could get my hands ready, the cake flew across our round table, landing icing-down on the kitchen floor.

"Shit," she said. "Do you think your parents wanted to serve that?"

"I don't know," I replied. My mom, the woman who

was known for her tuna casserole, would definitely consider serving Entenmann's to guests, right?

"Well, we better get busy," she said, as she picked up the cake and scraped every bit of icing off of the floor with a knife. Together, we re-iced the cake, and, frankly, it looked better than it had in the first place.

"Voila!" she said. "Ready to serve." We both began to laugh hysterically.

"We never talk about this, OK?" Sandra said. And we never did. Even when my parents and their friends ate the cake later that night.

She had a recklessness about her, a wild streak that gave me bursts of excitement and energy. She pushed the limits of reasonable behavior with a style I wanted to emulate. A joie de vivre, of sorts, that could throw mud in the faces of my detractors.

My bond with Sandra continued to grow through the years, and we would spend weekend afternoons together watching piles of thrillers that we had rented from the local video store. And, every now and then, when her parents were out of town, she would host keg parties in the courtyard of their house. One in particular was hilariously eventful.

"You can come over for five minutes before you go to bed," she said. "It's an adult party, but I know my friends will get a kick out of you." My parents let me walk next door briefly, and Sandra introduced me to all of her college buddies. It was all laughs and merriment until the phone rang.

"Shit," Sandra announced. "My mother and father are on their way home – three hours early. Fuck!" Sandra's parents were older when they had children and were Baptist country folk whose hot nights included a buffet at Morrison's Cafeteria and bed by 9:00PM.

"Everyone needs to help clean up, and get out within the next five minutes," she screamed. With that, I watched an entire keg of beer get poured into the courtyard garden, washing over the twenty turtles that Sandra's nutty mother had been nursing for years. I don't know whether or not the reptiles even had time to enjoy the alcohol buzz before drowning, but I was happy I was under a curfew. Sandra's mother's turkey chin must have hung even lower than usual when she caught a glimpse of her floating babies. Hopefully, she took solace in knowing that they went out having a blast.

I looked up to Sandra; she was a rule breaker who knew how to have a good time. She introduced me to rock and roll (Meat Loaf was her artist of choice), foul-mouthed comedians and adult-themed films that helped shape my already mature tastes in entertainment. My nature was to be considerably more risk averse than Sandra, so I was thrilled that she would let me pal around with her. I could live vicariously through her "take no prisoners" attitude without getting myself in hot water at home. And, even though my classmates had no frame of reference for the types of music and movies I tried to talk about with them, I felt cool and elite.

"No one at school has heard of Meat Loaf the singer," I told Sandra.

"That's because they're young, stupid and know nothing about anything," she said. "You're ahead of the curve."

As it turned out, Sandra's brother – who was older and lived in California – was gay. They never spoke about his homosexuality; in fact, for years, their family referenced him in terms of only his "black roommate." The interracial nature of his west coast living arrangement was what stood out as unique in their minds. Clearly, something didn't add up for them.

Math was never my subject either; I preferred the kinds of problems that I could talk my way out of or that had multiple answers. Likewise, my mother hired Carol O'Neill, a teacher at Highland Elementary School who had a thriving side career tutoring students who were similarly perplexed by numbers. About 5'1" and weighing in at more than 225 pounds, Carol was almost a perfect circle. Or, applying what she taught me about basic geometry, she was 360 degrees topped with a thinning, side-feathered mullet and so little make-up that even K.D. Lang would shudder.

Initially, our relationship was solely about fractions and long division. Carol came to our house twice a week in her faux wood-paneled minivan, working with me for a couple of hours each session. She and I would sit at a round folding table in the guest bedroom, completing whatever homework had been assigned by my primary teacher. I wasn't good at paying attention to material that didn't interest me, which made Carol's job particularly hard. She had to come up with ways to keep me focused.

"I want to see if you can get through this entire worksheet," Carol said one afternoon, hopeful, I think, that she could get home at a reasonable hour.

"What's in it for me?" I joked.

"How about a broccoli and cheese baked potato at Wendy's?" Carol wasn't kidding.

If someone attempted to incentivize me today with a food item from the dollar menu at a fast food chain, he or she probably wouldn't be in my life long enough to tell the tale. In 1985, I ate for comfort and was bought much more easily.

"Sure," I said, excited about both the melted cheese product and the thrill of winning it, so to speak. I raced through the math exercises as though the entire Wendy's franchise was at stake, missing only one question in my haste to collect the prize.

"Wow. Great job," Carol said. "Imagine if you worked like this all the time!" I could imagine it better with food hanging in the balance.

I ran outside to Carol's van and settled in the passenger seat before she could even walk to the car. I remember noticing her sensible attire: a pair of khaki pants and a red, Polo-style shirt. She wore a Target uniform before even they knew it would become their signature. It was definitely cutting edge when looking through the rearview mirror of time.

Wendy's was less than two miles from my house, and we were eating our potatoes in a matter of minutes. Over two spuds and a Frosty (I negotiated for the dessert treat during the car ride), I began to ask innocent questions about Carol's personal life.

"Are you married, and do you have kids?" OK, I wasn't exactly Barbara Walters, but I didn't care what kind of tree she thought she'd be.

"I was married but not anymore, and I have one son," she answered.

"How old is he?" I continued.

"He's an adult. He's in the armed services, stationed in Europe," she said.

I knew there was something nontraditional about Carol, and my questions poked at the differences that I perceived were just beneath the surface. She reminded me of my Aunt Lorraine, who to this day resembles what Chaz Bono probably hoped to look like after his transitional procedures. Nothing was ever said concretely about Aunt Lorraine's sexual orientation when I was growing up, but let it suffice to say that the back of her jeans had enough excess fabric to make wide turns – not to mention her oversized flannel tops.

"So you live by yourself?" I asked.

"No," she answered casually. "I have a roommate."

"Who's that?" I pressed on.

"My friend Rosa. She's a teacher's aide at school."

I knew just whom Carol was talking about. Rosa was a middle-aged, Mexican woman who was a dead ringer for Linda Hunt in *The Year of Living Dangerously* – only not as bouncy and with a less stylish hairdo. Barely five feet tall, her skin was ravaged by pockmarks that were difficult to ignore when looking at her directly.

"How long have you been roommates?" I asked. Carol looked at her watch.

"We have to get going. You need to get home, and so do I." It was evident that she wanted a subject change, but I continued my line of questioning as we got back into the van.

"Who's your best friend?" I inquired.

"Probably Miss Abrams," Carol told me, without thinking too long about it. Miss Abrams was an administrator at our elementary school and had such an intimidating style that most of the kids steered clear of her. With a salt-and-pepper buzz cut, reflective shades that never left the bridge of her nose and a pleather motorcycle jacket, Bonnie Abrams could make anyone hard pressed to decide whether she was a Chippendales dancer or one of the Village People.

"She seems kind of 'hefty,'" I remember saying.

"What does that mean?" Carol asked.

"You know, 'hefty.'" I repeated. At 10, the word applied to Miss Abrams. It conjured the idea of a masculine exterior, similar to those that Carol and Aunt Lorraine carried.

In hindsight, it's surprising that Carol ever returned to my house to tutor me, let alone continue a friendship; I grilled her but good. Over the course of that year, though, our relationship blossomed, and our time together became more about sharing activities and food than talking about her personal life. We went to movies together almost every weekend, attended book signings and even took a day trip to Disneyworld in Orlando. We enjoyed each other's company and drew strength from the security of our friendship. I never pressed her further about her romantic inclinations, and she accepted my unapologetic affinity for theater vocalists throughout high school and college. I think we both knew what we needed to after an hour-long car ride to Miami to see a Sandra Bernhard concert when I was in twelfth grade.

We were kindred spirits because we were silently coping with inner unrest. Carol would sometimes talk about having to preserve a certain image because she was a schoolteacher, which implied to me that there was someone suppressed beneath her double extra-large tunics and drawstring balloon pants. While I couldn't relate to the same degree, I knew that there was a part of me that needed to stay similarly out of view. The sad fact was that she reinforced what I feared – that I would likely need to keep my true identity bottled up into adulthood. Yet, at the same time, I was comforted to know that I wasn't alone and that there were other people who shared my struggle.

Our relationship survived all of my school years but ulti-mately lost steam once I began my life as an adult in New

York City. Carol visited me in Manhattan one time, staying at my east side apartment for a few days of theater, food and sightseeing. That was the last time I saw her.

Carol became less and less diligent about staying in touch, and her seeming disregard for my well-being – after a dozen years of friendship – felt like an abandonment. Her son had fathered her first grandchild, which likely accounted for a divide in her attention, but I had a suspicion that she still wasn't prepared to reveal her true self to me. Because I carried my own secret sexual identity, I understood her hesitance, but her disappearing act seemed an extreme way to handle things.

I wonder sometimes whether she thinks about me and how my life unfolded. I am certain that she sensed my homosexuality, and I am curious as to whether or not she became open about hers. Unless, of course, I had it all wrong and she just happened to be an overweight fashion nightmare with a boyish-looking Mexican roommate. It's possible.

What was almost impossible to understand, though, was the force of nature who was about to turn my life upside down. At age 12, my entire being was changed by Sylvia Bastaja, a woman whose unconditional love taught me about the limitless capacity of the heart. A woman whose unwavering passion taught me about tenacity and perseverance. A woman whose personal demons would break me forever.

HARD TO SWALLOW

The hard contact lenses rested on her eyes like glass discs, magnifying the empathically crystalline blue of her irises. They seemed to easily process everything they were observing and reflect an understanding softness that was almost uncanny. And yet, the glass shields, even in their transparency, masked a pain and sadness so deep that no visual aid could detect them. My 20/15 vision – almost strong enough to pursue a career as a sniper – was marred by a lack of emotional experience and the staid professionalism that Sylvia projected at the beginning of my pre-high school years.

Roosevelt Junior High was a concrete, urban jungle with outdoor, catwalk-style hallways and a student body that was labeled, politically, as "diverse." Today, it would undoubtedly be the scene of enough gang violence and gymnasium shootings to keep CNN in business, but, in 1987, it was where I spent my days. The grounds were at the center of one of the most crime-ridden areas of West Palm Beach, and a racial balance was accomplished by bussing in students from various white neighborhoods in Palm Beach County. In fact, the school bus that transported me each morning passed two other public junior high schools during the hour-long ride.

"Why can't I go to a private school?" I asked my parents, prior to the start of my seventh grade year.

"It's important to be around all different kinds of people," they answered. "And Roosevelt has some of the best teachers in the county."

That part was true: the county had assigned some of its strongest educators and administrators to Roosevelt. Yet, what good was that if you were beaten to death or shot prior to graduating? I found the logic to be questionable, but, as usual, Mom and Dad asserted their parental authority at the expense of my nerves.

The only thing I could do was attempt to look like I belonged. I tucked the hems of my ash-colored, acid washed denim into a pair of colorful high-top sneakers and layered my shirts within inches of good taste. My color-coordinated, sleeveless tee was tucked perfectly into my Chess King jeans, and the button down over-shirt hung loosely at my sides. My spiky hair – with highlighted tips, natch – was the crowning glory of a look that was so undeniably 80s that Debbie Gibson would have felt ahead of her time. With that wardrobe, there was no choice but to have a highly visible profile, and my homeroom music teacher recognized my flair. She asked me to stay after class for a few minutes at the end of the first week of school.

"Josh, the principal asked me to choose a student from

one of my classes to read the announcements each morning over the PA system," she said, "and I think you might be the perfect candidate." She had clearly sensed my unease with other students and was giving me a sense of purpose.

"That sounds like fun," I replied quickly, feeling special that she had identified me.

"You'll have to go right to the main office when the bus arrives each morning, so there won't be time for talking to the other kids before the bell rings," she continued. This was an opportunity to be in the safety of the school office with the secretaries and administrators; I wouldn't have to mill around the school courtyard until the gates were unlocked for the other students at 8:00 AM.

"I would love to do it," I confirmed, and Monday morning, I reported for duty. I had no idea that the start of that second week of school was destined to bring another change that would forever alter my sense of being.

Sylvia joined the staff one week into my seventh grade year, spearheading the gifted program. A tall, Norwegian looking blonde, she had a shapely figure that was accentuated by the closest thing to a Diane Von Furstenberg wrap dress that a teacher's salary would allow. With hair styled into loose curls that was just shy of what I called a "network helmet" – the look favored by the women on broadcast television – Sylvia's face was particularly round and nuanced by large pores that made her skin a focal point. She wore a floral scent that was potent but not overbearing, a sweet rose that trailed her as she moved around the room, and had a pronounced scar on the inside of her upper left arm. Her movements were graceful and fluid; she walked with a regal flow that held my gaze every time she got up from her chair.

"We need to dive right in," she said sternly on her first day. "We have already lost a week, and there's no time to waste." She meant business.

Until her arrival, the class was led by a substitute teacher who had done very little during his stint in Room 202. He was biding his time, knowing that Sylvia would arrive in a week. He ignored the county curriculum and relied on rounds of Pictionary at the chalkboard to pass the two hours a day he had our attention. Naturally, none of us was complaining, but there was nothing enriching about the geography and English lessons that he wasn't offering.

At home, my father helped me study all of the photo-copied maps and legends that Sylvia provided for a quiz the next day. It was an overwhelming amount of material, but I did my best to prepare for the challenge. Unfortunately, I still couldn't manage to score more than a "C" on the test, similar to the others who had surprisingly low grades, as well. These were advanced students who were accustomed to receiving "A's," so this sharp turn caused alarm among the kids and their parents.

"It looks like no one took this exercise too seriously," Sylvia admonished. "You better get in the game quickly or find a class that moves at your speed."

Between the low grade on my first quiz and the pressure to "step up," even after studying all night, my anxiety was in a tailspin. Sylvia's style was forceful and rigidly unsympa-thetic, but my parents ignored my worries. Or, at least until I received a low grade on her second lightning quiz.

My father was extremely competitive when it came to just about anything but maniacally so when school grades were involved. In fact, he had instilled such a drive in my sister that she held a 4.0 at every school she attended. I think he had the same plans for me, which, of course, would be a problem with Sylvia in the way. Never mind that she was wreaking havoc on my psyche; my folks could live with that. Fucking up my GPA, though, was another matter altogether.

Within two days, my parents were at school for a face-to-face meeting with Sylvia. I didn't really see the point; in my mind, it would have been best to have me moved to another classroom. But, she won my folks over by assuring them that her MO was to start out tough and lighten up as the semester progressed. She also relayed a story about her son who teetered on the edge of a nervous breakdown after receiving a lower than usual grade in one of his college courses. Sylvia explained that experiencing failure – early on, when the stakes were lower – was important in helping people cope with life's more significant ups and downs. Apparently, two of the Sabarras saw her logic, and my hopes of a transfer were crushed.

While I was struggling for the first time academically, I was also trying to make sense of the changes in my body and my heightened awareness of sex. It all felt so overwhelming, and nothing was more embarrassing than my father being asked to give a "birds and bees" talk to the entire population of boys at Roosevelt Junior High School. It made perfect sense in that he was an urologist, but it was difficult to find a comfort level with my dad discussing wet dreams and morning hard-ons in front of my classmates. The afternoon of the school-wide assembly, the teachers were responsible for separating the boys and girls and sending each to their appropriate lecture rooms. Naturally, I got the requisite taunts from the kids.

"Josh, shouldn't you be with the other group?" one boy laughed.

"Yeah," said another, "I don't think you even have a penis."

It was one thing to be marginalized and bullied by my peers, but I still didn't want my parents to know it was happening. I wanted them to be proud of me, and I would have done anything to keep them from catching wind of how disregarded I was by the other children. Five years earlier, my counselor at Camp Shalom had become the first person to shame me for being who I was, and there was no shortage of brutal teasing from classmates since. I felt that I was unlovable, a person who was so strangely different from everyone else that people could detect my inadequacy just by looking at me.

It was true, my adult female friends – Della, Sandra and Carol – enjoyed spending time with me and seemed unaffected by the weaknesses perceived by others, but, in my mind, I didn't have the security of their unconditional love. My parents and my sister represented that safety. They made it clear that nothing could change their feelings for me, but I worried endlessly about whether or not their love could be impacted by knowing that my peers thought I was such an abomination. My family was my life boat, the only people in my world who thought I was special and worthy of affection. I was terrorized by the nagging thought that they would eventually notice – perhaps at the suggestion of someone at school – that I wasn't worthy of the deeply loving support they provided. I woke up in fear every morning, almost crippled with anxiety. My heart felt like it might beat out of my chest, and my stomach was clenched in knots. Would that be the day that my family learned about the outcast living among them? And, what would happen if they did? Would they be as outwardly disdainful as the kids at school? Would they send me to a boarding academy? I needed to be able to count on their life raft, because my ship didn't feel like it was built strong enough to weather storms.

So, as the boys walked into the school auditorium, I averted my eyes as not to look directly at my father. I sat stoically in my seat, looking down at my lap like my life depended on it. I had to make certain that my dad didn't witness any interactions that would give me away.

"Good morning, everyone," my father began. "I am Dr. Sabarra, but I am probably better known as Josh's dad."

Fuckity fuck fuck. In case everyone hadn't put two and two together, my father finished the equation for them. The kid who they all made fun of had a father who was a "dick doc," a "pecker checker" and an "erector inspector."

The boy to my right was laughing so hard he could barely speak. "Your dad looks at dicks all day, too. I guess it runs in the family."

My face turned an abnormally bright red, and it felt like my skin was on fire. It was almost as if acid had been sprayed across my cheeks, my neck and my shoulders, burning me to the bone. For the next 45 minutes, my father proceeded to explain why nocturnal emissions occur, the reason we wake up with erections and how those erections can be slip-covered to avoid various diseases and unwanted babies.

While it was mortifying to learn about puberty, private parts and porking from my father – not to mention in front of my schoolmates – it couldn't have come at a better time. Especially since Sandra introduced me to my first pornographic film the weekend before.

"You can't tell your parents," Sandra whispered into the phone, "but I rented a dirty movie called *Caligula.* Do you wanna see it?"

"Where can we watch it without getting caught?" I asked.

"My parents are at church this morning. Come on over. If we see them pull into the driveway, we will finish watching it tomorrow." She still lived at home.

I ran next door and sat on the couch next to Sandra. For two and a half hours, I watched Malcolm McDowell and Helen Mirren in the most boring historical drama ever to hit the screen. Until, of course, the sex orgy towards the end of the movie.

"Oh my God, that's hot," Sandra said, as we watched erect penises slide in and out of vaginas until they erupted.

"What's that?" I asked, pointing to a creamy ejaculation.

"You mean the cum shot?" Sandra asked rhetorically.

"The white stuff, coming out of that penis. What is that?"

"That's cum," she answered. "You haven't jerked off yet? That's what sex is all about: the cum shot, baby!" Sandra's appreciation for a good, sticky climax coincided perfectly with my father's presentation at school. The gooey semen I saw in *Caligula* applied to most of the topics my father covered, and I couldn't wait to experiment at home.

Two nights after my dad's talk at school, I locked the door to the bathroom that I shared with my sister. Sitting backwards on the cushioned toilet seat, with my legs spread facing the underside of the seat cover, I began to rub the head of my penis against my right thigh. As my erection became more and more rigid, I could feel a build-up unlike anything I had ever experienced. With my right palm firmly on my shaft, I increased the speed of the back-and-forth motion until I thought my body might explode. I was scared for a moment, not knowing what it would end up feeling like, but the pleasure and intensity reached a boiling point before I could give it any more thought. I shot my first load of semen all over my leg and the toilet seat.

After catching my breath for a couple of moments, I used tissues to wipe up the dripping jizz before a panic light began flashing in my head: what if I accidentally left evidence behind? What if I didn't clean well enough, and my sister got pregnant from sitting on the toilet seat? Because of my father's speech, I now understood exactly where babies came from – and, while Florida is geographically the South, it's not the part of the South that looks favorably upon inbreeding. My OCD reared its ugly head, signaling the beginning of a masturbation cleaning ritual that I would continue for 10 years. (By the way, just the idea that the OCD acronym is not in alphabetical order always gave me anxiety. CDO?)

I never subscribed to the idea that one could have too much of a good thing, so my twice-a-day jerk-off habit required a large supply of rubbing alcohol. Each time I came, I immediately wiped the semen from my body, flushed the waste and reached under the bathroom sink for a paper towel. After soaking the Bounty with 70% Isopropyl, I wiped the toilet and its cover four times, hitting every open surface. I would then clean myself in the bathtub, after which I would repeat the four rounds of alcohol disinfection, making sure that there was not one drop of bodily fluid in the basin. There was no rationale to the "four wipe-down" process – but it was an even number and seemed to leave all of the bathroom components sparklingly sterile. It didn't dawn on me that my mother might question the excessive use of paper goods and alcohol, but I think she wrote it off to my signature need for order and cleanliness.

Once the floodgates opened, as it were, I had to find masturbatory inspiration. All I could get my hands on were underwear catalogs that came through the mail, and I grabbed them the minute they fell through the slot in our front door. If I could tell the model's religion by looking at the outline in the bulge of his briefs, he became my passion for that month. It wasn't until a few years later that a friend gave me some *Penthouse* magazines, which, at the time, had male/female pictorials. I was able to fold the pages in such a way that I could see the man's penis without the interference of any offending labia. It looked like "organ origami," but it kept me cumming for a few good years.

One related concern – which also sprouted from the health talk at school – was the wet dream. I worried every night before bed that I might ejaculate while I was sleeping, revealing something about my sexuality to my mother. After all, she did the laundry, so anything left in my shorts would cross her desk, so to speak. Likewise, I invented what I called a "dream catcher:" toilet paper folded into a rectangular pad that I placed at the front of my underwear before hitting my pillow. This way, if I had any dreams about the male models in my catalogs, the resulting ejaculation would land in the disposable toilet tissue as opposed to my cotton briefs. Unfortunately, on many occasions, the paper would twist during the night, leaving me with the wrong kind of blue balls by morning.

I knew that my sexual interest in men was not the norm, but I didn't realize that the frequency of masturbation was entirely unrelated to my homosexuality. In the natural, youthful narcissism of adolescence, I believed that I was the only person so deviant in my passion for sexual release and that my mother would somehow be able to "discover me" by finding cum on my sheets or in my underpants. The semen wouldn't indicate that I was a healthy teen whose body was functioning as it should have been; rather, it would have revealed a dark secret about my true desires. The pressure to hide any evidence that threw a spotlight onto my real self became so great that I continued to create obsessive rituals of self-protection. For example, folding the toilet paper I placed inside my underwear each night a certain number of times (eight, for the record) provided a tiny amount of ordered comfort.

By this point, my parents had stopped pushing me into after school activities and sports programs. My sister's high school career was in full swing, and being the valedictorian, a cheerleader, the student council president, a member of the homecoming court and the prom queen was enough to keep all of us busy without the added complications of anything that might interest me. Masturbation became my favorite pastime, and playing with my penis gave me the good feelings that I wasn't getting from friendships with other kids or the periods between snacks. Essentially, I was on my own without much human attention until my relationship with Sylvia took a surprising twist.

"Are you finding the map reading a little easier, Josh?" Sylvia asked as I was leaving her classroom on a Friday. It was the first time in the four weeks she had been at Roosevelt that she addressed me directly.

"I think so," I answered tentatively, surprised at her pleasant tone. Until that point, she had seemed unapproachable.

"Is there anything I can do to help? You are doing very well in my English class; it's just that one part of the geography curriculum that seems to be tricky for you."

"I suppose I need to spend more time looking at different kinds of maps," I said. "My dad is helping me at home."

"Why don't you bring your lunch to my room on Monday, and I can show you some tricks. Does that work?"

By Monday at noon, Sylvia and I were sitting at a table in the back of her classroom. She reviewed various maps with me, making me more confident in my ability to master the skill and more comfortable with her personality and style.

"You see," she said, "you had it in you all along. You're better at this than you thought." With those words, I started to see the softness in her circular face. "What do you like to do in your free time, Josh?"

"I love to go to the movies and to the theater," I said enthusiastically. My parents had taken me to Broadway shows every time we visited New York, my first experience being Jim Dale and Glenn Close in *Barnum* when I was five.

"I love the theater, too," she said. "Have you seen anything good lately?"

"Well, I saw a tour of *Les Misérables* during our last vacation in California," I answered, "and it's coming to the Broward Center for the Performing Arts in a month. My grandmother hasn't seen it, so we are planning to go together."

"That sounds terrific. I have always heard great things about that show, but I haven't had the opportunity to see it. Maybe I should look into taking myself to the theater." There was a loneliness in the way she responded, a defeated affect that pulled at my heart. She had just moved to Royal Palm Beach from Pennsylvania, and I got the feeling that she didn't have any local friends. I hesitated for a moment before saying anything.

"You know, you could always come with my grandmother and I," I offered sincerely.

"You mean with 'my grandmother and me,'" she said, correcting my grammar. She was a stickler for the use of perfect speech and, in a short while, turned me into an expert. Within months, I was able to use every punctuation mark correctly and provide the grammar rule that governed its use. Not many 12 year-olds could tell you how to appropriately punctuate two independent clauses joined by a coordinator.

"That would be lovely, actually," she said. "Do you want to talk to your parents and grandmother about it first?"

"I will talk to them tonight, but I know they won't mind at all." (See what I did there? The comma before the "but?")

"I am really happy you asked me," she said. She was so genuine in her reply; I sensed that I had lifted her spirits. The vacancy I saw in her piercing stare only moments before had transformed into a light sparkle that felt positive and hopeful.

Our relationship shifted in that moment. No longer were we on opposing sides of the classroom. We sat next to each other for the first time, and she became tangibly human as opposed to the off-putting authoritarian I met in August of 1987. Side by side, an inextricable bond was forged between two lonely people who needed each other's love.

"I was thinking," Sylvia continued, "Roosevelt doesn't have a student newspaper. How would you feel about working on that with me?"

"You mean writing articles?" I asked.

"Yes, and designing the layout. More like an editor's job, but we would do it together."

I was thrilled by the idea of having a project, let alone an endeavor that gave me something to focus on beyond jerking off at home. We began to work on the first issue the following week, writing small pieces about the various extracurricular clubs and students who were involved in interesting activities outside of the classroom. I spent every lunch hour in the guest chair next to Sylvia's desk, where we would eat our sandwiches and talk about school and our families.

"Why did you move to Florida," I asked one afternoon as we were typesetting copy for *The Roosevelt Reporter*.

"It was time for a change," she said. "It gets cold in Pennsylvania in the winter."

"But what about your kids?" I continued.

"My kids are grown; they're in their 20s. They don't need me the way they used to. Plus, I get the summers off, so I can fly back to see them." She never mentioned a Mr. Bastaja, and, for some reason, I got the idea that he was a subject she didn't want to cover.

"What about you, Mr. Sabarra?" she asked. "What's your story? Who are your friends here at Roosevelt?"

"I'm not really close with the other students," I said. "We don't have the same interests." That was how I framed *their* lack of interest in *me*. I realized that I didn't want Sylvia to know that other kids made fun of me relentlessly, the same way that I wanted to keep that information from my parents.

"What do you mean by that?" she persisted.

"I am into entertainment, and they're more into sports and the outdoors," I answered.

"I see," she said. "But surely there are some other students who like the same things you do." She was hitting a nerve, and my fidgeting revealed a great discomfort with the topic.

"It's nothing to worry about," she said. "I like entertainment, too, and you have me." We smiled, and she leaned in to give me a hug. There was an understanding in that embrace; a warmth that made me feel comforted. Sylvia knew that deeper rivers ran beneath the surface of my skin, and, while her arms were around me, I got a sense that she was navigating some rough waters herself.

That Saturday we went to the theater felt particularly special. I dressed in my nicest shirt and slacks and straightened the house in preparation for Sylvia's arrival. In my eyes, it was as if a celebrity was visiting our home. I was always fascinated to see teachers outside of the school environment; I somehow couldn't process the fact that they were real people who led real lives beyond the school walls.

I was standing at the front door as Sylvia pulled into our driveway. She and my parents chatted for a few minutes about how she was adjusting to life in South Florida and how making new friends in a new city was difficult. By the time we were ready to leave, my mom and dad had asked her to attend a family barbeque the following weekend. There was a discernable upturn in her demeanor upon accepting the invitation, a lightness that added a bounce to her walk back to the car.

We jumped into Sylvia's white sedan and made our way to Delray Beach to pick up my dad's mother. Over tuna melts and fries at the local deli, Grandma Elaine regaled Sylvia with stories about my childhood. It was a good thing that the sandwiches were big enough to keep our mouths busy, because my grandmother didn't stop talking long enough for Sylvia or me to get a word out. Thankfully, the rise of the theater curtain silenced the incessant chatter.

Les Misérables was as moving and emotional as I remembered. I was so taken with the musical melodrama the first time I saw it in Los Angeles, and the South Florida production was equally as affecting. As tears began to roll down my cheek during the finale, Sylvia put her right arm around my neck, rubbing my shoulder for comfort. Her eyes were watering, too, and, without words, we knew we were there for each other.

The school year rolled on, and Sylvia and I became closer and closer. My parents began to include her in more gatherings at our house, and she was an honorary family member by the time spring melted into summer. I felt an emptiness when she left to see her children for a couple of months, but I filled my time watching movies with Sandra and taking day trips with Carol. At night, I would read the weekly letters that Sylvia sent in her absence, before there were cellular phones and e-mail.

When she returned from Pennsylvania in July of 1988, we were inseparable. We had missed each other terribly and made up for lost time over meals and shopping and movies. The school year got off to a smooth start without the growing pains that I had experienced at the beginning of Sylvia's tenure; we had a short-hand now and knew when to relate on a student/teacher level and when to interact as close friends. Although, we did cross into a little gray area with a dirty little secret I had discovered about one of the school administrators.

A tough-talking dean – who was known as much for being strict as she was for her stylish wardrobe and high-rise heels – had a link to the adult entertainment industry. Her sister was a *Playboy* centerfold who had transitioned into hardcore porn films when her modeling career stalled. One benefit to my morning announcement gig was that I was able to overhear the conversations of many of the faculty members; apparently, the sister had a fan base among a small group of male teachers. I was fascinated by the idea that I knew someone who was connected to the sex industry, even before I understood what it was all about. In addition, it took the bite away from the dean's hard-as-nails veneer.

"Can you believe that?" I said to Sylvia the day I learned about the dean's sister.

"That's wild," Sylvia responded, her eyes darting around the room uncomfortably.

"It's more than wild," I said. "It's scandalous. It should be the front page of *The Roosevelt Reporter*." My passion for gossip and tawdry tell-alls was taking root.

"I don't think it's something we want to talk about, and we certainly don't want other kids to know," Sylvia warned. "Let's just park the conversation here." Although she was mature and professional in how she dealt with the information, it tickled her that it was so fascinating to me; I could tell. When we were not in school, she would allow me to belabor the subject and laugh about it, but she kept her distance from it otherwise.

In January of 1989, just around the time of my birthday, I performed an anniversary service of my Bar Mitzvah at Temple Beth Midrash. My parents invited mostly family and hosted a small luncheon following. Naturally, Sylvia was in attendance.

"That's quite an achievement," she said, handing me a beautifully wrapped box. "I want you to wear this in good health." I opened the gift in front of her, holding the light yellow sweater against my skin.

"I want you to think of me whenever you wear it," she said. "You promise?"

"Of course," I replied. "But I see you just about everyday, so I always think of you." She gave me a half smile and a hug, but there was a distance in her touch. A cool breeze rushed past us, blowing her hair and pleated blue skirt to the left as she walked through the parking lot to her car.

"I'll see you at school on Monday, OK?" The color of her outfit and the wind gave her an ethereal glide, an other-worldliness that I took note of as she positioned herself in the driver's seat. She closed the car door without taking her eyes off of me and pulled out of the restaurant parking lot as the lunch party disbanded.

The following week was uneventful, characterized only by the usual homework, studying and exams; the days passed until it was finally Friday. I whizzed by Sylvia's room early in the day to say a quick hello and found her standing at her classroom door. The teachers were required to patrol the hallways between class periods as a security measure. When I looked into her eyes, which seemed glassy and distracted, I zoned in on the contact lenses that appeared to be floating in the pools between her eyelids.

"I am not feeling well," she told me, "and I probably won't be here for our class period today."

"Is there anything you need?" I asked

"No," she said. "I just need to rest at home." Her eyes teared a little bit more, and she reached her hands out. I took them into mine, making note of the perfectly shaped nails that had been expertly pressed onto her own.

"Have a good day, and behave yourself, OK?" she said, tightening her grip on my fingers. I was about to be late for my next class and let go of her hands, allowing them to fall to her sides like lifeless stems that had been burned from a flower by the sun.

"I'll call you tomorrow," I yelled back, thinking that we would have our usual weekend chat. She nodded and wiped her wet eyes.

I called Sylvia's home on Saturday, and I got no answer. Sunday, the same thing. When I arrived at school on Monday morning, I reported to the front office, as usual, to begin reading the day's announcements. I ran to the secretary's desk to ask if Sylvia had checked in.

"Not yet," she told me, "But she'll be here shortly." There wasn't a worry in her voice, and life at Roosevelt appeared to be business as usual.

I went about my day until it came time to attend Sylvia's classes. When I got to her room, a substitute teacher was standing at the podium. He announced that Sylvia was home sick and that the next two hours would serve as a study period. I had barely removed my textbooks from my JanSport backpack when the school secretary walked into the room.

"Can I borrow Josh for a few minutes?" she said to the substitute, who couldn't have cared less what was happening.

She escorted me down to the principal's office, making small talk about her weekend as we passed through the halls. As she pushed open the door to the general conference room, I saw my parents sitting around a table with all of the school administrators. I had no idea what was happening.

I sat down just as my father started to speak, his voice cracking.

"Sylvia," he said. "She passed away. Honey, her heart gave out, and she just couldn't make it."

"What?" I asked, laughing in disbelief. "What did you say?"

"Sylvia. She's no longer with us." My father's eyes were swollen and red; he tried his best to hold it together but was torn apart by the shocking news that he himself had heard only 30 minutes before.

It was as though my body was sitting in the room, but I was looking down at myself from the ceiling. My mother started to talk, the principal followed and then another administrator jumped in. I couldn't hear anything but echo-like sounds as moments of my final interaction with Sylvia flashed through my head like a strobe. My silence collapsed into heaving tears as I tried to make sense of everything. Sylvia's watery eyes and tone of voice suggested that she knew she was saying goodbye. Her hands in mine would be the last time we would touch, and "behave yourself," were the words I would carry in my heart for the rest of my life.

I stayed in bed for days, trying to balance myself through wide emotional swings. At moments, I became furious with Sylvia. How could she be gone? She knew I had no one else but my family and that I needed her support. Then, guilt for feeling angry would burn through my body like deadly vapors followed by plunges into sullen loneliness and despair. My parents came into my room to talk to me, and I would stare into the ceiling, listening but not speaking.

When I finally returned to school after being self-sequestered in my bedroom, I was rattled to hear constant chatter among the student body. Many of the kids knew about my special relationship with Sylvia and were even more tentative about addressing me than usual.

"Are you OK?" one girl asked. "I heard Mrs. Bastaja killed

herself." The room started spinning. The color drained from my face, and my ears began to ring. I sat down on the nearest concrete bench to prevent a fall.

"Didn't you know?" she continued. "I thought everyone knew. Your mom and dad didn't tell you?" No. No, they didn't.

I confronted my parents that night, and they admitted that the "heart" story had been concocted to protect me. Apparently, Sylvia had slit her wrists in the bathtub and drank a poisonous liquid to ensure that she wouldn't survive. To make matters worse, her suicide had been planned: her grade book was up to date and displayed neatly on her kitchen table; her keys were lined up on the counter; and a note was left at the scene. I was never able to read it nor did I have access to anyone who knew its contents, but my 14 year-old brain kept thinking over the words that may have been in that final letter.

The note that I imagined lived in my head for weeks. I could see Sylvia's artful penmanship perfectly lined on a piece of her signature stationery, explaining why she befriended me when she had planned to leave me behind all along; she owed me an answer. I must have been in the forefront of her mind, regardless of the insurmountable darkness that brought a razor to her arms. In the aching red of the bath water, discolored by hopelessness and desperation, she likely regretted her choice, I thought. It was probably just a moment too late for her to realize what she'd done to me and reverse course.

Mired in my self-centered youth, I believed that I should have been her most pressing consideration, and I struggled with the idea that perhaps I wasn't worth living for. The other kids had disregarded me, and, ultimately, so did Sylvia.

Maybe my peers had been right all along. It was hard at that age to understand that Sylvia had deeper problems and was driven to her final act by demons that didn't even know I existed. In those days, the idea of professional psychological support was not conversational; the school provided nothing but a hapless guidance counselor, and my parents seemed to feel that their own words of support were sufficient.

The only things I really knew were that my best friend, Sylvia, was gone, and that the other adults in my life who were closest to me were not laying all of the cards on the table. I began to expect that people would disappoint me. I started to develop a "guilty until proven innocent" perspective and was particularly angered when people withheld the truth in attempt to not upset me. In my opinion, dishonesty was always worse than the truth. A lie of omission was no better than a lie of commission, and this tragedy, both harrowing and life-altering, instilled in me a need to be honorable and upfront with everyone in my life from that day forward.

I learned bits and pieces of backstory by chatting with the handful of teachers who had been friendly with Sylvia at school: she had two children, both of whom still lived in her hometown in Pennsylvania. Supposedly, their father had been horribly abusive to Sylvia, at one time throwing her down a steep flight of stairs. The odd scar on her left arm was from a wound that appeared when she came back to consciousness. She later met a married man with whom she began an affair, but, knowing that it didn't feel right, moved to Florida to escape her past. The gentleman followed her to Royal Palm Beach, throwing her new life into the very same tailspin she was running from. This woman, whom I idolized and taught me everything I know about grammar and writing, was fragile; she had real adult problems that she never shared with me, maintaining the illusion of strength. It dawned on me that it was easier for her to keep up appearances around a youngster than it might have been with adult friends.

Years after Sylvia's death, I located her son and reached out to him by phone. I wanted him to know what an impact his mother had on my life, and I was hopeful that he might be willing to talk about who his mother was before I met her. He never replied to my messages, leaving unfinished business that still haunts me.

Underneath it all, she was a flawed person who drew joy from her pure friendship with a 14 year-old boy who would never forget her. In two short years, she touched my life forever, and there isn't a week that goes by that I don't think of Sylvia. I know she would find pleasure in my personal and professional evolution. And, every now and then, I pull the pastel sweater from a bottom drawer in my closet – the yellow, braided pullover that she gave me as a gift shortly before she passed away. I still can't let go of the last tangible piece I have of our friendship. Time faded the rose scent that lingered on the dyed cotton, and it ravaged the pale color that looked so nice against my milky white skin. But, in a turn of kindness, it left sharply detailed memories woven into its enduring fabric. The sweater will never be able to explain the pain that drove Sylvia to suicide, but its calming softness reminds me – nearly three decades later – to love wildly with all of my heart. The story that runs through the body of that knitted material, at once beautiful and heartbreaking, has kept me alive when black shadows have threatened to eclipse my light. Sylvia's gift, as it turned out, wasn't a sweater at all.

"Behave yourself, OK?" floods from my chest into my

ears sometimes, often during moments in which I would give anything to have Sylvia by my side. At those times, I can feel the warmth of her hands in my palms, and I imagine the wisdom she'd offer if she were in the room. Sylvia sent me into adulthood with a deep, almost indescribable pain that left a piece of my soul eternally hollow. But, at the same time, she filled my heart and my mind with a hard lesson in love that I would trade only to have her back.

TAKE A LOAD OFF

"Do you really need that?"

The jumbo slice of red velvet cake was decadently moist, and its whipped cream cheese icing? To die for.

"That's your problem," my father continued. "You don't need the cake. Order sorbet instead."

Scientifically speaking, he wasn't wrong about the nutritional value of frozen fruit in comparison to a baked dessert; the cake at our neighborhood restaurant was highly caloric and contained enough fat to stop a fast-beating heart. What he couldn't understand was my unique relationship with food. I did, in fact, *need* it. I was its prisoner.

I felt loved by my parents and my sister, but, in my mind, that was their emotional responsibility – after all, I belonged to them. Food had no obligation to me and yet was unconditional in making me feel whole and satisfied, even if for only the fleeting moments that it lingered on my tongue. And, it let me have control; I could decide how much of it I wanted and when. I had the power, and I made the rules – the food was happy to oblige. Unlike my classmates who were relentless in teasing me about my sexuality, pecan pie was accepting. It comforted me after a verbal battering, filling me up and hugging me with its buttery crust. And cheesecake? Well, there was nothing more dependable and empathic than a thick slice of creamy chocolate swirl. It understood what I was going through and assuaged my sadness and anxiety with its intoxicating richness.

Sweets weren't the only foods that rallied around me. Their savory friends – pizza and Chicken McNuggets made up the "inner circle" – never let me down. Not surprisingly, French fries were particularly helpful; the salty goodness could melt away a couple of hours of pain. Nothing made the word "faggot" sound less lacerating than a plate of golden potatoes fried to perfection. Whether they were curly, shoestring or of the steak variety, their crispness in my mouth replaced, for a few minutes, the parts of my self-esteem that had been chipped away by cruel epithets.

Food was my solace, my support system outside of my immediate family. It didn't care if I wanted to fuck a man, a woman or a moose. It simply wanted me to be happy – and it worked overtime.

"I *do* need the cake," I told my dad, "it's December; the sorbet is too icy."

"Have the cake. But, remember it next time you don't want to tuck your shirt into your pants because of your stomach. Or, when you buy an extra-large t-shirt to cover your chest."

The food had been so good to me; how could I turn my back? And, where would I find those moments of peace when the stomach that had been ripped out by my school "friends" felt empty to begin with? My soul was trying to survive at the expense of my body.

Because the sensory satisfaction that came from putting desirable foods into my mouth lasted merely moments, I began to increase my intake. The frequency of my snacking was directly proportional to the frequency of positive feelings. And, it wasn't as though carrots and celery sticks masked the internal hurt; only the sweets and salts were up to the job. The more I ate, the more I numbed myself to the shame.

As my small, 5'8" frame ballooned to a "startlingly" chunky 175 pounds, my distended belly eclipsed my feet; my chest gave up its natural contour in favor of protruding breasts. My legs were never anything but skinny, making me look like, I thought, a Cambodian refugee or one of the children Sally Struthers collected money for through her toll-free number. Eventually, I was living in a grotesquely misshapen body that became an outward representation of the unlovable person who was locked inside. Or, at least that's the person I saw in my reflection.

I was not obese. Photographs taken through the years showed a mildly overweight teenager who could have benefitted from some physical activity. My mirror harshly yelled another story. It told me that my body was as abnormal as the feelings that were stirring inside it, the sexual feelings that bubbled below my skin. Those feelings that other kids picked up on but that still made little sense to me. Kids usually made fun of physical differences – "fatty boombalatty," "fire scalp," "midget;" no one could escape if he was heavy, a redhead or short in height – but they were somehow able to see through my body to the emotions under the surface.

I attempted to harden myself by not looking past my exterior. Instead, I obsessed over my weight. I looked into every window or piece of glass that I walked past, staring closely at the unattractive ball of fat that was gazing back at me. In my mind, I had become such a freakishly fat person that even my father was unforgiving in his comments about my food intake.

The truth is that I was a little pudgy, not dissimilar to just about every adolescent going through hormonal changes and growth spurts. But, my classmates' unwavering contempt for my romantic inclinations continued to fuel poor eating habits that soothed my insides. My father would then harangue me non-stop about my food choices and quantities, leaving me nowhere to hide. I was figuratively beaten down at school and then punched some more at home for trying to comfort myself. I was a hostage to food. I needed it to feed myself emotionally even though its upside had a price. It offered a temporary salve for the internal hurt but left me with a body that called even more attention – both inside and outside of home – to my differences.

There was nowhere to turn. I couldn't tell my parents why I was eating so erratically; in fact, I wasn't sure myself at the time. I didn't have a close school friend to confide in, and there wasn't an objective adult who recognized the problem. Everything I felt inside was trapped beneath a bulging exterior that was as unattractive – or so I was told – as the human heart that was aching to be different, to be better.

I didn't feel deserving of positive attention from those around me. After all, my body type was far from appealing

– I certainly couldn't up the beauty quotient in a group. My peers outwardly recognized that I was beneath their respect because of my homosexuality, and over the years, I had come to believe them. Since my summers at day camp, my worthlessness had been drilled into my head; my caustic sense of humor masked a self-esteem and body image so low that I couldn't find a way to climb out from underneath them.

There was seemingly no end to the cycle; I was stuck inside a body that disgusted me and everyone else who saw it, I thought. I was already scorned because of my feminine interests and tendencies, and my flabby abdomen – replete with "man boobs" and cleavage – ensnared me in a spiral of self-hate. My excess weight made me even less likeable, and my resources for change were limited. I could do little but suffer in silence, as not to beg questions or concern from my parents.

At one point, I attempted to grab the reigns by closely monitoring my food intake, hopeful that some willpower would give way to a slimmer appearance. The anxiety, though, was more immediately quelled by satisfying foods than by the possibility of an incrementally better body. I fell under the hopelessness of my situation. I simply wasn't born with the strength of those who pull themselves up by their bootstraps – the fearless people who, at all costs, morphed into beloved personalities.

Every night, I dreamed about rubbing shoulders with the exciting luminaries I read about in the entertainment tabloids. They were smart, talented and good-looking people who understood my value as a person. They appreciated and embraced my differences, but only during my sleep. Inevitably, the sun would rise, and my alarm would go off at 6:00AM. I woke up, disappointed to be back in my own skin.

After a bath – during which I'd sometimes doze for a few extra minutes, hoping to revisit that night's Hollywood premiere party – came the challenge of choosing which shirt was large enough to conceal my unattractive body. I had also taken to wearing tight undershirts in an effort to further flatten my chest. No matter the Florida heat, the physical discomfort was more palatable than the true shape that was beneath my clothes.

Movies and Hollywood magazines became my escape. I ran to the cinema any chance I could get, losing myself in the excitement of people whose lives were extraordinary and seemingly without troubles. I wanted to be one of them, and I dreamed about it for the entire two-hour running time of every film. I was an odd-shaped outsider who didn't look like any of the glamorous stars I read about in *People* and *Entertainment Weekly*, but that didn't seem to matter in the dark.

Cher and Dolly – not surprisingly, two of my celebrity idols – had both defied the odds. They overcame hardships and their nontraditional physical attributes, transforming themselves into glittering representations of Hollywood legend. Like many gay boys and men, I found strength in their perseverance and the idea that reinvention was a path to being adored. I longed to be accepted, which didn't seem likely in light of my closeted sexual interests and now chunky shape.

During a summer vacation, my family drove up the east coast of the country. We stopped at an amusement park called Carowinds, which sat on the border of the two Carolinas. I loved the idea of riding a roller coaster in one state and then walking over to a funhouse in another. What I didn't love was standing in the baking sun in a shirt that was three sizes too big. I was attempting to hide my physique in excess fabric, which my mother noticed as she saw me hunched in a shaded corner.

"If you're really self-conscious about your chest, we can look into having something done about it. You could run with a trainer or even have surgery, if need be," my mom said.

For a moment, I was devastated; even my mother thought I needed surgical intervention. Plus, I was never into the idea of running unless, of course, I was being chased or an ice cream truck was going too fast for me to catch up.

"Are you serious?" I yelled. "You think I am fat enough to have surgery?"

"I just know that your shape bothers you," she said. "I want you to feel good."

As quickly as the suggestion threw my head into a spin, I became intrigued by the novelty of going to sleep looking one way and waking up looking another. Maybe this was the answer to everything. I would be heading to college in a few short months, and, if I acted quickly, no one at the university would ever know what the old Josh looked like. I was deathly afraid of needles and medical attention, but I disliked my body so much that the self-loathing eclipsed my trepidation. I could quite literally look like a different person before meeting a new group of peers – and plastic surgery had a glamorous patina that worked for Cher and Dolly, after all. Perhaps people would like me because I was similarly "cutting edge."

The day after we returned from our vacation, we made an appointment with a family friend who was, conveniently, a cosmetic surgeon.

"What is most concerning to you about your appearance?" he asked, without judgment.

"My chest," I replied. "I have to wear big shirts or layered clothes to cover my boobs."

It had been nearly a decade since I had removed my shirt in front of another person, but I knew that this was my chance to fix the part of my body that had been plaguing me. I slowly pulled one arm out of a sleeve, holding the body of the shirt in front of me while I removed the other. The doctor had to pry the size XL tee from my fingers. He asked me to remove my pants, as well, leaving me in front of him wearing nothing but cotton tube socks and underwear. I didn't know where to put my hands. My instinct was to cup both sides of my chest with my palms or wrap my arms around myself to cover as much of my midsection as possible. The idea of standing nearly naked in front of someone with the express purpose of pinpointing unattractive areas of my body was unnerving.

He lifted a black Sharpie marker from his coat pocket and removed the cap. "I need you to stand still and straight," he said calmly. I was fidgeting. With quick strokes, he began drawing a series of straight and dotted lines across my chest and under my arms. His black marks pointed to everything that I hated about my body.

"I am going to make small incisions at the bottom portion of your nipples," he explained, "essentially lifting them up so I can remove tissue and fat from underneath. The scars won't be visible because they'll heal along the underside of the nipples. No one will even know you had anything done."

"So, will I be able to wear any type of shirt I want after the surgery?" I asked.

"That's the idea," he said. "But you'll still need to work on it by yourself a little bit. Nothing can replace diet and exercise."

He took photographs of his markings and made copious notes inside my patient chart. When he put his pen down, I bent over to reach for my shirt and jeans.

"You know," he said, "let me take a look at something."

I stood up again while the doctor leaned to the left side of my stomach and then the right. With his thumb and index fingers, he gently squeezed my love handles.

"As long as you're under anesthesia," he said, "how would you feel if we removed some of the fat from your sides?"

"Are they that bad?" I asked.

"I've seen worse," he admitted, "but I'd go ahead and do them."

As he continued to grab the fat, I tried to focus on objects at the far corners of the examining room – a jar of marking pens, a bio-hazardous waste bin, a glass container full of cotton pads. My eyes darted around wildly, trying to settle on an image that would take my head out of the room. Here I thought I had a clear idea of what was wrong with my body – but the doctor had found even more. I wanted to disappear, or, at the very least, fall through the floor. There was so much ink on my torso that I almost couldn't see the flesh tones underneath. I was a flabby mess, and even the surgeon thought I had stopped short of hating my appearance enough.

My surgery date was set for two weeks after the initial consultation. On one hand, I was excited about shedding the parts of my skin that made me self-conscious, and, on the other, I was a nervous wreck about the mechanics of the procedure. The anesthesia, the intubation, the blood, the recovery

– and, of course, my underwear. It may have been more than a decade since the end of my Camp Shalom experience, but I hadn't moved beyond the uneasiness of removing my clothes in front of anyone. Knowing that a surgeon, two nurses and a cute anesthesiologist could be staring at my penis was a top concern. Also, I had never been under general anesthesia before and had no way of understanding where exactly my level of consciousness and bodily function would fall. What if I got aroused during the procedure when the doctor or a male nurse touched me? Surely, they would suspect that I was gay.

I told my parents that I didn't like the idea of laying completely naked on the operating table, a concern that they chalked up to my signature modesty.

"Josh, they're used to seeing people naked. They'll be busy performing a surgical procedure, not looking below your waistline," my mother assured me.

"My love handles are *at* my waistline," I reasoned. "They'll definitely be focused on my groin."

"So, do you want to cancel? Don't complain about your chest if you decide to back out." In her own way, Mom knew how to win a battle.

"Fine, but I want my underwear on the entire time. If they get ripped or dirty, we can just throw them away," I said.

"Dad will let them know," she assured.

My dad had taken the day off from his own practice to be at the plastic surgeon's office with me on the day of the operation. I heard him talk to the doctor and the nurses about my underwear, relaying my sensitivity about being undressed in front of other people. To lighten the mood, he delivered the message in a spirited tone that actually made me feel even more insecure.

"Josh would feel better if his underwear stayed on during the surgery," my father announced, as a nurse was placing the IV needle into my hand and starting the drip. "No one gets a peek at the 'magic schmeckle!'"

If the IV flow hadn't started almost simultaneously, I probably would have passed out on my own. "Magic schmeckle?" Was he serious? My biggest fear was that my schmeckle would perform some levitation tricks while I was knocked out, and my father had just called everyone's attention to it. Fortunately, my next memory was waking up to the hazy lights of the operating theater.

My right eye strained to open, as though large magnets were attached to the upper and lower lids. The weight and the force felt oppressive, but I mustered every ounce of my reserved energy to peek through. Rather than blindingly bright, the industrial light bulbs hanging from the ceiling in a circular steel fixture were a gauzy, dim yellow outlined with a cotton-white halo. As the left eye opened with similar difficulty, I was able to make out a couple of human figures, scurrying around the periphery. My ears began to tune up in concert with the murky visuals, processing voices that sounded like a needle moving through warped vinyl.

I turned my head slowly from side to side, trying to get my bearings. My upper torso was swaddled in sterile fabric, and, alternately, the lower half felt chilled and exposed. Sore and scratchy, my throat was raw as I attempted to wet my mouth with saliva that tasted like melted plastic and tar. My right hand, taped and stiff with an intravenous needle, clung to the steel table beneath my back while my left arm was stationed at my side.

The voices became gradually sharper and louder, but, in

my blurry haze, I was too disoriented to identify the sounds and faces. Time had stopped for an undeterminable stretch, and I was trying to put all of the pieces together in my mind. As a current of cool air ran up my legs, I was jarred into the moment.

"Where's my underwear?!" were the words that, I thought, were forcefully coming from my lips. What seemed like a scream was a whimpering, inaudible inquiry.

"Josh. Josh. Josh." I heard a female voice repeat my name over and over.

"My underwear," I strained. "Where's my underwear?"

"Josh, we're done," the woman repeated twice. "We're done."

"I am supposed to be wearing underwear." Despite my physical condition, I was fixated on a missing pair of white briefs.

"Josh," she said, "there was too much blood. We had to remove them and wrap you in a towel."

With that, a voice I recognized filtered through the room.

"You're fine, Josh. Everything is fine. I have a clean pair of underpants in the waiting room, and we'll get them on you as soon you wake up a little more." As always, my mother was prepared with a change of clothes that would make me comfortable – only right I thought, since she *was* the person to suggest this first procedure that would begin my addiction to plastic surgery.

The recovery was a bitch. Anesthesia often causes varying degrees of nausea, and I wasn't spared even a little bit. With a lined trash can next to my bed, I leaned over every twenty minutes, heaving with dry contractions. There was no food in my stomach, and my body was making sure of it – three times per hour. The discomfort was exacerbated by my fiery throat; the breathing tube necessary for general anesthesia had rubbed the skin in my mouth to a burning wound. I was unable to relax because of the discomfort, and my entire body had become a battered looking black-and-blue. I lay in bed like a bandaged mummy, simmering in the almost unbearable pain. What had I done to myself?

Every joint felt as though it hadn't been moved in years, like all of my connective tissue had atrophied. Even areas of my body that were untouched by the surgical procedure were tender, and the slightest movements took marathon strength. I had no energy reserved and wasn't able to recharge with a night's rest. Always a stomach-sleeper, the liposuction on my chest required that I lay on my back around the clock. Unable to sleep in that position, I lay awake, conscious of every cut, stitch and bruise.

The bleary-eyed exhaustion from the anesthesia and the body trauma – not to mention two weeks of sleepless nights – seemed virtually impossible to get through.

I reasoned that I had gotten what I deserved; the extreme discomfort was the physical manifestation of my emotional unrest. This was the price to pay for being less than everyone else. As much as I could, I tried to think ahead to the end result: the death of a body I didn't like and the birth of a new person.

As days passed and dark bruising mellowed into a yellow discoloration, the results of the surgery started to become evident. My attitude shifted from "Why did I go through this by choice? I suppose I deserve it" to "Why didn't I do this sooner?" My tits had flattened into a somewhat contoured chest, and there was a little less love on my handles – nuanced changes that became an incentive to drop pounds by altering my diet on a regular basis. Glimmers of confidence began to emerge, in no small part because of the attention I received from the few friends I saw before heading to college.

"Josh, you look fantastic," one friend commented, over a dinner of fresh salads.

"Doesn't he?" her twin sister added. "He looks like a different person."

A different person? The three words I had been wanting to hear came at a very painful price. But, clearly, the cosmetic procedure was the answer.

"It's like you have been transformed," they agreed. "Amazing. Wish we could get some cottage cheese removed."

"Well, it worked for me," I replied. "Go for it!"

"Oh, I don't have the guts to go through with something like that," one said. "Plus, it's really expensive – for the rich and famous!"

The guts? Was there something strong inside me that I didn't realize was there? Perhaps there was a drive, a force that compelled me to prove the critics wrong. A more appealing body shape would certainly keep my father's jabs to a minimum, and the celebrity glamour of my plastic surgery just might make me seem more exciting to the new people I'd be meeting at college.

With the last of my compression bandages in the garbage, I went off to Syracuse University with fitted jeans and cotton-knit shirts that would never have flattered me pre-surgery. Instead of gaining the "Freshman Fifteen" – weight that new students are said to put on because of their unlimited meal plans and alcohol consumption – I lost nearly 35 pounds. I counted calories like I was in a hot game of "Deal-a-Meal" with Richard Simmons, strictly adhering to an eating regimen that would supplement the liposuction. By Thanksgiving, I had become dangerously thin.

"Look at your wrists!" my father scolded when I flew home to celebrate Turkey Day in Florida. "You have no fat on your body. Your body needs *some* fat."

In June, I was a pudgy, 175-pound eighteen year-old whom, we all agreed, needed surgical intervention, and in November, I was Karen Carpenter. I'd try to order sorbet, and, in an almost unreal turn of events, my dad tried to get me to have ice cream instead.

"You weren't happy when I was overweight," I said, "and now you're not happy that I am thin."

"Thin is one thing; emaciated is another. Can't you just settle on 'normal?'"

Normal. I wanted so much to be normal that I electively put myself through weeks of agony to achieve a slimmer body type. The students at college never saw the beefier Josh – and they seemed more wrapped up in their studies and new friends than in my sexuality. I didn't need to rely on food to cradle my emotional insecurity as much as I had during high school.

Being told I was too thin made me secretly secure; it meant that I had room to binge for a week or two – without getting "fat" – if I ever again needed to call on the embracing comfort of food for moral support. A twist in my brain told me that it was not OK to look undesirable because of excess pounds but that being gaunt – essentially, the problem in reverse – was a more socially acceptable issue. Nevertheless, I agreed to lighten up on the militant willpower I had applied to my eating habits, striding into the new year at a healthy

135 pounds. I jumped on a scale twice daily for the next five years, making sure that I stayed within 10 pounds of the "new normal."

After graduating from college, when I was already employed at my first job and had been maintaining a slim body shape, I read about an advanced liposuction technique that was better at sculpting specific regions. I had been happy with the work I'd had done previously, but I still wasn't brazen enough to remove my shirt at the beach or a pool. I wanted my chest to be perfect, and I knew that the first round hadn't quite done the job. My OCD and its related appetite for perfection fueled a conversation with my parents.

"Ultrasonic Assisted Liposuction (UAL)," I said to my mom on the phone one evening. "That's where results come from."

"You don't need more surgery," she said. "You got what you needed the first time."

"It's not perfect, though. I still won't wear some of the hipper clothes, and I will never take my shirt off in front of someone," I told her truthfully. Once I had healed from the first surgery and a couple of years had passed, I determined that my chest was 40% better than it had been prior to the procedure. I wanted it to be exactly 100%.

"You're dealing with the human body, Josh. Nothing is ever 100%," my mother warned me, sensing that my personality was starting to drive an obsession.

"Well, it can be much better. I want to find a different doctor, someone who does the UAL and is more aggressive about results."

Ultimately, my parents agreed to underwrite Phase 2, this time to be done by another colleague of my father's in

Palm Beach. I waited until November for the consultation, knowing that it would be much easier to have a revisionary operation in the winter months. Note to those considering lipo in the summer: the necessary bandages are a beast in the heat of July.

During the Thanksgiving break, I dragged my mother to an upscale mall in Boca Raton, and I purchased three shirts that I wanted to be able to wear following my next surgery. I brought them with me to the consultation, and I insisted that the doctor and his nurse allow me to try each one on, fashion show-style.

"Can you both see why I won't wear this?" I asked, pointing to my nipples. My boobs are too prominent." They looked at each other and back at me, nodding in agreement.

"How about this one?" The second piece was a black, form-fitting shirt from Saks Fifth Avenue that was so thin it was sheer. "I need to be able to wear this." In that particular case, it was the idea that I *could* wear the top and feel comfortable. It was an extreme choice in clothing that I would likely not be bold enough to make, but I wanted to be clear about my expectations.

"That shirt requires confidence more than it requires surgery," the doctor told me. "I can make your body fit the shirt, but whether or not you actually think it looks good on you is another story."

He was clearly skilled at assessing the mindset of potential patients, and he was onto something with me. My runway show helped him determine that I had a specific result in mind and that I expected a perfect end product. He was intuitive enough to realize, though, that I was uncomfortable with who I was on the inside and that I likely wouldn't feel good in the second shirt even if my body was sculpted to supermodel standards.

"You have to believe in the results and *feel* like you look good in that shirt before you step outside in it," he continued. "I can give you a gorgeous chest, but I can't implant the confidence."

At that age, in my early 20s, I hadn't processed the cumulative impact of how much I was bullied because of my sexuality. My self-esteem didn't survive the verbal beatings I had been getting since I was seven, and my attempt to make my outsides beautiful and glamorous was the way to bring it back to life now.

"I'll be confident once I know that I have done everything possible to make my chest look perfect," I said. If anything in my life wasn't perfect, it certainly wasn't because I didn't do everything in my power. That controlling component of OCD gave me the misguided sense that I was always steering my own ship. And, taking a page from the first surgeon's book, I picked a couple of other areas on my body to target. "Let's not waste the good anesthesia; how about a little more work on my love handles and a 'tightening up' of the stomach?" I beat him to the punch and pointed it out before he could open his mouth.

"I was actually going to mention that," the doctor said. "Might as well fix it all."

After many consultations with various doctors, I learned that plastic surgeons typically have egos the size of the tummies they tuck. Conversations began with back-handed compliments – "I've seen worse" or "There isn't much I would do" – and ended with a list of procedures that the doctor could perform to improve upon God's gifts. Each one of them supposedly held the skilled scalpel that would change my life. Regardless, I was back on the operating table one week prior to Christmas, during a holiday break from work. I had become friendly with the surgical nurse because of my endless questions about the procedure and its risks and had already told her that my underwear needed to stay on. She was amused by the request but reassured me that she wouldn't touch them – or peek underneath.

As I came out of the anesthesia, I reached immediately for my briefs, which were soaked and blood stained – but still on my body. I seemed to snap back to myself much easier than I had with the original surgery, and my overall recovery was markedly quicker. Within two days, I was up and about, making an eventful trip to the grocery store with my mother.

I had layers of foam strapped tightly to my body, held close to my skin by a "compression undershirt" that was designed to make lipo procedures more effective. The padding extended down to my pubic area, which made fitting into my jeans a challenge. Using a strong rubber band, I extended the button loop, allowing the denim to hang onto my waist without actually being fastened properly. It wasn't ideal, but it would do for an hour – or so I thought.

Happy to be out of the house after two days of bed rest, I slowly walked the store aisles with my mother. As we rolled up to the deli counter with our cart, my mother asked me to place her order for sliced meats while she ran to the produce section for lettuce. When the butcher handed me the packages, he smiled awkwardly.

"Thank you," I said, staring back at him.

"You may want to check everything. I mean *everything*," he replied, almost in a whisper.

"I am sure it's fine, but thank you." We had been shopping at the same store for years. I wasn't really worried that he'd confused turkey with ham, but he seemed serious.

As I turned the cart and began to walk away, I felt a piece of fabric brush the back of my knees. I looked down to find that the rubber band around my waist had broken, and my pants were around my ankles. In the middle of the super-market, I was in my underwear. I didn't feel the jeans fall because of the layers of fabric pressed against me. Unable to bend, I moved as quickly as possible to the "Chips and Crackers" aisle and hid myself behind a Cheetos display until my mother found me.

"What are you doing?" she asked, looking startled.

"Taking a whiz on the floor," I yelled sarcastically. "The rubber band broke, and my pants fell down at the deli counter."

There was nothing to do but laugh – and lift my jeans, of course. I held the waistband up while we finished shopping and didn't leave the house again until we'd pur-chased an oversized pair of pants that accommodated all of my padding.

During the months following my second surgery, I con-tinued to wear the compression garments around my chest in an effort to maximize the results of the operation. I dressed in larger clothes to cover the bandaging, actually making me look like I had gained a significant amount of weight. Secretly, though, I was shopping for all new clothes, lying in wait for September. Just two weeks into the fall, I revealed my brand new body in some knockout clothes that were pre-viously off limits. More form-fitting, slim-line shirts as well as some knitted pieces had been folded into my wardrobe, along with some new leather belts that called attention to my shrinking waistline.

Friends flooded me with compliments, responding so enthusiastically to my new look. The constant positive attention was like a drug. For the first time in my life, I felt OK with how my body looked – and it didn't matter to me if people knew how I had achieved it. In fact, I loved the glamorous brand of drama that was associated with plastic surgery. At that time, the average person didn't just pop onto an operating table the same way he would jump into a barber's chair – so my extreme makeover seemed like a conversation point; it made me more interesting, I thought.

"You're fascinating," an acquaintance told me. "It's kind of fearless, going under the knife like that."

"Well, a couple of cuts in exchange for a better looking body? Why not?" I replied, somewhat distracted by the music in my ears.

"I'd have climbed on that operating table with you," she said, "if I knew my figure would turn out as perfectly as yours."

What more could I do to keep generating this heady feedback? It started to become clear how people got addicted to surgery. I actually likened it to childbirth: it didn't exactly feel fantastic while it was happening or during recovery, but the results were good enough to get me to do it a second (or third) time.

Two years later, I again got antsy to make some physical changes; I needed an ego boost. This time, I wanted to remove the bump in the bridge of my nose. I always looked like my mother's side of the family, and this rhinoplasty would have me favor my father's. My parents weren't in love with the idea of a third surgery, but I was insistent – and played the guilt card.

When I was two, my father had been pushing me in a swing at a local playground. My laughs and smiles encouraged a greater height and faster pace, which would have been fine had I not let go of the side chains. As my small hands unclenched, I went flying out of the rubber seat, hitting a large tree, face first. George of the Jungle had nothing on me, and I had a face full of splinters to prove it. My nose was broken, and the skin on my cheeks required multiple stitches.

"Had Dad not been so careless when he was pushing me on that swing, my nose may have looked normal," I told my parents. "Perhaps it healed differently than nature intended."

"I doubt that," my mother said, "but I'm not going to argue. You want to fix your nose, fix your nose."

That was easier than I expected. Wow.

Once again, I made a Thanksgiving pilgrimage to South Florida, where I identified one of the top "nose guys." During our initial meeting, we discussed the logistics of the procedure and what kind of results I could expect.

"You don't have a bad nose," the doctor said, "so it's not going to be a dramatic change. But, your profile will be cleaner, and I can definitely improve on what's there." Via computer imaging, he was able to render an "after photo," showing me how my face would look following the surgery. To my eye, it was much better.

"How hard would it be," I asked, "to touch up my chest with the lipo wand while I am already under anesthesia?"

"Easy to do," he replied. "But, what's wrong with your chest?"

"It's not terrible, but I am hoping it could be just a little more contoured."

Even though my second lipo delivered results that were remarkably better than where I had started, I still wanted it to be perfect. I probably would have lived with it had I not decided to go in for the nose job, but this was another chance at getting it just right.

"Sure, I can do that easily," the doctor said. "Again, it will be only slightly better, but I can do a little bit."

My third cosmetic surgery went smoothly, and I was pleased with my new nose. I was more affected by the alteration than I had imagined, though. For years, I had been used to seeing my facial features and my profile in reflected images and photographs. Now, I saw a new person every time I passed a mirror – a stronger, more angular face. No one would make fun of the man on the other side of the glass now; his polished exterior seemed sharp enough to slice metal. Another positive? I knew I didn't plan to have biological children, so the original schnoz wouldn't show up on someone else – always an amusing, tell-tale sign that a parent has had some "upgrades."

It was amazing that my fear of surgical complications was again upstaged by my need to look as good as I possibly could and to generate attention – no matter the financial, emotional and physical costs. In fact, by 24, I had become so accustomed to cosmetic interventions that Botox and tissue fillers were all on my general maintenance program.

Down the line, an injection mishap would leave the left half of my top lip numb, which definitely changed my perspective on the tug-of-war with Mother Nature. I had become the friend whom everyone asked for insight into the latest "new beauty" offerings, as I was a field expert who had tried everything. While I had, for years, worn my plastic surgery addiction as a badge of glamour, I was jarred back into reality when faced with unwanted, permanent side effects. I began to take stock of the work I'd had done, running through the catalog of positive feelings that accompanied other people's reactions to my cosmetic alterations. I came to the conclusion that the return on investment just wasn't good enough; I was rolling the dice with my health by searching for an ultimately unattainable outcome of physical perfection and approval.

With the wisdom of years, I also understood that my addiction to cosmetic surgery – and all of its related drama – was a "borrowing of self" in a way. The real person who was living inside my body, who could be acknowledged only in my head, was able to wear a shell that the people outside seemed to find exciting and important. The surgeries were part of my armor, protection from the people who had been beating the real Josh down for years.

Aside from the occasional injections of Botox, I moved beyond my interest in cosmetic procedures. Sure, I liked my new nose, and my body was definitely well served by liposuction, but the surgeries did not turn me into a new person. The positive attention that came part-and-parcel was superficial; what I really craved was similar attention for being the person I was underneath the nips and tucks. He wasn't out yet.

THINGS CUM UP

What Spanish Cultural Day at Forest Hill High School meant to the student body was nothing more than Cool Ranch Doritos and a jar of tomato dip.

"¿Quién va a llevar la tortilla chips?" Ms. Hudson asked.

"I'll bring four bags," I said. I always made sure there were enough crispy triangles to keep the class snacking for its entire 55 minutes; otherwise, we might have actually had to learn a foreign language.

"I can grab the salsa," Andy Webber offered, equally as averse to following the lesson plan.

"¡Perfecto!" Ms. Hudson replied. A good-natured dingbat, she was easily convinced by our honors Spanish class to shelve the conjugation textbooks in favor of a daytime fiesta.

"Should we run to the grocery store after school to get the food?" Andy whispered towards the end of our class period.

"I'm sure my mom can give us a ride," I answered. Fortunately, the supermarket was within the two-mile radius that my mother's anxiety disorder would allow her to drive.

Andy was a tall, lean blonde with soulful, blue eyes and a runner's body. His expertly trimmed hair sat on top of a round face, and his shaded stubble made him look more like an adult than a teenager. He wore knee-length board shorts year-round – not out of the ordinary in Florida – and I was mesmerized by the hair on his legs. Thick and defined, his calves were dusted with blond wisps that gave *me* a tingle every time the wind brushed past them. I often daydreamed about what he would look like naked; I was certain that he had a full bush of pubic hair, considering that the rest of his body had not only met puberty but welcomed it in.

From the store's front register, after the Doritos, salsa dip and sodas had been scanned and paid for, I noticed that Andy left the checkout lane. He was discreetly milling around the exit.

"Paper or plastic?" the bagboy asked. My eyes moved from Andy to the groceries on the conveyor belt.

"Paper *in* plastic," I said, never wanting to commit to one environmental detriment over the other. As I looked up, I realized that the teenager bagging the food was a classmate.

"Are you and Andy spending some quality time together?" he said with a sneer. "It looks like the two of you might be working up an appetite." He moved his tongue back and forth against the inside of his right cheek, simulating what it would look like if an erect penis was pushing in and out of his mouth. He was probably the same football-playing meathead who had scrawled the word "fairy" across my brown paper math book cover.

I averted my eyes, not looking at his face while he placed the snacks inside double bags. It seemed like an eternity as I stood there, my body tense with embarrassment. The school sports star was making fun of me, implying that Andy and I were likely to be trading blowjobs before washing the semen down with corn chips. I wished Andy hadn't been distracted by the vending machines at the electronic doors; I would have felt less like a vulnerable, open target with a show of friendly support.

"Why'd you walk away?" I asked Andy, when I raced to the exit as soon as I grabbed my bags from the school jock.

"I wanted to see what was in these machines," he said. He pointed to a line-up of quarter-hungry, glass canisters that featured glittery stickers and small bouncing balls for the toddler set.

"Did you see who was bagging the groceries?" I continued.

"No, why?" he replied, looking away from me. It crossed my mind that Andy might be lying. I had only a few seconds to feel sick to my stomach because, otherwise, I would have to explain my flushed skin and queasy unease to my mom.

"Oh, nothing," I answered. "Let's find my mother; she's waiting in the car outside." I decided to believe that Andy was, in fact, interested in the toy machines. After all, he had a younger brother, and perhaps he was going to be thoughtful enough to buy the four year-old a gift.

Andy and I met at Roosevelt Junior High School, and our friendship survived the transition to ninth grade. An athletic boy's boy, he had a surprising interest in independent films and the performing arts that drew us close. Throughout the weekdays, he would be busy with the basketball and track teams, but we'd spend the weekends at each other's houses watching movies and eating pizza. Part of his appeal was that he was the kind of friend I was *supposed* to have – a male who was my age and who was discernibly heterosexual. It wasn't until a rainy Saturday at the end of our sophomore term that I was faced – head on – with the unhealthy nature of our relationship and the subsequent, years-long impact it would have on my social and sexual development.

"You have to get your dad to take you to *The Rocky Horror Picture Show*," Sandra told me. "It plays in downtown West Palm Beach every Saturday at midnight." My former babysitter and next-door friend was still introducing me to all things hip and cool. My first orgasm was inspired by the *Caligula* screening in her parents living room, so I had every reason to believe that her latest suggestion would yield similarly exciting results.

"I'm going to see if my father will go with Andy and me this weekend," I said. "Is it really dirty?" I wanted to make sure that it wouldn't create uncomfortable viewing with my dad or the high school athlete I secretly wanted to kiss.

"It's not dirty," she said. "It's more of a rock musical with some racy scenes." Sandra gave me the lowdown on the interactive experience – I gathered a spray bottle, newspaper and uncooked rice – and my father, Andy and I enjoyed Susan Sarandon and Tim Curry in the cult spectacle.

At 2:30AM, on the ride home from the movie theater, my dad stopped his white Chevrolet Celebrity at a traffic light, coincidentally just alongside the Forest Hill High campus. In the adjacent lane, a car chauffeuring two kids from our school came to a stop at the same red light. Andy and I both noticed our classmates.

"Don't those kids go to our school?" I asked.

"Um, I'm not sure," Andy mumbled as he leaned down to reinforce his shoelaces.

"Look inside that car," I said. "I'm pretty sure I see those guys in the halls every day." Andy didn't move from his crouched position, his head below the back door window. In that horrifying instant, I experienced a humiliating jolt: he was ashamed to be seen with me. The food I'd eaten at the movies moved into my throat as I flashed back to the grocery store two months earlier. Andy didn't want the bagboy to see us together – I knew it then but didn't want to process the hurt – and his loose laces were a cover for the embarrassment that was attached to his association with me. Other than a handful of chubby girls and my adult pals, Andy was the only age and gender appropriate friend on my rag-tag roster – and he wanted to hide me as though I was a garbage bag that had to be out of view when guests visited. I was his dirty secret, the friend whom he enjoyed spending time with but who could tarnish his reputation as the campus golden boy.

From the driver's seat, my dad couldn't tell that the small amount of self-esteem I had left had been asphyxiated in the back of the car. The air was heavy; breathing in and out seemed like a Herculean undertaking. I turned my face to the side and purposely banged my jaw into the glass of the rear passenger window. The physical pain, I thought, might talk my mind into ignoring the expanding sickness in my stomach. I clutched my midsection with both hands as I knocked my head into the glass a second time. The dizzying effect of the blow anesthetized me for the remaining 10 minutes of the ride home.

"Thanks so much Josh and Dr. Sabarra," Andy said as we dropped him at the front of his house. "I had a great time tonight." We avoided eye contact in silent acknowledgement of what had happened.

"You're welcome, Andy," my father replied. "Happy to have you join us anytime." I wanted to scream otherwise from the open car door, but nothing came out – I felt like I was in "kidnap mode." There was a phantom gun to my head, and I couldn't yell, "Help me! I'm back here!" for fear of being wiped out entirely.

Throughout high school, I was bullied and teased relentlessly, but I made every effort to keep it quiet. I didn't want to perpetuate the idea that I was gay by suggesting it to people who may not have thought about it in the first place. I put all of my energy into maintaining a 4.0 grade point average and ingratiating myself to the staff, which, in turn, also got me ridiculed for being a "teacher's pet" and an "over-achiever." (I always hated the term "over-achiever" because it made the case that one person could achieve too much. The label was probably coined by less productive individuals who wanted to feel better about their own inadequacy. To this day, I prefer to be known as an "achiever," when applicable.)

When there was any kind of gossip or scandal, the faculty knew just who would have his finger on the pulse of the story. On one occasion, I was called out of a class – mid-hour – by another teacher who wanted confirmation of a rumor she'd heard. Word on the street was that one of the school's sleazy coaches was, um, practicing splits with the head cheerleading adviser; it was the talk of the semester. I hadn't actually seen them doing anything questionable together, but I'd gathered enough information from their respective teams to satisfy the inquiry. There was little question about whether or not the coach enjoyed cheerleading.

My investigative skills – had I lived in Cabot Cove, Jessica Fletcher would have met her match – made me the perfect intern for *The Palm Beach Post*, the county's leading daily paper. I studied the masthead and identified the name and phone number of the weekend arts section editor.

"I'm interested in volunteering," I said, once I got him on the phone.

"We don't really have an internship program," he answered, "but I appreciate your call. You sound like a go-getter." Even at 14, I understood "no" to be only the beginning of a negotiation.

"You couldn't use a pair of hands to help file paperwork?" I pushed. "I'm not asking for a dime in return." I desperately wanted a purpose, an after school activity that met my interests and didn't include other students.

"This isn't a place for kids," he said. "The newsroom is an adult environment." That was exactly what I'd hoped for; an escape to a place where I would be better understood and appreciated.

"I get it, but a few hours a week after school won't kill anyone. I promise I'll make it worth your while." I wasn't caving in, and the editor was too much of a gentleman to hang up on me.

"OK, you win," he said ten minutes later. "I am going to try you out. $5.00 an hour to file press releases and stock photos."

Six months into my journalism gig, the editor recognized my interest in writing and asked me to draft a weekly entertainment events column. Thrilled to have a byline at 14 years-old, I jumped on the opportunity, and, shortly thereafter, was writing broader feature stories. My articles made me an almost-celebrity in the halls of Forest Hill High School, where teachers and parents commented on the pieces I had written each week. The attention and wunderkind status helped to patch the holes left by the teenage boys who tore me down until the day I graduated. There was a validation – a lightness in my otherwise pounding chest – that came from the adult recognition. Maybe the kids were wrong, and I did, in fact, have value? Perhaps I *was* special, and acceptance was waiting just beyond the walls of high school.

■ ■ ■

Harry Greenstein wasn't exactly waiting for me at Syracuse University with open arms. In fact, attached to his stocky, trunk-like body were two abnormally small upper limbs that bounced up and down with the slightest movement. He was a 5'9", Jewish T-Rex, and I was his roommate.

"I'm so happy that you're a member of the Tribe," Harry said when we first met, using the guttural, Hebrew "chhhh" that could've been confused with his clearing phlegm from his throat. "Ve can valk to Shul together." He looked and sounded like the shuffleboard players at my grandparents' condominium complex. More than half of his words were old-school Yiddish, and his voice had the sing-song lilt of an immigrant just off the boat in 1919.

"How do you know I'm Jewish?" I continued. Tradition-ally, people pegged my last name as Italian, plus I hadn't gotten around to the nose job yet.

"I can tell," Harry answered. "Ve look like ve come from the same stock." Lord, I hoped not; he was right out of *Jurassic Park* – and, on his way to becoming an Orthodox Jew.

"What country are you from?" I asked, curious about his

thick accent. To my ears – and having grown up in South Florida – he could have been from Boca Raton.

"Vhat are you, mishuggah? I'm from right here; Syracuse!" he announced, flailing his mini-arms like propellers.

Harry woke up at 6:00AM each morning, chanting through a rigorous, ritualistic prayer process. I was already about to strangle him with his own Tallit for disturbing my sleep, but, when he coughed up a not-so-endearing pro-nouncement about our dorm mates, I realized I might need thicker rope.

"You know ve have two faygalas across the hall, yes?" he said.

"Two what?" I didn't know bupkis about Yiddish.

"Two faggots," he said, this time in language I was all too familiar with. "Just vhat ve need, right?"

Shit. It seemed that the more evolved, open-minded students who flocked to places of higher learning were paired with other roommates. I was stuck with a hairy homophobe who barely spoke English.

Across the hall were Darren and his roommate, Oliver, both unusually attractive sophomores who had developed a romantic relationship during their freshman year. Darren was a tall, all-American Adonis who was politically active on campus, and Oliver was a quiet, small red-head with a muscular body and freckles for miles. I had not been around gay people my age, and I was fascinated by the couple; they were so open about their sexuality.

It wasn't always a beautiful day in the gayborhood, however. As outwardly harmonious as their relationship appeared, Darren and Oliver had stormy fights every night – knock-down, drag-out battles that would make Liz and Dick look like amateurs. It was a real-life daytime serial, and my right ear was glued to the door of my room. I couldn't turn away because it wasn't ordinary drama – it was *gay* drama, and I was intrigued.

One Saturday night, for two hours, I listened to screaming, then sobbing, then silence, then screaming, then furniture falling, then sobbing again. What came next? From the sound of it, Darren. Following their epic emotional and physical brawl, I was an ear-witness to a very loud make-up fuck. Until that point, I had not seen, heard or been around anything related to gay sex, so there was something thrilling about the scene. As I listened, I pictured what must have been happening with every scream and wailing grunt. I thought about their sweaty bodies, wrapped in each other, having the kind of physical contact I'd dreamed about. I locked the door and grabbed a tissue, jerking off to the sounds of my two fellow residents going bump in the night.

Darren and Oliver gave me hope. The turbulent nature of their romance held no appeal, but their unapologetic attitudes about their sexuality gave my psyche a boost. I observed two young, gay men who were accepted by almost everyone around them. People like Harry stopped me from dipping my toe in the water, but, because of the couple across the hall, I could see a future – as distant as it might have been – in which I'd be able to live authentically.

The following weeks found Harry getting stranger, spending very little time doing schoolwork and the bulk of his hours laboring for radical student organizations on campus. Like Barbra in *The Way We Were*, he had the nose, the frizzy hair and the whole activism thing down. Too bad there was no blond, handsome Hubble who had the hots for his roommate. I could see myself brushing shaggy strands of tousled hair from Robert Redford's forehead.

The crazy level escalated to the point where Harry was barely speaking English. Add to that six-foot snow banks and temperatures below minus 30, and I was on the first Delta Express to a warmer climate. I longed for *orange juice* more than I wanted to be an *Orangeman*. I left Syracuse at the end of my first semester, making tracks so quickly that I didn't even have time to wave goodbye from the tarmac. I looked forward to a six-week break before starting my second semester of college on a more tropical campus in Coral Gables, Florida. The University of Miami was bending over backwards to get my tuition money: they even promised a single dorm room – no whack-job roommate! – with a coveted private bathroom. The heavens were smiling on me, as was the familiar and welcoming Florida sunshine.

My parents lived only 60 miles from the University, and I took advantage of the proximity. I drove home every weekend so my mother could re-stock my food supply and do the laundry, but, by the time I reached my junior year, I'd engineered a class schedule that had me at school only three days a week.

"Don't you want to be around other students?" my mom asked.

"All they do is party and drink," I said, which wasn't untrue. But, I was isolating myself for altogether different reasons.

"You don't need to get caught up in that," my mother affirmed. "I guess you're better off coming home when you don't have classes." Her faint smile made me unsure of whether she believed what she was saying or just enjoyed having her baby at home.

I didn't sit idle during the down days; I completed assignments diligently and interned during the school year for a Miami-based public relations firm. What I didn't do was have a traditional college life: no parties, concerts, friends or lovers. The feelings of shame and worthlessness that were the residual effect of the camp counselor and Andy Webber and Harry Greenstein kept me clinging to the safety of my parents. I felt protected and comforted in my childhood home; no one questioned my sexuality, teased me or made my personal life a topic of conversation. College was a tour of duty, something I had to endure to ensure professional success. What I really wanted, though, was to press some sort of fast-forward button that would flash me through undergraduate school and into the *real* world. Funny, then, that I'd wind up in the middle of a fictional soap opera – literally.

I had been a daytime TV aficionado growing up; our housekeeper patterned her work day around which serial was on the tube at what time. She cleaned our home three days a week on the following schedule: the living and dining rooms during *The Young and the Restless*, my parents' suite while watching *The Bold and the Beautiful,* the three other bedrooms throughout *As the World Turns* and the large family room during *Guiding Light*. Essentially, I was raised on the CBS line-up, following the housekeeper around to wipe the spots she missed while distracted by the goings on in Genoa City. Who was better suited to be an intern on one of the soaps?

In addition to journalism, I was interested in exploring film and television production as a possible career path. Like I'd been with the editor at *The Palm Beach Post*, I was tenacious in sending letters and making phone calls to the internship coordinators at all of the daytime dramas, all of which were up and running during my summer breaks. Three of them offered me positions, but *Guiding Light* was New York-based – much easier for my parents to underwrite considering that public transportation was more accessible in Manhattan.

The behind-the-scenes drama was even pulpier than what was on the air. One ingénue was rumored to have been having an affair with her on-screen love interest, who, in a wave of guilt, confessed his infidelity in front of his entire church congregation. Even wilder was the young hunk hired to play a cross-dressing villain whose method acting threw him over the edge mentally. One afternoon, while shooting a big scene that included the entire cast, he stripped off his clothes and ran around the studio butt-naked.

My sister, Nancy, who was in law school at New York University, had a crush on one of the *Guiding Light* heart-throbs – even when we were teenagers – and she started to suspect that I might, too. She came to visit the set one after-noon and enjoy the beefcake scenery, and she noticed that my eyes were locked in the same direction as hers.

"You know," she said, "if you're gay, it's OK. I just want you to know that it wouldn't change anything." My sexuality had never been questioned by a family member.

"What? What makes you think I'm gay?" I shot back, worried that I hadn't been discreet enough when glancing at the shirtless actor and that Nancy might mention it to my parents.

"Nothing in particular," she said. "I just wanted to let you know that I wouldn't care." My palms began to feel clammy, and I could feel a halo of sweat dripping from my forehead.

"I can't believe you would say that to me," I replied.

"Why? It's not like it's something bad," she said. In my experience, she and the couple at Syracuse were the only people who shared that sentiment.

"I'm not gay, and I don't want to talk about it anymore," I said. She never brought it up again.

The cast and crew of *Guiding Light* became like a second family, and I learned in a matter of weeks how hours of television could be churned out like factory work. They were a quirky bunch who adopted me without any uncomfortable questions, welcoming me back each winter, spring and summer break. At every opportunity, I ran *towards* them and *away* from the tiny bit of a campus life I had established. They offered the camaraderie, support and fun times that everyone else seemed to experience during summer camp, high school and college. The showbiz gypsies embraced me, and it was clear that my place in the world was with them.

Likewise, I wanted to marry my journalism experience with my passion for entertainment, and my supervisor at the soap opera suggested splitting the days in New York between CBS News and the daytime show. With a couple of phone calls and a letter of recommendation from *Guiding Light's* producers, she secured a part-time internship for me with Helena Stern, the network's head talent booker.

"You have a remarkable background," Helena said, while we sat in her office on 57th Street and 11th Avenue. "Pretty amazing, actually."

"Why is that?" I asked.

"I've never met someone your age who has already written for a newspaper, interned at a PR firm and worked at a national daytime television show," she answered. Until she said it out loud, I hadn't realized what I'd accomplished. "Most college kids are getting drunk and partying."

"I was never invited to the party," I said. An overweight woman in her late 30's, I had a feeling she could relate to being an outcast.

"Just as well," she replied, "because you're going to have the time of your life with me. In fact, the fun starts tomorrow."

"What's tomorrow?" I asked excitedly, already taken with Helena.

"Our interview with the Queen of Soul," she replied.

"Are you fucking kidding me?" The words slipped out of my mouth before my head could process them. Helena laughed, charmed by my excitement and enthusiasm.

"Meet us at the Delmonico Hotel at 3:30PM tomorrow," she said with a smile, "and don't use the word 'fucking' when you greet Ms. Franklin in the lobby."

When I first arrived at the hotel and got into the elevator, I noticed that each floor number had been covered with black duct tape. Odd, I thought, but I hand counted the buttons until I pressed what I calculated to be 19. When the car reached the correct level, the doors opened, revealing additional duct tape obscuring the floor number indicators at the sides of the elevator panel. I stepped out into the hallway, noticing that similar black tape had been placed over each room number; at that time, the rooms were identified by the floor number and a letter of the alphabet – 19A, 19B, 19C and so forth.

I walked into the interview suite – 19F, but, of course, only the "F" was visible – and headed right over to Helena. She was chatting with Roz from Arista Records, the label releasing Aretha's new music collection, and I jumped in to alert them to the duct tape situation.

"Aretha isn't here yet," I said, "but the elevators look a little shabby; they're covered in black tape."

Roz, who was a publicist for the record company, gave Helena and me a sly smile and explained that the tape had been her handy work.

"Ms. Franklin doesn't like heights," she said. "This way, she won't realize that the interview is happening on a high floor." She seemed very proud of herself, but I looked at Helena in disbelief. Was this bitch putting me on? Helena and I used all of our willpower to stop from laughing, but we weren't going to challenge the representative from the label.

I took my post in the lobby and greeted Aretha immediately upon her entrance. She gave me a bright smile and was particularly warm when she realized that I was a college intern. We stepped into the elevator, and I saw her grasp the handrails, braced nervously for our ascent. As the old, New York elevator forged upward, I saw a look of bewilderment flush through the Queen's puffy cheeks. It was initially a combination of confusion and concern, but her eyes shifted from fright to fury right in front of me.

She walked out of the elevator, stopping in front of room 19A – er, "A" – to stare at the duct tape. After a dramatic 30-second pause, she moved to "B," making her way down the corridor and stopping for a prolonged period in front of every single door leading to the makeshift interview studio in 19F. Before Roz could get a word out of her mouth, Aretha reached forward and angrily ripped the tape from the silver plate affixed to the door.

"I knew someone was playing games with me," she barked.

Um, really, ReRe? You don't say. I had to hand it to her,

though. She did the interview like a professional before storming into the hallway and proceeding to walk down 19 flights of stairs. I had never seen someone that big move so quickly, but Roz had forgotten to show Aretha some R-E-S-P-E-C-T, and Girlfriend wasn't having it.

"I'm glad *that's* over," Helena said. "One singer down; one more to go this week." She thanked me for my help and walked me out of the hotel lobby.

"What day and time do you need me?" I asked enthusiastically.

"Oh, don't worry about it," she said, "it's very early on Thursday morning, and I don't want to ask you to get up." A grin was breaking through her words.

"Who is it?" I asked.

"Honestly, don't worry about it. You need your rest. Dolly Parton will just have to get by without you." A few drops of urine actually leaked into my underpants.

"Did you say, 'Dolly Parton?'" I was stunned. Dolly's larger-than-life personality and rags-to-riches story captivated me the moment my parents first played "9 to 5" on the family stereo. As a young kid who was confused by feeling different, her music and upbeat persona gave me a sense that everything would turn out OK.

"I sure did," Helena winked. "I had no idea you'd be this excited." She was onto me. Apparently, it was obvious that I'd have an affinity for the diva icons.

I was on a "Dolly Diet" for the next two days, eating almost nothing and sleeping very little. In my head, I rehearsed repeatedly how my interaction with the country superstar would unfold, and I hoped that she'd live up to my expectations. My nerves were stirred by a mix of excitement and fear of disappointment; at that point, I hadn't met many celebrities, let alone one who meant so much to me.

"I bet she'll be awesome," my friend Sandra said when I called from New York to tell her about my week. "She always sounds so down-to-earth on talk shows."

"I hope you're right," I answered. "I will be devastated if she isn't what she seems."

"You understand how cool this is, right?" Sandra asked. "People would love to have your life right now."

"You think so?" I was beaming with an ear-to-ear smile.

"Hell, yeah," she said. "Schmoozing with famous people? Everyone dreams about that. You're actually *doing* it."

When I was introduced to Dolly at 6:30AM the following morning, she was in full hair and make-up and surprisingly animated for such an early call time.

"Nice to meet you, Josh," she said, as she showed me into her dressing room. "Your friend Helena told me that you're a big fan."

"Yes, and we have the same birthday," I blurted out, stumbling over my words as though I was just learning to talk.

"If you were born on January 19th, you can't be all bad," Dolly said. "Have you had breakfast?"

Over corn muffins and a fruit platter, we chatted for an hour about our shared Capricorn traits, how one of her first hit singles was called "Joshua" and how she might restyle her wig for an appearance later in the day. By the time we'd finished eating, there was a connection between us that felt like home. It was as though she knew how important the moment was to me and was determined to give me every ounce of her energy.

"You take care of yourself," Dolly said, as we snapped

some photos and parted ways. "I have a feeling our paths will cross again."

"Nothing would make me happier," I replied, and I meant it. She pulled me in for a hug and then held my hands in hers before she left the room. It seemed as though I was the only person who mattered to her that morning, and her gracious warmth, for a short period, erased everything I was told was wrong with me.

The gay icons marched through my life in single file that summer, like an A-list Pride Parade that only I'd been invited to. Cher, decked out in a ripped black jacket and a neon red wig, introduced me to See's chocolate lollipops (still my favorite treat); looking as supreme as ever with her untamed hair and giant hoop earrings, Diana Ross stopped to chat in the name of love; Bette Midler, bubbly and petite, was, indeed, divine. Hopefully, the legendary songstresses weren't jealous of Denzel Washington and Matthew McConaughey, who also got to hang out with me that June and July.

"I promised you the time of your life," Helena said on my last day as an intern at CBS News. "Did I deliver?"

"Beyond what I imagined," I answered, holding back tears as I hugged her goodbye.

"Honey, you're such a special guy," she said. "I plan to be in your life forever."

"Are you giving me your word?" I asked.

"I haven't failed you yet, have I?" she replied. And she hasn't to this day.

I returned to Florida to complete my senior year of college, but I was less present than ever. At night, I thought only about chasing the Hollywood spotlight. Even though the glow wasn't mine, it had thrown a desirable heat around me that lit a fire in my stomach and made people around me take notice. Students who chatted with me casually before class time were dazzled by my stories of glamour and celebrity; my associations with the rich and famous made me interesting to them.

"I am obsessed with him," a fellow student said when I told her about the morning I'd spent with Denzel Washington over the summer. "Is he as hot in person?"

"He's a handsome guy," I answered, still not ready to confirm her assumption about my sexuality.

"I wish I had the chance to meet him," she said. "You're so cool."

"I am?" I questioned, feeling equal parts fantastic and fraud.

"Totally," she continued. "Hanging out with movie stars is *the shit*."

Based on other people's reactions to my internship experiences, I believed her. I just had to figure out how to make a living doing it.

HARD FOR THE MONEY

Davey Wilson was the first underhanded Hollywood blowhard to fuck me over. The pear-shaped bobble-head nearly ruined my career before it started.

"I hate to lose you to the west coast," Davey lamented, on my last day of work in the New York publicity office of a major movie studio. The company's internationally revered family brand was the perfect place to begin building a resume.

"I'll be only a phone call away," I chirped, "and we'll still be working together." It was the kind of bullshit that passed regularly between Davey and me, an artful game of disingenuous conversation. The only thing he hated to lose was the opportunity to tear me down, and if I never saw his fat ass again, it would have been too soon. After two years in the east coast satellite office, I was anxious to move to Los Angeles. The strategy and marching orders all came from studio headquarters, and the publicists in New York were simply soldiers who executed battle plans. I needed to be on the other side of the country if I eventually wanted to be a decision maker.

Initially, the job in Manhattan was a dream-come-true. Not only was it a first-class training ground that would undoubtedly set me up for an illustrious professional life, but it was associated with one of the most respected banners in the entertainment industry; everyone I knew was dazzled by my launch into the real world. And, it was a big enough crow to feed Mallory Silverberg two meals.

"What's Josh going to do once he graduates from college?" Mallory, a neighborhood "Gladys Kravitz," asked when we ran into her at Lord & Taylor in the Palm Beach Mall. It was during my senior year of college, and I was home for the weekend running errands with my mom.

"He wants to go into the movie business, doing the ads," my mother answered. They were talking about me as though I wasn't in the room, and my mom still had no understanding of the difference between publicity and advertising. Not surprising, considering that she and my father couldn't even get the name of a movie right – they weren't sure if *20,000 Leagues of Their Own* was a baseball comedy or an undersea adventure.

"It's not actually advertising," I tried to explain, "it's more about positioning a piece of entertainment in the media." Mallory, whose beady eyes were scrunched around a pelican beak, looked me up and down like I was speaking Greek. She turned back to my mom.

"Well, I hope he's good at waiting tables," she said, tossing an air kiss. She hit us with her plastic garment bag as she sauntered into the shoe department, her long, tie-dyed skirt dusting the floor. Mallory, as it turned out, deserved more of a *thank you* than a *fuck you*; her dismissive thoughtlessness represented a challenge. I was determined to prove her wrong.

As I was about to graduate with a dual degree in Motion Pictures and Psychology, I listened to my classmates talk about their plans to land "regular jobs" locally until industry opportunities presented themselves. They were passive and resigned to waiting for luck to roll their way. None of them had bite marks from Mallory Silverberg, though.

I mobilized just days after the department store encounter, purchasing *The Motion Picture Almanac*; it provided me with all of the movie studio addresses, the names and titles of the current players and the history of each company. I created a longhand database on a legal pad, noting pertinent information about every person I planned to target. I designed my own stationery with matching, printed resumes – my CV was robust for someone not yet out of college, considering the internships – and purchased Alfred Hitchcock postage stamps that matched my letterhead. My polished presentation, I reasoned, would catch the attention of the kinds of public relations executives I wanted to work for. I was half right.

Davey Wilson was one of a handful of studio flacks who recognized that I was uniquely qualified for an entry-level assistant position as soon as my cover letter and resume landed on his desk.

"Would you be willing to come to New York for an interview?" he asked by phone, a month before my graduation ceremony. "You have an impressive background for someone just starting out."

"I'll be in the city for my sister's law school commencement in two weeks," I said. "Would that work?"

"We can wait until then," Davey said, "but, if the interview goes well, we would need you to be here two weeks later. We have a big animated feature opening in mid-June, and it's all hands on deck." Within a month, I was standing on my first red carpet.

That premiere was less of a screening and more of a star-studded, city-wide event. Fifth Avenue had been shut down for an electrical light parade that began at Central Park and ended in front of the theater, and the line of press and photographers took up two blocks of 42nd Street. The spectacle was like a theme park in the middle of Manhattan, and I was tossed onto the biggest thrill-ride. Throngs of fans and onlookers were penned behind stanchions on the opposite end of the street, and I was on the VIP side of the velvet rope. Anyone would have been happy to trade places.

"I'm going to need you to escort talent down the carpet," Davey said, "and then get them seated in the theater once they've talked to all of the journalists."

"I've never done that before," I responded. "Is there anything specific I need to know?"

"Sorry, no time for a tutorial today," he answered. "Use your instincts."

I had been pushed, head first, into my Hollywood fantasy, but I didn't feel prepared. What if my instincts weren't as sharp as I hoped or what Davey expected? What if I made a fool of myself in front of a celebrity, bungling the entire premiere? It was like being in the middle of the Atlantic Ocean with no life vest. I stepped to the side of the red carpet onto a shaded piece of sidewalk, taking four or five deep breaths. After a few minutes, the reality of my situation became crystal clear: if I didn't at least try to execute my assignment, I'd be embarrassed and likely fired. There was no choice but to return to my post and dive in.

Thankfully, adrenaline made me a superstar. The flashing lights, the energy of the crowd and the pumping music stampeded over my insecurity and thrust me into cruise control. I worked that red carpet like a pro with one celebrity after another. I introduced them to each media outlet, monitored the questions for relevance and appropriateness and then moved the stars along to another journalist after a couple of minutes. It was as though I had been raised on a press line.

"You're fantastic at this," Peter Gallagher said when he finished talking to the media and walked to his seat in the theater. The star of *sex, lies and videotape*, *The Player* and *While You Were Sleeping* was enjoying a hot moment in Hollywood.

"You really think so?" I asked, looking for more validation. "This is actually my first event."

"You'd never know it; you were born to do this." A movie star had recognized my skill and savvy, and I wanted to call my mother right from the middle of the media line. I glowed with Peter's compliment for the rest of the evening.

It took me three months to settle into my job and new life in New York City. I shared a two-bedroom apartment on Sutton Place, a tony and uptight east side neighborhood, with my sister, which made the transition from Florida easier. Nancy and I were extremely close, and having her to come home to made me feel like I wasn't entirely on my own. Sure, I'd left the family nest, but my sister was a safety net underneath the big city high-wire. She and I would sit on our couch and talk every night about my transition into the workforce; she understood my worries, as she had recently joined a prominent Manhattan law firm – her own first professional experience. I was grateful to have Nancy's support and counsel because hitting my stride at the office was not as easy as the first premiere event would have had me believe.

The New York publicity team was basically a co-ed fraternity of a dozen 30-somethings, and the few assistants fell at the bottom of the hierarchy. My days were spent clipping articles about the company out of magazines and newspapers, copying them and distributing them to the staff on both coasts. In addition, I would type memos, run errands and maintain file cabinets full of paperwork and publicity photographs. While I knew I had to pay my dues, I felt like a meaningless part of the operation when the group would attend screenings of upcoming film projects, leaving me to answer their phones.

"These screenings are not for assistants," Davey announced on a weekly basis. "Support staff needs to keep the office running." There were four administrative employees; only one was required to hold down the fort during a two-hour film. Davey and his team of publicists seemed to delight in being exclusionary; it was the professional equivalent of hazing.

On occasion, the higher-ups would have me assist them at offsite events, such as a press day or a celebrity talk show appearance. Even in those moments, I was repeatedly reminded of my station.

"Josh, I need you to go get bottled water for Anne Bancroft," Davey said. She was co-starring in a film the studio was releasing and was conducting interviews with select journalists at the Regency Hotel in mid-town.

"Where would you like me to go for that?" I asked innocently.

"Where do you think we are? Guam in 1930? There's a fucking drug store on every corner." Embarrassed, I walked out of the room and scurried to the nearest Rite Aid. When I returned with two large bottles of Evian, I was met with a raised eyebrow and a downturned mouth.

"Nobody likes Evian," Davey snarled. "Go back and get another brand." Apparently, Poland Springs did the job; there were no complaints when I delivered the replacement water.

"Now that you finally got it right," Davey said, "I need you to sit in the hotel suite during Ms. Bancroft's next interview while I run back to the office for an hour. Do you think you can at least handle *that*?" It sounded like he'd lost faith in me entirely because I didn't know to purchase the correct label of water.

Before Davey left the hotel, he introduced me to Anne, who carried herself like celluloid royalty. Her salt-and-pepper hair was shoulder length, and her low heels were the perfect complement to her tailored pantsuit.

"I'm Ms. Bancroft," she said, holding her hand out to shake mine. "You're very young."

"Nice to meet you," I replied, without baiting the conversation about my age. She was a bona fide screen legend, and moments like that were what got me through the boring days in my office cubicle.

"I'm going to do this next interview in the front room," she said. "I won't need any help." She clearly didn't take to my youthful charm the way Dolly and Cher did only a year earlier. She wasn't bitchy or outwardly rude but rather old school Hollywood: casually pleasant and guarded at the same time.

"No problem," I answered, "I will wait in the sitting area. If you need anything, just let me know."

"I'll be fine," she said, seemingly certain that there was nothing I could possibly do to facilitate the press day. "Oh, and one other thing. My husband is going to be calling."

"If the phone rings, should I answer and knock on your door if it's him?" My disappointment in Anne's indifference toward me turned into giddy excitement. It seemed that I might, in fact, have a purpose during the next hour *and* possibly get to talk to comedy genius Mel Brooks.

"No!" she said forcefully. "Don't even pick up that receiver." I was taken aback by her vehement response. "I'll answer all calls myself."

"No problem," I said with a mock cheerfulness that belied the feeling of rejection that stirred in my gut.

"I don't need my husband hearing another man answer the phone in my room," she continued. Not one other person had ever perceived me to be a romantic threat to a straight man, but Mrs. Robinson wasn't rolling the dice.

For two years, I juggled similar professional assignments; some were thrilling, others dispiriting. Days with Harrison Ford and Michelle Pfeiffer left me euphoric and passionate about my career choice, but 5:30AM call times to sit and clip newspapers, for hours on end, in the basement of the office pushed me right back down to earth.

"What's Harrison Ford like?" my friend Carol in Florida asked on the phone one night.

"He's really nice," I answered, "and very easy to work with." Phrasing it that way made me feel important, as though I was in the trenches alongside better and more interesting people than the average folks back home.

"I work alongside a bunch of boring teachers," she said. "It's pretty cool that you are creating an exciting life for yourself."

I hadn't told her about the stretches of time I spent typing memos and answering phones for Davey, so, to her, my life had a glamorous appeal. In order to move up the food chain, though – and to be living the life I'd led Carol to imagine – I was going to have to move to Los Angeles. The publicity staff at the company headquarters was more than double the size of that in New York, similar to the structure at competitive studios. Job turnover was more frequent, as were opportunities for employees of one studio to defect to another.

For weeks, I mulled over a location change. Into the late hours of the morning, I'd sit on my bed, wiped out, making lists of pros and cons. I considered the logistics of being in California – needing a car, the cost of living, having no immediate family around – against the ease of staying in New York – my sister, a couple of friends, and a shorter plane ride to my parents in Florida. On paper, staying put fell more into my comfort zone, but the sparkle of Hollywood obscured my outlook. The idea of more celebrities and more red carpets, and likewise, more for family and friends to like about me, had an irresistible pull. Moving would put me in the middle of the action; after all, I knew I had more to offer than being a bench warmer while the rest of the team was at a movie screening.

"Are you sure you want to do that?" my mother asked when I told her about my idea to move. "You don't really have anyone to rely on in California."

"I know it will be lonely and isolating," I said, "but if I don't do it, I'll be a glorified secretary for the next ten years."

"You know Daddy and I will support whatever decision

you make," she said. "Go talk to your boss tomorrow, and just know that we're behind you 100%."

Davey, unfortunately, wasn't so quick to embrace my proposal of a transfer.

"I understand that you want to advance," he said, "but I'd like to keep things status quo at the office here."

"I am planning to move to LA with or without a job," I bluffed. "So, if you can't find a spot for me on the studio lot, I'll pound the pavement when I get to California."

"So, is this your two-week notice?" he asked.

"I guess it is," I said, surprised at how ballsy I was. Having my parents as back up – financially and emotionally – gave me a "fuck you" confidence that paved the way to Los Angeles.

"In that case," Davey said, "let me do a little research. Maybe we can find a lateral job for you." Two days later, he signed a leave-of-absence form and gave me the details of my new gig; I would be assisting two LA-based publicists.

My mom and dad flew cross-country with me, helping find and furnish a one-bedroom rental in Studio City. My silver Mazda MX-6, which had been parked in my parents' Florida driveway since I'd left home, was shipped via truck, and, within two weeks, my life in La La Land was organized. I had four days to explore the city with my folks before reporting to work.

"Hey, Josh, how are things at home?" Davey asked when I answered my cell phone; I was in line to purchase new linens at Bed, Bath & Beyond.

"Great to hear from you," I said, "but it's probably too soon to call California home."

"California? Aren't you at home with your family in Florida?"

"I start work in the LA office on Monday," I said, "how could I possibly still be in Florida?"

"About that," Davey said, "I never actually committed to the job transfer. I thought I was just giving you permission to take some time off."

"What are you talking about?" I was stunned. "We discussed all of the details before I left New York."

"There isn't a job for you in California. If you want to continue your employment with the company, you'll have to be in New York on Monday."

I dropped my basket of sheet sets and bath towels and sat on the floor to the side of the cash register. I felt a panic come over me.

"Is this a joke, Davey?" I couldn't believe what I was hearing, but, considering that the maturity level of the New York staff didn't rise above college freshman, it wasn't far-fetched to think that I was the target of a prank.

"I'm afraid not," he answered. "You must have misunderstood me."

"We both know I didn't misunderstand you, Davey," I said, trying to hold myself together; my anxiety flared into anger. "I have an e-mail trail of our conversations."

"Not much was ironed out over e-mail," he replied, "but I have to let you go now. Someone just walked into my office. Hope to see you Monday."

By the time I relayed the phone call to my parents, I had the colorless pallor of the cement floor beneath me. I'd heard all of the tales about unscrupulous Hollywood executives who stopped at nothing to keep their jobs, but I was devastated that my Los Angeles welcome mat was woven with such a trite story.

"I think you should print those e-mails," my father said, "and we will take Davey and the studio to court."

"There's no point in that," I answered. "No one will want to hire me if that's my introduction to the industry."

"You're right, Josh," my mother continued. "You'll find another job, and we'll laugh about this in a couple of months."

Within 20 minutes, before my head even stopped spinning, the phone rang again. This time, it was the head of human resources.

"I just got off a call with Davey Wilson," he said, "and I understand that there are some e-mails detailing your transfer to LA. Is that correct?"

"Yes," I said. "Were you not aware that this was happening?"

"None of it was cleared through the appropriate channels, and Davey is in some hot water. Can you please forward the e-mails to me?" I sent them immediately, and my job was reinstated one hour later.

"I'm really sorry this happened," the human resources executive said, "and I hope this won't impact your enthusiasm for the company." He was your typical HR drone, vomiting company lines like he had a case of the Tinseltown Flu. "We're so happy to have you in LA, and I will see you for orientation on Monday." Apparently, Davey had his head handed to him for not getting the proper approvals and attempted to avoid the corporate consequences by throwing me to the wolves.

My colleagues at studio headquarters were seasoned, professional adults who taught me the strategies behind effective public relations. They introduced me to opinion-making press contacts and gave me many opportunities to be more involved with events and movie campaigns than the higher-ups had allowed in New York. But, while I appreciated my new work environment, I couldn't get rid of the bad taste Davey left in my mouth. I felt less invested in my job because of the insecurity he instilled; Aladdin's carpet could have been pulled out from under me at any moment – Davey had already demonstrated the trick.

I woke up to my first earthquake on the day of the press junket for *The Insider*, an Oscar contender about a tobacco industry whistleblower. The lead cast – including Russell Crowe and Al Pacino – was set up in hotel rooms that had been transformed into small production studios, and press from across the country filed in, one by one, to interview the stars in four-minute blocks. My job was to make sure that the journalists got the most out of their time with the talent, and I hustled everyone in and out of the interview suites with an admirable efficiency. Unfortunately, I wasn't sure that I was a match for the Australian gladiator's bad behavior.

"Josh, why are all of these journalists still waiting to interview Russell?" one of my bosses asked. We were about to break for lunch.

"He arrived more than 30 minutes late," I replied, "and he has been taking cigarette breaks between every interview."

"You need to fix this," my boss said. "We can't let one of these press people leave without a Russell Crowe interview." She didn't seem to be the least bit concerned that his production suite smelled like an ashtray in spite of the movie's anti-tobacco message or that his smoking was what was taking time away from the media. I learned quickly that many of the senior staff members had purchased the emperor's new clothes from consignment shops; they wanted to keep their jobs and used smoke and mirrors to demonstrate their value to studio chiefs. They weren't necessarily skilled or talented but rather lucky to have failed upward.

"Would you like me to ask him to stop with the cigarettes?" I questioned. He was a new Hollywood name, but he already had an A-list attitude. I didn't really want to go toe-to-toe with him.

"I don't know what to tell you to do," she said, "but you have to figure out something." She must have thought, as a 24 year-old assistant, I was more capable of solving the problem than she was – a compliment and a conundrum at the same time.

With the help of some co-workers, I was able to maneuver the schedule to please everyone, and the day ended successfully. The same could not be said for the movie's premiere at the Academy of Motion Picture Arts and Sciences only days later, at which Mr. Crowe appeared to have enjoyed a considerable amount of alcohol; he yelled at his staff in front of guests and media before leaving in a limo with a female co-star.

"I can't believe that," my mom said, as I relayed the details of the premiere on my drive home. "I guess it's fun to be in the midst of all the tabloid drama."

"I suppose so," I replied, "but it's really stressful and frustrating, like trying to corral 80 toddlers." My celebrity encounters since transitioning from intern to full-time employee weren't the same kind of fun. I was no longer the cute college kid who charmed the stars simply by being in the room. The stakes were higher because the pressure was now on me to clean up – sometimes literally – their messes. However, the glittering lights made me interesting to people around me (my friends and family loved the excitement of my day-to-day existence and the "inside" stories), and I wanted to cultivate their enthusiasm. I couldn't wait for the day that I would move up and be even more appealing to people without having to shovel shit from spoiled celebrities. So, when Shelly Stafford, the head of publicity at a rival studio, called late one afternoon, I was ecstatic to step outside for a conversation.

"I've heard from some friends at your office that you're quite the powerhouse," she said.

"That's nice to hear," I answered calmly, trying to sound composed. Inside, my stomach was doing cartwheels; my reputation had made its way to someone powerful.

"Can you come in early next week? I want to talk to you about a lower management job at our company." She got right to the point.

When her assistant showed me into her office – a cream colored palace appointed with ornate furniture and freshly cut flowers on every surface – Shelly, who was notorious for being a nasty bitch, was sitting with her back to me.

"Are you willing to work 24 hours a day?" she yelled out over her shoulder, not swiveling in her chair even the slightest to look at me.

"I'm happy to do whatever it takes to get the job done well," I said as I stared at her back. Her head was tracked with obvious hair extensions that were due for tightening, and a Barney's price ticket poked out from the back of her neck. I had a feeling that she was the type to wear something once or twice and then return it – not the kind of woman whose protruding clothing tag was an oversight.

"That's a good answer," she said, her eyes still fixed on the computer screen in front of her rather than the job candidate behind her. "I can pay you $50,000.00 more than you're making now, and you'd have to start in two weeks. Do we have a deal?"

She didn't have to ask twice; I accepted the offer before she even laid eyes on me.

"Wow," Shelly said. "You look like a baby." She had finally turned around and stood up to show me out of her office.

"I hear that a lot," I said, "but I have the experience and the drive to do this job." I felt as though I had to excuse my appearance by up-selling my capabilities.

"I am counting on it," she said as she walked me to the door and closed it behind me without a goodbye or a hand-shake.

Two years into the job, I was promoted to mid-level management. By age 27, I was the director of my department and earning a hefty six-figure salary. Friends whom I'd left behind at my first job marveled at what they saw as a lightning-fast rise to executive status.

"You're hitting it out of the park, aren't you?" one former colleague said over Chinese chicken salads at Mo's in Burbank. "Do you love the gig?"

"I am working around the clock," I replied, "but it's nice to not be answering someone's phone anymore." I wished I could have responded to her question with a resounding, "Yes!"

"I dream of that day," she said, "I can't wait to have the disposable income that you do." She had noticed my new Lexus SUV when I arrived at the restaurant.

I still felt like a half-baked person who was an undesirable outsider, but the perception of my success gave me a mis-guided sense of acceptance. Growing up, I was a pariah, the kid everyone teased for being different. Now, my advanced career and access to the glitterati made me uniquely alluring to those who envied my Hollywood lifestyle. Thankfully, no one was around to hear my boss beating me down each day or to observe my second holiday season at the company.

"I haven't signed the department Christmas cards," I said. "Did they get mailed out already?"

"That ship has sailed," Shelly answered tersely. "You should be focused on your work and not a stack of greetings."

"This is the second year in a row that I haven't been acknowledged on the cards for vendors and press," I said. "I want them to realize that I'm an important part of this department."

"Maybe your third year here will be the charm," she said, raising her voice, "and perhaps you're not as important as you think." She was the living, breathing definition of the word "cunt;" Shelly knew I was her star employee but treated me like a gnat that could be flicked away by a well-manicured finger.

"Speaking of important," she said, "we need to walk across the lot to a filmmaker meeting." We were set to talk with the executive producer of a documentary film that the studio was promoting; it was in contention for an Academy Award and was a labor-intensive project.

"I didn't realize you were bringing *him* to this meeting," the producer said as we walked into her bungalow office.

"He's spearheading the campaign," Shelly answered, "so I figured he would need to hear whatever you wanted to say."

"So be it," she said, rolling her eyes. "Here's the bottom line: Josh is too young and inexperienced to work on my movie."

"Has anything fallen through the cracks? I think the campaign has been first-rate," Shelly said. She had my back only when it reflected positively on *her* department.

"Everything has been great so far," the producer continued, "but I have a gut feeling that I can't ignore."

"I'll have to take some time to think things over. Let me sleep on it, and I'll get back to you tomorrow. I'm not sure that taking Josh off of this project is in your best interest." By that, Shelly meant that it wasn't in her own best interest.

"You're going to keep working on this film," Shelly said as we walked back to our offices together.

"That may not be the best idea," I replied. "If she has a preconceived idea about my age and experience, maybe it would be better to assign someone else."

"You're the best person I have," she said. "She'll know that by the end of this project."

"So, I'm the best person you have on staff, but I'm not important enough to sign the holiday cards?" I asked, still hurt by the slight.

"Exactly," she said. "Don't bring it up again."

I worked at the company for another year, planning and executing publicity campaigns for some of the world's biggest movies and television series. Some days, I was lunching with the producer of *Entertainment Tonight* and then having dinner with the editor of *US Weekly*, all with the purpose of generating media interest in our projects. It was just as likely that I'd be watching over the set of a *Vanity Fair* cover shoot as it was that I'd be meeting with a famous film director to discuss how he could more effectively speak about his movie with journalists. Box office success, unprecedented home video sales and awards recognition fueled my drive and gave me a sense of professional satisfaction. All that, coupled with the fact that family, friends and colleagues who were dazzled by my meteoric trajectory, made the bitter pills of soul crushing bosses easier to swallow.

Davey Wilson and Shelly Stafford were socially accept-able bullies. They were no more evolved than the school kids who terrorized me as a youngster. The only difference? Their behaviors weren't designed to single me out; they treated everyone with similarly dehumanizing disregard. Having been marginalized for so many years, though, it was hard to not take it personally. I had allowed myself to be a second-class citizen at work so that I could maintain the approval of those in other areas of my life. Everyone wanted to know about the films I was working on – *Harry Potter and the Sor-cerer's Stone, The Lord of the Rings, Toy Story 2, Kill Bill* and *The Notebook*, among many others – and I was compelled to keep delivering gossip and war stories in order to feel worthy of their attention.

My career advanced quickly; I was a senior vice president with my own luxury home and a Porsche by the time I was 30. I had closets full of designer clothes and enough shoes to make Imelda Marcos feel underprivileged. I didn't, however, have the sense of self to enjoy the material rewards on my own terms.

How was it possible that I still felt lonely and insecure? I seemingly had it all – the spoils that accompanied my monetary compensation and the VIP access that was tied to my senior-level title. What no one saw from the outside, though, was a man who worked around the clock without the time to cultivate meaningful friendships – and without the courage to be himself. My sexuality was still simmering below a well-dressed surface, creating a stifling pressure. My job and its perceived glamour masked a real, live human who was bursting to get out of the closet.

I called my friend Renée on my way home from a work event that I had produced at UCLA's Royce Hall. The program included dramatic readings and music from the film *Cold Mountain*, a historical drama I was tasked with publicizing. Much of my night had been spent in a small, backstage greenroom chatting with Nicole Kidman, Jude Law and Sting. Nicole was luminous, with almost translucent skin that made the cascade of strawberry curls around her face seem too perfect. Jude's receding hairline couldn't stand in the way of his good looks, and Sting was, well, Sting. It didn't come cooler in my eyes than Gordon Sumner.

"Why don't you ever bring me to any of these things?" Renée asked when I told her about my night. "I would kill to have your life." I understood where she was coming from; at one time, I had dreamed of escaping behind the silver screen.

"It's not as exciting as it seems," I answered. "It's not *my* life. Nicole and Jude and Sting don't come home with me." I paused for a moment and considered the words that had come out of my mouth. It wasn't, in fact, my life. Just over a decade prior, friends were ashamed to be seen with me; now they clamored to be on my arm.

"I don't care what you say," she replied, "it's pretty awesome. You're the coolest person I know."

OPEN WIDE

"It might turn you on to know how many ways you can fuck someone in that shower," Norm said, as he proudly showed off the interior of his itty bitty bathroom; he was giving me the grand tour of his one bedroom apartment in West Hollywood. I could see the whole place from the front door, but I didn't want to rain on his parade.

Norm's living room and bedroom, which made up the remainder of his, um, humble living quarters, were draped in fringe and fabric and accented with candles in a variety of shapes and sizes. It looked like a place that Stevie Nicks would live if she lost her money and was forced to settle in Gay Town, USA.

"It's a great flat, isn't it?" he asked. He traveled internationally for work and had a tendency to pepper his language with foreign terms and phrases. It was a bloody annoying affectation, but I was so charmed by his Italian good looks that I "kept calm and carried on."

"It's definitely cozy and homey," I said. I always had a hard time lying outwardly, so I responded in a way that was truthful, even if it wasn't a direct answer to the question. And, frankly, I wanted to steer the conversation back to sex play in his powder room.

"The idea of two people in your shower is kind of hot," I said, "but they would have to be Mary-Kate and Ashley Olsen to fit in together." The seamless glass cubicle was so tiny that I don't know how Norm even fit his own hulking, 6'1" frame inside.

"Very funny," he said, "but, trust me, it's easy for two men to get close in there."

"They'd have no choice; one would actually have to be inside the other," I quipped. Norm was dark and gorgeous – albeit somewhat smarmy – and I was hard at the idea of being pushed up against him under a cascade of hot water. I imagined my small hands running through his thick, black hair until they worked their way down to his crotch.

"That's exactly how it would happen," he said, "because all three of us couldn't be in the shower together otherwise."

"Three? Are you expecting someone else to join us?" I was confused.

"Me, my big cock and you. If I push myself right in behind you, it would work out fine," he answered with a sexy smile. I could feel my dick sticking to the front pouch of my Armani boxer-briefs. It was our sixth date, and I was hopeful.

"I think I might like that," I answered playfully. "Are you feeling like you need to rinse off?" I was scared about what it would it feel like to be fucked and whether or not I would be able to keep from cumming too quickly, but my fear was outweighed by the fully extended excitement in my pants.

"I'm kind of wet already," Norm winked. Despite my profound insecurity, I was certain I wasn't misreading his signal; my arm reached toward his hip. With his eyes boring into my hand, he took a giant step back and moved closer to the front of his apartment.

"I really enjoyed dinner tonight, and thank you for coming over to see my place," he said, giving me a quick peck on the lips and motioning towards the exit. He didn't have to walk me to the door because it was only steps away from any of the three rooms.

"Are we saying goodnight?" I asked, surprised at the abrupt end to the evening. His innuendo implied I would get a ride on the log flume.

"I'm really tired, and I have to get up early to work out tomorrow," he said. In porn films, plumbers jump into bed with their customers when they first meet and cops don't so much as read someone his rights before getting the perpetrator on all fours. How had I met the one gay man in West Hollywood who didn't want to bend a willing guy over – especially since I'd waited 31 years for that moment?

In the years leading up to that night, I had ignored advances and blocked stares from members of the same sex. I'd rehearsed a script that the camp counselor and Andy Webber had written across my mind, and I settled into the idea that, to be worthy of people's approval, I had to be closeted. I engaged in only "safe activities," those that would include my single, female friends and would not put me in a bar, dance club or around gay people. Limiting my interactions with "wildcards" – people who would openly make assumptions about my sexuality or ask questions about my romantic life (or, in my case, the lack thereof) was also part of my routine. Those I kept close sensed my unease and followed my lead; they avoided the subject.

Work obligations had thrown me into uncomfortable situations at times, as much as I tried to avoid them. At an awards show in Hollywood, I was seated next to a handsome, middle-aged man who was nominated on behalf of a project he'd produced for the studio I represented. As we made friendly small talk – I was half his age and looked even younger – I could feel his hand brush against my thigh.

"Do you like how that feels?" the producer whispered. My entire body tensed up, and I quickly pulled my leg from his grip. I felt heat on the back of my neck, as though everyone's eyes were on me. The room would know I was gay.

"How what feels?" I asked, pretending to be oblivious to his advance.

"My hand so close to your hot dick," he said.

"Sorry, it's kind of loud in here. I can't really hear you." I was tap dancing on a Cheerio, and I wasn't going to be able to keep it going.

He moved to the very edge of his seat and put his lips right against my ear.

"I bet you would be able to hear me if I tied you to a bed and had my way with you." That came in loud and clear, and I wanted out of the room like yesterday.

Uncomfortably stuffed into black-tie evening wear, I fidgeted in my seat like a trapped badger. Moving as far away from the producer as the 24-inch width of my chair would allow, I looked around the room erratically. The other guests were laughing and engaged in their own conversations throughout the two-minute commercial break, and I was thankful that no one appeared to have noticed what was going on in my row. In my head, all of their attention was on me. When the presentation continued, I breathed for a moment; I had ten minutes to figure out how I was going to escape when the lights came back up.

"I have to run to the bathroom," I said, the minute I was able to stand. "I'll be right back."

"Can I go with you and hold your junk while you pee?" he asked. I moved away so fast he probably didn't realize that I'd actually heard him. My first instinct was to switch seats with a female colleague who was seated farther back in the auditorium, but I didn't want her to know what was happening. Instead, I found my boss and told her that I was feeling sick; I needed to get home before my stomach rumblings became projectile. I wasn't lying.

When the crowd was seated again, I walked into the empty restroom. In the mirror closest to the door, I stared at my pale face. The blood had rushed from my cheeks. I splashed cold water into my eyes and then dried them with an industrial paper towel that felt like sandpaper across my skin. My mother was expecting me to call on my way home, and what was I going to tell her?

"Is it over already?" my mother asked. "I didn't expect to hear from you for another hour." Even though she was on east coast time, she always waited up to make sure I got home OK – as Jewish mothers do.

"I left early," I said. "I wasn't feeling well."

"Was there someone to cover for you?" My mom knew

that I wouldn't leave a work event prematurely unless I was on a gurney.

"Yes, there were plenty of people from the studio there."

"Who were you sitting next to? Anyone interesting?" I was hoping the question wouldn't come up, but my mother liked to discuss details.

"One of the producers of a movie I am working on," I replied.

"Was he someone who could be helpful to you down the line?" she continued. She was always looking at the big picture.

"I don't think I'll be in touch with him again," I answered. "He made me a little uncomfortable." As much as I didn't want her to know what occurred, I also needed to get it off my chest – and no one was closer to me than my mom. On occasions when someone assumed that I was gay, I felt that I had to tell her – in the event that the person got to her first. It wasn't rational; she lived 2500 miles away and would never have a reason to be in contact with anyone in my Rolodex. Nonetheless, I wanted to reiterate that I liked women and did not plan to veer from my career path because of dating distractions. My professional life was an easy cover.

"What did he say to upset you?" she pressed.

"I think he might have thought I was attractive." I down-played his interest.

"I hope you made it clear that you're not his kind," she said.

His kind? If she meant "lecherous pig," I was, in fact, not his kind. She didn't know, however, the carnal nature of his desire for me. Instead, she used the phrase "his kind" to mean "gay." A shooting pain went through my forehead, creating such a dizzy spell that I thought I was going to throw up on my Dolce & Gabbana tuxedo. She didn't realize that her words were punching me deeper into the closet.

"I'm glad I left. I'll be able to get to bed early," I said, shifting gears. I became an expert at the art of the subtle subject change, a conversational technique I employed when sexuality was a topic – as it inevitably would be when I bought pornography for the first time during a business trip to New York.

The first publication I got my hands on was *Playguy*, a stapled monthly that included five or six pictorial layouts of naked men in every enticing position imaginable. On second thought, some weren't even imaginable until I saw them.

Immediately upon leaving the store, I was haunted by the fact that the cameras at the newsstand captured my purchase on tape. Never mind that no one would ever know who I was or would be able to report it to my parents, but I was in a panic. There was no going back; the evidence had been recorded. I called my mom, naturally.

"You won't believe what just happened," I said.

"Nothing bad, I hope," she answered.

"I was shopping at the newsstand next to my hotel, and I inadvertently picked up a gay porn magazine with my stack of newspapers," I said. There was nothing inadvertent about it, but at least I was able to tell her my version of the story before the clerk at the store called. I was certain that he had searched the security tape, had the authorities identify me and was ready to drop the bomb on my folks.

"Take it back; maybe you can get a refund," my mother suggested.

"It was only $8.99," I replied. "So it's probably not worth

the time." The pages were already a little sticky; I'd had it for an hour before the phone conversation. Let it suffice to say that a return was out of the question.

"Just throw it away," she said. "You don't want that lying around. Someone might get the idea that you're a homosexual." Other than the maid who may have spied the magazine in my bag, I wasn't sure who that someone might have been. Regardless, my mom didn't want people to think that her son had a sexual interest in men. The tone with which she spoke the word "homosexual" had the formality of a diagnosis – and it sounded as though she'd be embarrassed if others believed me to have the "disease."

As worthless as I felt at the harsh words of schoolmates and homophobic adults, nothing crushed my spirit more than the thought of the most important person in my life feeling ashamed of me. It wasn't as if I were a criminal, a bad person who made the choice to execute a shameful act. Who I was on the inside was entirely out of my control; my sexuality was as natural to me as my eye color. Nevertheless, I helped keep her illusions, and nobody saw the internal bleeding.

I continued to buy porn secretly, graduating from magazines to movies within a year. I was so fearful that my true self would be discovered that I was particularly diligent in discarding the adult video sleeves and DVD inserts; there was no way that visitors to my home could possibly stumble upon them accidentally. As an extra security measure, I hid the actual discs in packaging for legitimate films. *Fill My Ass*, for example, was hidden in *Terms of Endearment* binding, and *Homo on the Range* was disguised in a *Beaches* wrap. It didn't dawn on me that the melodramatic tearjerkers were as much a giveaway as *Men Who Fuck Each Other: Part 4*.

It also didn't dawn on me that a seemingly innocuous invitation to a Bar Mitzvah was a calculated, romantic set-up. Susan, a work colleague with a 13 year-old son, was a "wildcard" in sheep's clothing. She and I were friendly at the office, but our relationship didn't call for inclusion in a family event. Her gay, single friend Norm, however, was on the guest list, and Susan decided to host our first meeting – unbeknownst to me.

I noticed him the minute he walked into the synagogue. It was hard to miss his height or the spiky shock of hair that appeared to defy gravity and even more difficult to ignore his nearly perfect facial features. Across the aisle and seated three rows in front of me, I was able to glance at Norm throughout the service without anyone being aware of my divided attention. The party that followed had the two of us seated – not coincidentally – at the same table, and he was less discreet about focusing his eyes on me.

"Mr. Cute Guy over there is staring you down," the guest next to me said during dinner. "You should jump all over that." She obviously sensed that I was gay and likely thought I was too old to be closeted.

"Really?" I asked with a surprised inflection. "I hadn't noticed."

"Oh, honey, he has been ready to pounce all night," she said.

"I don't think so," I answered, looking down at my plate and laughing modestly. Norm was hot; his name was misleading. It wasn't possible that he could be interested in me; I was still the chunky fag whom other people didn't want to hang around, at least in my mind.

I excused myself from the table for what I'm sure my

seatmate thought was a bathroom break. After 30 minutes, she had to have realized I wasn't coming back. If Norm was, in fact, going to pounce, I had no idea how to handle it. And, if I had known that the invitation was a set up, I wouldn't have attended in the first place.

"Hi, Mom. I'm on my way home from the Bar Mitzvah." I had called her from the car, even though it was 1:00AM in Florida.

"That was a short party," she said.

"Yep. People left early," I answered. This time, I didn't walk close to the truth. I had a strangely pleasant feeling in the pit of my stomach, and no barb from my mother – even unintentional – was going to chase it away. I may have run from the dinner table like a Hollywood bulimic, but I left with a rapid heartbeat and an excitedly nervous belly. At 31, I developed my first crush.

The next two weeks became an emotional seesaw, ups and downs that were by turn maniacally exhilarating and pitch dark. The butterflies flew into my stomach for hours at a time while I thought about Norm's adoring eyes, only to be eaten by the snakes that wrapped my insides like a vise. Was Norm, at last, a gateway to self-acceptance? And, if he was, didn't I need approval from my family to walk through the arch? It was thrilling to think of where I could end up but agonizing to consider the journey.

My parents are very smart, scientific thinkers whose liberal outlooks have shaped my own left-leaning political views. They are outwardly accepting of everyone. My fear was rooted in one central question: would they be accepting of *me*? It's one thing to embrace the world when they're not family members. How close to home is too close for comfort?

I wasn't ready to alter the paradigm between us. I wanted them to take the same interest in my life that they had for 31 years, and I worried that I would be marginalized by my primary support system. What if they were embarrassed of me because of the "nontraditional" nature of my sexual orientation? What if our communication became infrequent or worse, nonexistent? I was unsettled and frightened by the fact that my sexuality could create an irreparable chasm in the foundation of our bond.

Finally, my need for romantic love and physicality was waging a battle with the terror of a familial fallout. For too long, I ignored every sexual impulse and denied myself high school hook-ups, college tumbles and one-night stands. I convinced myself I hadn't been openly dishonest with anyone about my sexuality because I never acted on it. Being "found out" and a shame to my parents was of more concern than being true to myself, and I started to feel crippled by it. The positive attention that came from Norm's small gestures of interest gave me the confidence to move in the direction of authenticity.

"What brings you here today?" my new therapist, Donna, asked. She was referred by a friend, as was my fitness trainer. I assembled a gay guidance team in anticipation of my new life.

"My sexuality," I said. The words, "I'm gay," had never come from my mouth.

"What *about* your sexuality?" she continued.

"I prefer men," I answered, "and I haven't told anyone yet."

"You don't think people might suspect that you're gay?" She said it. Gay.

"Probably; I don't think it will surprise anyone but my mother."

"You honestly think she doesn't realize?" It was hard for Donna to believe.

"She's a little naïve in that regard," I answered. "But you'd think she would have put two and two together when I wanted a Cher album for Chanukah at 12." I made my first gay joke, and it danced off of my tongue effortlessly. There was a freedom in not having to pretend that I was interested in the pop diva because of her skimpy outfits – and in being able to talk about my crush on Norm.

"You know that you can go on a date with him before you come out to your parents, yes? You can live your life and share what you want in your own time." Donna, in one hour, cut the binding that strapped me for so many years.

"I'm going to tell them tomorrow," I said. "I don't like the idea of being dishonest with anyone, let alone my family. If I am going on a date with a man, I need my parents to know about it." I wanted to see Norm without wasting another minute.

I called my sister the following morning, my voice muffled by nervous tears and their related congestion. Nancy had laryngitis and was able to croak out only a few lines and acknowledging noises. I gave her the news, and she, from what I could make out, was far from surprised. She was happy that I was ready to live a genuine life.

We conferred about the best time to tell my parents and decided to get on the phone with them together that evening. I was grateful for my sister's support and willingness to be on the call – considering that we were all in different states – but, honestly, how was she planning to help with no voice? Press 1 for "We Accept You," or press 2 for "Find Another Family?"

During the day, I was working on a film campaign with

sitcom star Paul Reiser and veteran actor Peter Falk. It was a small movie called *The Thing About My Folks*, a project aptly titled for my circumstance. Paul and I had lunch together that afternoon, but I was a bundle of nerves; and, of course, he had no idea that he was an innocent bystander on my coming out day. I don't know how I got through the meal or had a coherent conversation with Paul – not to mention how I dealt with an annoyingly ornery "Columbo," may he rest in peace – and the hours passed glacially until 6:30PM pacific time.

"What's wrong? Why are you both on the phone together?" My mother knew something was going on, aside from my sister having lost her voice.

"We want to talk with you and Daddy, all together, as a family." She yelled out to my father, who joined the call immediately.

"Who's in trouble?" my father asked.

"No one's in trouble," I assured them. "But I want to tell you and Mom something very important." They were silent. "I am..." I stammered a little bit. "I am like Aunt Lorraine."

"What do you mean, 'you're like my sister?'" My dad wasn't smelling what was on the grill.

"I'm not an overweight lesbian in Levis and flannel," I said, "but I'm gay." They were quiet. "Are you upset?"

"The only thing that would make me upset," my father said, "is if you weren't happy during all of the time you were sitting on this." I started to cry.

"Or, if you don't use protection," my mother added. "You have to be safe."

"That has nothing to do with being gay, Mom," I answered.

"I know, I'm just saying," she said.

"If you're 'just saying,' why didn't you 'just say it' years ago?" She didn't have an answer, but she had a question.

"You have never slept with a woman, right?" she asked.

"That is correct; I am a virgin." All of my cards were on the table – and I mean *all* of them – from that moment forward.

"So how do you know you wouldn't like it?" My dad, Nancy and I started laughing at the same time.

"Well, have you ever slept with a woman? Because, if not, how do *you* know that you're not really a lesbian?" Even my mother realized how stupid her question had been; nothing along those lines came up again.

There was only one thing that disappointed me about my parents' behavior during my coming out: the way they chose to deal – or not deal, for that matter – with my grandparents. At that time, my paternal grandfather and my maternal grandmother were still alive. Grandma Beverly died in 2006 just before I would meet my first boyfriend, Gavin, so there was never an opportunity to tell her who I was about to become. Grandpa Al was another story. My parents did not want him to know about my sexuality and went as far as to ask me, when bringing my boyfriend home for Thanksgiving, to visit my grandfather alone. They were worried that he would suspect something if he saw us together.

My chest ached because I'd been so proud of how they handled everything and then gravely upset by their attempt to throw a sheet over me. I understood that my grandfather was from a different generation, one that didn't accept homosexuality as freely. But, I had spent years being someone else, and I couldn't bear the idea of being asked to mask my identity to put others at ease. I would have been OK if my grandfather died at that moment from the shocking news because at least I could hold onto my integrity. When someone asks you to disguise who you are – and by the way, I wasn't planning to review the *Gay Kama Sutra* with Grandpa Al, just introduce him to Gavin – it crushes you into a million little pieces. It's like you're a damaged collectible that people want to trade in for a shiny, new model they'd be proud to display. I was devastated and refused to visit my grandfather without my boyfriend.

For years – starting with my summers at Camp Shalom – many people who suspected I was gay made comments and slurs. That was the reason I knew to keep it a secret and let my quick wit be my shield. When your own family reiterates the messaging of ignorant bullies, albeit unknowingly, the sting is hard to bear – especially when you're in your thirties and finally feel free enough to step into yourself.

The next Thanksgiving, Gavin was again with me in West Palm Beach, this time joined by adopted lesbian Aunt Lorraine. I was sitting at the dining room table – extended to capacity to accommodate every loner and misfit neighbor my father would agree to include – across from my Grandpa Al and my aunt. He would look over at me and Gavin, glancing back at Lorraine from time to time. Towards the end of the night, I saw him lean into his daughter.

"You know, Lorraine," he said, "I just hope that Josh is happy."

"He looks better than I've ever seen him," she answered. "I'd say he's happy."

He knew what he needed to know. What he didn't know before his death in 2009, however, was how terribly underestimated he was by my parents in this particular circumstance.

When Grandpa Al passed away, his estate was divided between my parents and my father's sister. What little was left – a small condo and an annuity – was evenly distributed among my father, my mother and Lorraine. My mom had always been there for my father's parents as though she was a biological child, and the will was specific in rewarding her warmth and loyalty. At the end of their lives, all of my grandparents' business had been tied up neatly with a bow, seemingly erasing the many years that they harbored resentment towards Aunt Lorraine because she was a lesbian. Their disapproval was cloaked in petty upsets, such as her not visiting as much as they would have liked during her college years. But, there was no denying that her sexuality was a pin in their hearts.

As the years went by, my grandparents took some bold steps towards accepting Lorraine as a gay woman. In fact, she would sometimes visit their home in South Florida, most often having her girlfriends in tow. A serial monogamist, Lorraine fell on the Melissa Etheridge side of the "Lipstick to Butch" chart, so I was always curious to see whom she would bring home to meet the folks. The entire cast of *Fraggle Rock* was represented at one time or another.

It must have been extremely difficult for Aunt Lorraine, coming into her own as an adopted child and a gay woman during the 1960s. She did the best she could to be true to herself, and my grandparents did the best they could with a limited political and emotional outlook that was reflective of the times. Over the years, fences were mended to a degree, but there was always an unspoken divide – which is why my parents didn't want me to reveal to Grandpa Al that I was gay. Their reasoning was that two homosexuals in the immediate family was adding insult to injury and that there was no need for Grandpa Al to go to his grave with that information. I was glad that it didn't quite work out that way and that his intuition told him that I was finally living a full life.

I took note of a couple of interesting things during my coming out. First was that I didn't have to come out only once. I had the conversation multiple times with multiple friends. I felt that it was important to tell the people who were closest to me that I was, essentially, starting a new life. Doing it over and over was exhausting; even I was tired of hearing my story. Second, I saw how much deeper my friendships with people became. There was no longer an elephant in the room. No wondering. No subject off limits. People who valued my friendship had previously tiptoed around me, never wanting to jeopardize our bond by touching a subject that I might find uncomfortable. Everything was out in the open.

One additional piece of the coming out puzzle also fascinated me: the idea that the process, in and of itself, meant that I was announcing to family and friends what I liked to do in the bedroom. To my knowledge, none of my straight friends had similar burdens: "Mom, I love to be tied up!" or "Hey, Sis, did you know that nothing makes me happier than having my clitoris stimulated with a vibrating rod?" weren't conversational sentiments among my heterosexual counterparts. I, on the other hand, had to accept the responsibility of announcing that I liked to have a man's penis in my mouth. I guess people were more comfortable knowing in advance that they might see me holding hands – or engaging in other common displays of romantic affection – with another male. But, nevertheless, it felt extremely personal and somewhat violating to have to talk openly about my sexual proclivities.

Coming into my own and being more open about my personal life also factored greatly into my professional growth. As a young executive, I was so tightly wound and had a one-track mind: all business, all the time. Because I had nothing else in my life towards which to channel my attention, I spent my days and nights obsessing over every detail of my work. Whenever I meet someone who is particularly uptight or a "stick in the mud," I am often the first to say that he or she just needs to get laid. My staff was most probably wishing that I would take my own advice.

While I fired a couple of assistants along the way – one would leave devil dolls in my office and start "hate pages" on Facebook – I considered myself lucky when it came to Ari, Lauren and Troy. All three of them were invaluable and supportive, but they would likely describe their time with me differently. Ari was my administrative assistant when I was initially coming out – which he didn't even know until he eventually surmised that the Gavin who was calling so frequently was more than a friend – and Lauren took Ari's spot when I promoted him. She had a front row seat for my transformation from an almost unbearably perfect robot into a more relaxed, light-hearted human being. Within a matter of two months, I became an entirely different person. I finally understood what it meant to have a life outside of the office, and it became crystal clear why most of my staff and colleagues didn't want to join me for all-nighters at the studio. Even the air seemed easier to breathe and my eyes saw everything just a little bit brighter.

My work ethic didn't change; I was still the boss who wanted everything lined up and in order. But, my less rigid style absolutely influenced the kind of executive I became throughout the years. I hired Troy when I started a new job after coming out – so he never knew the closeted Josh – and I have sometimes wondered what a conversation among my three superstar assistants might reveal. Each of them had the same boss in theory, but I was three different people during the periods that they worked for me. Unquestionably, they would characterize me as a highly skilled mentor who gave each of them opportunities to grow professionally. I have always been proud of that reputation. In struggling to find myself for so long, however, Ari and Lauren may have been short-changed by my stiff outlook. I am still in touch with all three and am thankful for the opportunity to make it up to them, hopefully with the same level of support that they offered me during a monumental time in my life.

I'd hoped that my time with Norm would have turned into something monumental. Prophetically, my first date with him – which doubled as my first date, period – was on Valentine's Day. We acknowledged the significance of the holiday and decided that, for us, it was just about getting to know each other – and Barbra Streisand.

Barbra happened to be sitting with her husband, James Brolin, at the very next table; it was a gay blessing. I actually thought things might work out because she was there for our first dinner. Barbra is, after all, the Lord of the Gays, right? (Coincidentally, it would be exactly five years later that I would go on a date with her son, Jason. It was on a Christian holiday, so it was fitting that the two of us would go out for Chinese food. Too bad that the General Tso's Chicken was spicier than he was.)

Norm and I continued to see each other for two months, but I became increasingly frustrated by the pace of the romance. He invited me out for an evening but would barely touch me. After 31 years, I was ready to kiss more than his mouth. He, however, was extremely reserved because of my lack of experience. He was keeping me close but wouldn't let our relationship move forward.

"I talked to my best friend," Norm said, "and she agrees with me. Being new to all of this, you can't possibly know what you want." *She* was your standard issue, zaftig fag hag.

"I'm not starting out at 20," I said. "I may be romantically immature, but I have life experience."

"I don't know if I can do this," he said. "I feel like you need to get out there and try things."

"I want to try *this* out," I said, "with you."

"That's sweet," he answered condescendingly. "You're adorable. But, I don't want to get attached and then find that you want to explore other men."

"So, you would prefer that I go out and have sex with a bunch of guys," I asked, "so I can figure out what I want?"

"That's not exactly how I would put it, but yes," he said.

We had one last date, the sixth, during which he showed me his apartment, made sexually suggestive remarks and sent me home with only a fast kiss. I knew that we had come to the end of the line, but I didn't understand how the experience would scar me.

I became afraid that others, too, would be concerned about the responsibility of "being the first." Norm had cast me as a carnival freak show attraction – trapped in the center of three rings – as opposed to someone worthy of being loved on his own merit. After having felt ashamed about my sexuality for so long and then at last finding the courage to live on my own terms – even if it did take me more than three decades – Norm's rejection was like a blow to my head. He made me feel like I still had baggage I would need to hide if I wanted to be accepted and loved by another man.

Living most of my adult life in Los Angeles, the porn capital of the country, it was no wonder that the adult entertainment industry would wind up finding its way into my world just as Norm exited.

I would buy a number of succulent plant arrangements for my house and front porch from a quaint nursery in Santa Monica. Run by a handful of young, handsome gay men, it was always fun to visit, and my parents loved to look around the store when they would be in town. During one of their LA vacations, my mom and dad were in the back of the shop, looking at a couple of rare cactus plants. Of course, I noticed that I could see a sexy pair of dark briefs under the tight jeans of the gentleman who was waiting on them; he kept squatting down to show them various pots and blooms.

When he stood up and turned around, I realized that I had seen his ass before – in more than a dozen of my favorite porn films. Only in Southern California would my gray-haired parents be chatting with Bradley West, an adult entertainer whose green thumb had been in places they wouldn't want to imagine. His true talents would have turned their gray heads white. And, guess who comes to my house twice a month to water, feed and tend to my garden? Yep, Mr. West himself. Nothing droops in his presence.

I fantasized sometimes about living out a scene from one of Bradley's movies. The gardener shows up at the door, adorably handsome in his cargo shorts, t-shirt and flip-flops, bending over to water the plants. I happen to walk onto the patio in my robe, and, well, the ending is no mystery. I wanted to be bold enough to make a move on Bradley, who, at 35, was hotter than ever. My fear of rejection and fresh wounds from Norm kept me from even making an attempt. Also, I didn't want to offend the poor man. I suppose, however, that even rubbing him the wrong way would have been better than nothing. I still had yet to get laid.

PRIORITY MALE

It was about to go down. Or at least I was.

After 31 years, it had all come to this moment. Since junior high school, I dreamed of touching another man's naked body, and I longed for someone who wanted to touch mine. Gavin and I walked into the bedroom, hand in hand, and flopped onto his queen-size mattress. I landed on top of him, a position that turned him on; I could feel it in his pants.

"This is new for me," I said, worried about my performance. Would I cum too fast? Would I not be rhythmic in my movements?

"It has been a couple of years for me, too," he replied.

"No, you don't understand," I continued. "This is actually my first time."

"That's OK," he said, "let's take it slowly. We're not in a

rush." My virginity didn't faze Gavin the way it concerned Norm, and the sense of relief was indescribable. His sensitivity and kindness told me that he was the right person to experience sex with for the first time.

"I just wanted to be up front with you," I said.

"We don't have to make a big deal of it," Gavin replied, stroking my floppy hair. "Let's just enjoy each other without worrying about anything, OK?" He made me feel safe and wanted, unlike Norm who treated me as an undesirable oddity because of my lack of sexual experience.

Gavin's attraction to me sparked a confidence that I hadn't experienced previously, a taste of sexual power that coursed through my body like electricity. The temperature in my chest rose to a boil, and my brain began to flip through the catalog of porn scenes it had watched throughout the previous 10 years of daily rehearsals for my opening night. As Gavin lay flat on his back, I straddled his crotch on my knees, removing my shirt and unbuttoning my jeans. My five buttons were stretched to their limit and needed a release as much as I did.

"What…what…what do you like?" I asked, looking away from Gavin's face and tripping over my words. It was a piece of the sex puzzle that made me nervous and embarrassed, simply because I didn't know what *I* liked. In the adult films I'd seen, one partner was typically the top, or active partner, while the bottom got poked in the ass. I had no idea which end I wanted to be on. (I eventually learned that I'm versatile and enjoy both, which is an asset; guys who are steadfast in their "top" or "bottom" roles don't usually consider dating men who are inclined the same way, which further limits the dating pool.)

"Do you want to fuck me?" he whispered as I leaned forward to kiss his thin lips. He didn't have to say another word; the next hour moved along as though I had been practicing for years. Thankfully, my diligent study of porno movies taught me the general run down – kissing, nipple play, a blowjob and then intercourse – and I gave Gavin a mind-blowing orgasm that ultimately splashed across his chest, his chin and the headboard. We had barely recovered and wiped down the furniture when I felt Gavin's hand brush across the bulge in my black Calvins, signaling a Round Two that was as passionate as the first.

Exhilarated but exhausted, I stood up and dressed, only half lacing my leather boots. I ignored my OCD's call to clean the semen from my chest more thoroughly before buttoning my shirt, and I pulled my jeans over the cotton briefs that probably should have been burned instead of washed.

"When can we do this again?" Gavin asked with a crooked smile as I finished dressing. I took the question as a four-star review.

■ ■ ■

I situated myself in the driver's seat and watched Gavin walk back into his apartment building just as tears began to fall from my eyes. I looked in the rearview mirror, watching my emotions flood onto my face. There was so much to process in my head: I had just experienced romantic and sexual intimacy with another human being for the first time. Gavin wanted *me*. He was excited about *me*. He was turned on by *me*. The boy who had been ridiculed for years, who ate too much cake, who was an outsider – finally felt desired by another man. The tears were no longer of sadness or feelings of worthlessness from the past; they were salty drops of joy, excitement and hopefulness that stung my cheeks altogether differently.

I turned on the music system for my drive back to the Valley. Appropriately, "All Fired Up" from Pat Benatar blared through the speakers, and my tears dried into feelings of power and accomplishment. If it hadn't been 3:00AM, I would have called every friend programmed into my smart phone to tell them what just happened. Thanks to my porn education, my first time was a homerun – nothing clunky and no misfires. I earned that trophy and a second turn at bat. Or, rather, a second turn *with* my bat.

Gavin and I met working for the same movie studio in 2001, never mind that we were separated by more than 8,000 miles. He was stationed in the studio's Australian offices while I was based at the Los Angeles headquarters, but he visited from time to time.

"Isn't Gavin adorable?" a colleague said to me, taking for granted that I was gay before I had come out. My heart nearly stopped in those moments, which popped up frequently, as though I had been caught doing something wrong. I worked hard to keep my sexuality a secret – being deliberately vague with pronouns even though they didn't apply to romantic situations – and I panicked when I thought I had been detected. It seemed like a failure on my part.

Gavin was, indeed, very cute. At our first meeting, I paid attention to his slim fitting jeans, his causal t-shirt and lightly worn baseball cap; he had a strong, masculine physique. His cheeks were accented on both sides by dimples, and his green eyes had an approachable kindness that was genuine and appealing.

Just after coming out, I was at dinner with a friend who had been Gavin's supervisor at the time we worked together. I saw the wheels turning in her head when I mentioned how hard it was to meet quality dates in Los Angeles. (I am fairly sure that dating is hard *everywhere*, but people apply that phrase to their own cities in an attempt to feel better about being single. Guilty.)

"Gavin moved to LA a few months ago," my friend said, "and we have stayed close. You two should reconnect. He's very social, and he could probably introduce you to a lot of people."

"Is Gavin gay?" I asked. He had no glaring affects that led me to think one way or the other about his sexuality.

"Absolutely gay," she said. "He is in LA on a diplomatic visa because he is promoting Australia as a shooting location for US filmmakers," she answered. "He is hoping to turn it into something permanent."

I had no idea how loaded that statement would turn out to be, but Gavin was in touch to set a lunch date before I had time to give it much thought. I paid for our first meal, and, as Gavin walked towards the exit in front of me, I got a full view of his perfectly round ass. He had two small globes that combined to create a perfect, shelf-like bubble butt. I couldn't take my eyes off of it, and, fortunately, my long coat obscured the hard-on in my jeans.

Our second date was a pleasant dinner at a neighborhood restaurant during which Gavin continued to charm me with stories about his parents in Sydney and his close relationship with his sister and her kids. I was sold.

"How often do you speak to your parents?" Gavin asked in his captivating Aussie accent.

"Every day," I responded. "I know that doesn't make me sound cool, but we're very close." I didn't want to admit that I sometimes spoke to my mother three times in an afternoon.

"I think that's great," he said. "It says something about your character."

We smiled at each other, and I felt the embrace of romance and approval. My stomach dropped to the floor, and I began to push around the roasted chicken and baked potato that were on my plate. My appetite disappeared, and my empty tummy filled with the proverbial butterflies that tricked me into feeling full.

"I am thinking that there should be a third date," Gavin said. "How about dinner and a movie this coming Saturday night?"

At last, I knew what it was like to have feelings for someone that went beyond friendship. It was as if I was bouncing on a cloud instead of sitting in a metal chair. In an instant, the world felt lighter because I allowed myself to experience the affection that I had robbed myself of for so many years. Gavin didn't see the seven year-old at camp who had been teased all summer; he was oblivious to the high-schooler whom others didn't want to sit with at lunch; he hadn't met the overweight, unlovable person who had been under the surgeon's knife multiple times.

I was careful to choose the perfect outfit for Date 3: a pair of tight jeans with a light blue, checkered button-down shirt. Navy, lace-up boots that extended halfway up my calves added an edge to an otherwise safe wardrobe choice. At that point, I didn't know that Gavin had a thing for men in rugged boots and uniforms; had I been aware, I probably could have surmised how the evening was going to end.

Encouraged by the ease and flow of our conversation during dinner, I was hopeful that Gavin would make some affectionate gesture during the movie. I purposely placed my arm on the elbow rest between us, letting him know – at least I thought – that I was open to holding hands. The 90-minute feature ended without so much as a touch, leaving me to question whether or not Gavin actually found me physically desirable. I drove him home, which was a short two miles from the movie theater, and, as I pulled up to the front door of his building, he asked if I wanted to see his apartment. Maybe I had been too hasty in writing off his interest.

"There's a great pool on the rooftop," he said. "It's really worth a look."

It was less the pool – particularly considering that it turned out to be a four-foot deep wading puddle – and more the thought of possibly seeing Gavin naked that convinced me to park the car and join him for a tour of his place. The pay-off turned out to be good.

"Isn't this amazing?" he asked, as he walked me around the pool deck that overlooked the city. "On a clear night or a sunny day, it represents everything I love about being in Los Angeles."

Before I could respond, I felt Gavin's lips on mine. He wrapped his hands around the back of my neck and began to kiss me passionately, his tongue darting in and out of my mouth. I had no idea if I was a good kisser, but I knew that my large lips gave me an advantage – and I was too caught up in my own head to give in to the worry.

It was my very first kiss and yet it didn't feel awkward. Gavin's warm mouth fit so naturally onto my lips, and the sensation called the rest of my body to attention. I was conscious of my nipples; I could feel their rigidity touching the fabric of my shirt.

"Let's go down to my apartment," Gavin said, taking my hand and leading me to the second floor. The musty hallway and its substandard décor would have made the Ramada Inn feel proud, but it didn't soften my hard-on. Neither did the hodge-podge of Ikea furniture that Gavin had purchased on Craigslist.

Gavin turned on the television and went into his galley kitchen to mix drinks while I watched *The War of the Roses* on an obsolete TV set that was flickering in the corner. Before I had time to get too nervous about what might happen next, he had returned to the living room sofa with refreshments and an eager tongue. We made out for a couple of minutes before he led me to his bedroom.

■ ■ ■

My relationship with Gavin fell into place effortlessly over the next couple of months. There was no chase; neither of us faked the "hard to get" scenario – and no one runs after a stopped bus. Rather, we relaxed into a routine that was comfortable. By the middle of that summer, we were officially a couple who spent nearly all of our time together. Even our sex life had settled in terms of frequency and range after only eight weeks (my 24/7 drive remained in high hear; Gavin's was far less aggressive), but I had no frame of reference for what an adult courtship should be. Gavin accepted me; he thought I was smart and funny and unique. In turn, I accepted his companionship without understanding that it was OK to want more. It would be almost three more months before the dark clouds of fall would shade our new relationship.

"I have to talk to you about something," Gavin said when I walked into his apartment after work one evening. "It's not good news."

"What could be so terrible with me on your arm?" I tried to lighten the mood.

"I got laid off because of a restructure at my office," he said. "I have no job as of today." He looked down at the floor, embarrassed and dejected.

"Honey, we will find you another job; we are both very connected." My attempt to make him feel better didn't work.

"I don't think you're getting it." He was sharp with me for the first time. "This job sponsored my visa. Without it, I have to go back to Australia. It's not just about the work or the money. I won't be able to stay here with you."

"Can't we have the visa renewed?" I asked, as though it was as simple as getting a passport at the post office. I didn't know anything about the process.

"I would have to find a job at a company that is willing to sponsor and pay for my papers," he said. "It's nearly impossible unless you are married to a US citizen or you're famous."

At that time, same sex marriage was legal in certain states, but it was not recognized by the federal government. It would be mid-2013 before the Supreme Court would catch up with the times and strike down the Defense of Marriage Act (DOMA), so my marrying Gavin during his visa crisis would have accomplished nothing. I tried to be optimistic regardless, but Gavin seemed ready to throw in the towel.

For the next couple of months, Gavin met with what felt like every immigration attorney in Los Angeles, and thousands of dollars later, we were able to secure an 0-1 Visa that would be valid for three years. That particular credential required that the applicant be a person of extraordinary ability in his field of expertise. For example, an actress – maybe, say, Kate Winslet – who lives in the UK can work in the United States through an 0-1 Visa. With that requirement, we had to create a dossier on Gavin that spoke to his unique capabilities. Oddly, "good blow job" wasn't on the list. I worked around the clock to build a profile for him.

My ambition and drive – coupled with my resourcefulness – saw us through Gavin's initial visa problems. I kept my eyes on the prize and pushed through every brick wall in our way. He, however, fell under what he perceived to be an unmovable boulder, counting on me for all of the heavy lifting. During that time, our relationship transitioned from a balanced union into a parent/child dynamic, and, while I liked being needed, there was nothing less sexy to me than a helpless adult. It would not have been so immediately concerning, in hindsight, had the storm clouds disbanded with the immigration reprieve.

Just days after Gavin's visa became official, he received a letter from the management of his apartment complex. The building had been sold, and the tenants were given three months to find alternate housing before the units went condo. Gavin was in no position to purchase his one-bedroom pad.

"I feel like I have a thunderstorm over my head," Gavin told me that night. "It's one problem after another; now I have to find a place to live. Since I am not working, I don't really even have the money to move."

"We got through the immigration issue; we can figure this out, too," I reasoned, trying to calm him down despite my own mounting panic. We had been together just under a year, and it disheartened me to see him so beleaguered. I confused being needed with being in love – a product of my romantic immaturity – and I was about to pay a price for not knowing the difference.

"You could always move into my townhouse." The words came out of my mouth before I ran them by my head. This was my first relationship, and I had never lived with someone as an adult. I wasn't ready for Gavin – or anyone, for that matter – to share my home, but I didn't want him to have to search for an apartment with other roommates. Feeling bad for Gavin was poking holes through my romantic interest in him.

"I want to be with you," he said as his eyes welled and he kissed me passionately on the mouth. "This will be good for us."

While the invitation to live with me solved Gavin's problems, it exacerbated mine. His visa, work and living situations weighed heavily on me, as though they were entirely my problems. Coping with the stress, especially considering my history of anxiety issues, was not easy. I often felt pinned to the floor by Gavin's misfortunes and the pressure to provide for both of us financially.

"It's more than I can handle," I said to my mother on the phone during a work break one late afternoon.

"Daddy and I will help you and Gavin out with extra money if you need it," she replied. "Don't worry."

"It's not just the finances," I said. "For the entire year we have been together, it has been one hurdle after another. I love Gavin as a person, but I am not sure I'm actually *in love* with him. I feel like I am a caregiver and not a partner."

"He is a good person," my mother said, "and he's kind. I would feel bad if you split up. What would he do?"

"I don't know," I replied, "I worry about him, too."

"So, maybe you just stay put. Things will work themselves out," she said.

Weeks after Gavin moved in, feeling temporarily secure with his visa status and the roof over his head, he purchased a 1995 Porsche 911. It was his dream car, and he was able to finance the $30,000.00 over a five-year period. He kept his old Chevrolet run-around car for daily use so he could maintain the sports car's perfect condition.

"Are you sure you want to strap yourself financially for this toy?" I asked, trying to make a statement. "You'll be making a car payment in addition to covering the insurance costs for the Chevy and the Porsche."

"I don't really own anything in this world," he answered. "This would be mine."

"I hear what you're saying," I said.

What I also heard was that the money that Gavin could be contributing to our life together – even if only $500 per month – was now going towards a piece of metal sitting in my garage. I was buying him a Porsche. Resentment is the one emotion that eats its own container, and I was feeling chewed apart.

"You're wrong to feel that way," one of my friends told me while I was venting over lunch one afternoon. "The poor guy needs to have his name on something."

"In a perfect world, that would be great, but I am supporting a 40 year-old adult," I replied. "It would be nice if he contributed to the house or the utility bills. Even just a small amount."

"You're not hurting for the $500 a month," she continued.

"It's not about that," I said. "It's about feeling like Gavin is present in this relationship."

"You know, Josh, you're not the easiest person in the world to live with – especially with your OCD. Not to mention, you are new to the whole relationship thing, and he has been understanding of that."

"Meaning what?" I asked. I knew where the conversation was headed. "I shouldn't expect Gavin to pay his way because he was kind enough to take on a virgin?"

"Yes; in a way, he took on a responsibility," she said. "His responsibility is emotional, and yours is financial. It's a wash." For a while, I listened to those voices, those of my own friends who supported Gavin's position over mine. Apparently, they agreed that I *still* had to pay for arriving at the fair freakishly late.

I remained more concerned about Gavin's well-being than my happiness; it was like having a noose around my neck all the time. He survived on my resources, and I put his needs before my own. We coexisted that way for a few years. I knew that, in his heart, he was grateful, but he rarely articulated it. I also knew that I needed some excitement to help lift me out of the depression I was falling into.

One evening while thumbing through a local Los Angeles weekly paper, I noticed ads for escorts in the back pages. I looked through every one of them, reading carefully their menus of services. After a couple of nights of consideration, it came to me: what if we hired a hooker for a three-way? And, even better, what if he was a porn star whom we both drooled over – a gay man's fantasy?

I had an appointment to see my therapist the next day,

and I mentioned my threesome idea. She explained that such escapades usually open a Pandora 's Box.

"Once you crack the bedroom door, Josh, all hell can break loose," she warned.

"I understand that," I said, "but how many men do you know who are 34 years-old and have had sex with only one person?"

"That's somewhat nontraditional, I agree," she said.

"I just wish I'd had a year or two to play the field before meeting Gavin," I continued. "His sexual interests are so limited. I want to try other things."

"Have you talked to him about it?" she asked.

"I mentioned it a number of times. He said he expected my curiosity to rear its head eventually."

"Right, and has he been amenable to trying new things?"

"No," I answered. "Our sex life always sticks to the same flavor – vanilla. That's why I think hiring a 'third' would shake it all up."

After another half-hour of discussion, she and I decided that it might not be such a bad idea in my case; she felt that I had been very systematic and thoughtful in arriving at my decision:

1) It would be a business transaction; there would be no emotional connection to the third party.

2) I would be able to control the proceedings, from safety to specific activities.

3) Gavin would never have to wonder what went on between me and another man because he would be in the room.

4) The third party wouldn't have to leave satisfied. Only Gavin and I would have to enjoy it.

It all added up to me, so I gave Gavin my "indecent proposal" that evening. He was very considerate about it, and he understood why it was something I felt I needed to do. He expressed concern that I might want to do it all the time if I enjoyed the experience, but I assured him that we would communicate openly and that, if it wasn't working for either one of us, we would discontinue the practice. He ultimately agreed to go along with my plan. I went online immediately, and searched Rentboy.com for our lucky winner: porn star Chandler Roberts was to be the test run.

The night of our adventure, Gavin began nursing a glass of vodka on the rocks, trying to relax and let go of his reserved upbringing; he was nervous, and I was high with excitement. Chandler showed up right on schedule, and we had a terrific evening. I juggled both men with the fluidity of a pro, and I know for certain that everyone was satisfied. What I also knew for certain was that I had tasted the fruit – literally and figuratively – and wanted more.

I went through a roster of three-way partners, all at about $300 a pop. Online, it's easy to find your favorite adult actors, and I had them all. There was Jace, an Argentine athlete with a body that looked like it had been chiseled in stone, and Tyler, a blue-eyed blonde with tattooed arrows pointing to all of his pleasure zones. Too bad he wasn't among the first; by the time I got to him, I was no longer in need of directions.

Colton Storm was one of my favorite porn models, and I came across an online bulletin advertising his services. His rates were somewhat higher than his colleagues' because of his superstar status in the adult business, but I forked over the cash in exchange for a birthday treat to myself. Colton was up for anything other than kissing, an issue that came up a few times when hiring men for sex. He was willing to put his mouth anywhere on my body or Gavin's – and I mean anywhere – but drew the line at touching lips; he wanted to save something intimate for only his boyfriend. I had heard about a similar practice in a movie starring Julia Roberts and Richard Gere, but I thought that was just a Disney fairytale. Apparently, however, *Pretty Woman* provided real-life hookers with a guideline.

Colton became a regular for us. That was, of course, until the night he announced his retirement.

"I'm not going to be able to work for you guys anymore," he said.

"Why is that?" I asked, not as disappointed as I think he expected.

"I found Jesus," he replied.

"You found him tonight?" I continued, trying to stifle a laugh.

"It sort of just happened," he answered seriously, "but I found him."

"Is that who you were looking for on your hands and knees?" I blurted, no longer able to hide my amusement. After searching every crevice of Colton's body that evening, I was able to find only the places that Jesus *wasn't* hiding.

There was never an ounce of jealousy when I would watch Gavin engaging with our hired three-way partners. In fact, I was relieved that the rentboys were giving me a break for the week and satisfying Gavin – even to a small degree. Because he was primarily a bottom, we erred on the side of caution (safety first!) by not allowing anyone but me to top him. He wasn't getting full-on intercourse the way he would have liked it, but he was getting a sexual release for which I didn't have to do much. I had become bored with our limited sexual repertoire, and bringing these men into our bedroom served a dual purpose: I got to experience fresh meat, and Gavin got off with little energy on my part.

He complained frequently that I would spend too much time talking to the hookers, and there were definitely a few evenings during which my interest became more conversational than sexual. How these men got to where they were, in a position to have to be selling their bodies, fascinated me. A few of the guys we hired were true hustlers, slick street talkers who had scripts memorized. They were working to "put themselves through medical school" or to "pay for the care of a sick relative." I could always see Gavin roll his eyes when those types of stock answers would pour out.

Other men in our bed, however, seemed earnest in the telling of their stories. One gentleman in San Francisco – I liked to sample the flavors of different cities – was fluent in five languages; he moaned in all of them. He had a high sex drive and was turned on by the idea of selling it. Likewise, he used all of his work money for his culture and language courses, eventually transitioning into – get this – a government job.

By a certain point, I had experienced sex with more than 30 men – even though Gavin was always present. I thought for a moment that I had gotten it all out of my system and that I had explored enough bodies and positions to solve the sexual mysteries that loomed in my head. There was still a missing piece, though, and after a couple of months, I started to get some clarity. I felt that I had to take things a step farther. I needed to feel what it would be like to have a sexual connection to a man without Gavin in the room. At the time, I wrote it off as delayed exploration and needing to do some "romantic research." What I later realized was that I was looking for something beyond sex. I didn't feel a passion for Gavin, and I was searching for more than a warm body. It wasn't easy to come to terms with that, but there was no denying my awakening.

At the same time, Gavin's visa was on its way to expiration, and the clock was ticking, just as it had three years earlier. Not even one lawyer was confident that we would be able to make magic happen a second time. Guidelines had become more stringent, and our days together seemed numbered. Part of me felt that a natural end to our relationship might be just what the doctor ordered, but I also wanted to help Gavin get settled in the United States once and for all – he was a project that I needed to complete. So, I finally pressed him on the simplest solution: he would have to marry a woman. Gavin was a very honest person but also frustrated by the fact that he could not marry me and have the same rights to be in the country that his straight friends who married women enjoyed.

The search for the perfect wife was on. Many of our friends were public people who couldn't put themselves at risk of exposure. Others were too scared to take the plunge. Some, however, knew "spinsters" whom they thought might be willing to tie the knot with Gavin. One of my friends sent her lesbian pal on a "date" with him, and another acquaintance attempted to pair Gavin with a divorcee who was down on her luck. Nothing was panning out until a friend of Gavin's introduced us to Chloe. A plucky, 20-something music student, she was the perfect mix of ladylike lesbian and "fuck the system" warrior. Her rebel yell was amplified by her sexy girlfriend, her washed out leggings and her vintage rock-and-roll t-shirts. She was moved by our passion to maintain our relationship – she didn't know that things were rocky because we hadn't discussed it ourselves – and angered by the inequalities experienced by gay and lesbian people.

We were very careful about nurturing a relationship with Chloe, courting her the same way hopeful adoptive parents woo birth mothers to hand over their children. We had many "get to know you" meals together, and Gavin became the thoughtful and considerate suitor whom he should have been with me for nearly five years. Even at the beginning of our relationship, Gavin was never one to go out of his way to demonstrate his affection, and, with Chloe, he had blossomed into the model boyfriend. How could she refuse?

Chloe agreed to marry Gavin, and then began the challenge of planning and documenting a ceremony. His job was to live with Chloe for a few days at a time so that they could learn each other's habits and routines. Gavin knew what kind of toothpaste she used, what she ate for breakfast, her coming and going patterns; there wasn't a detail they didn't know about each other by the time they wed. In addition, they would go on day trips to various locations in California so they could take pictures with different backdrops and seasonal surroundings.

Gavin was spending quite a bit of time with Chloe, all of it necessary to maintain the "legitimacy" of their relationship. I wasn't the least bit jealous of the hours he was away from me. In fact, I relished the moments that I had my house back, all to myself. Rather than missing Gavin, I missed the quiet moments in my bedroom – the moments before the walls would absorb the sounds of our endless arguments and the fracturing of the last pieces of glue that were holding us together. The romance was over.

He chose a wedding date a few weeks after all of the other arrangements with Chloe were finalized, and formal invitations were designed and printed – including gold foil overlays and custom envelopes. Lush floral sculptures added some matrimonial authenticity to the proceedings.

Watching Gavin get married was easy; there was a sense of relief. I sat upright on a white, wooden folding chair that was arranged among a small cluster of mismatched furniture to the right of the wedding processional aisle. Around me was our close circle of friends and family who came for moral support and to help populate the photographs. Gavin – who looked dashing in a brown suit, pinstriped with lavender – was in a sweaty panic; his bride, Chloe, had equally frayed nerves that presented themselves in her giddy laughter.

The ceremony happened in a small Hollywood, storefront chapel – popular for low-cost weddings and those of the shotgun variety; the "McDonald's of marriage," so to speak – sandwiched between a pawnshop and a check cashing business. It looked like the location of a crime scene more than a wedding destination, but it was available on short notice and provided enough of an atmosphere. Draped in white fabric and accented by bouquets of fake roses, the 500 square-foot room sat 20 guests in front of a raised platform. It had a 1980s sitcom feel to it, which was fitting.

Over the months leading up to the wedding, we had folded Chloe into our lives. By the time the ring – a piece of cubic zirconia that Gavin had purchased in the costume jewelry department at Bloomingdales – was actually on her finger, she felt like part of our family. The formality of the marriage, however, came with some emotional side effects.

We climbed into bed early following the reception, as Gavin and I were both exhausted and drained by everything that had led up to the day. Essentially, we had produced a studio premiere-level event – complete with the fanfare that would go into the release of a blockbuster movie – so that my partner's marriage to a woman would go off without a hitch. It was a strange kind of tired. I laid in our king-size bed, feeling Gavin's right leg pressed against my left. The warmth of his skin was comforting to touch, but, in my mind, I was a million miles away. Nothing had changed in terms of our living arrangement or our day-to-day routines – we would both get up at 7:00AM the next morning for a new workday, just like always – but somehow the bridge over the emotional distance between the two of us had shattered into a million shards of splintered wood.

I felt that Gavin and Chloe's marriage certificate represented more than the legality of their union; it was a baton passing, of sorts. On paper, Gavin was now someone else's responsibility, and he appeared to be extremely comfortable and committed to his new bride. I felt like a weight had been lifted and that I had been liberated, so why was my heart sinking? A piece of me knew that I should be happy that we had, for all intents and purposes, solved most of Gavin's problems. But, now that I was no longer running on the adrenaline of the race against Gavin's expiring visa, I was forced to come face-to-face with my relationship – which was devoid of romantic love.

GROPE THERAPY

When someone begins a statement with the phrase, "I am not the kind of person who," no matter what follows the qualifier, he or she is, in fact, that type of person. I was not the kind of person who would have an open relationship.

"Are you telling me that you want to see other people?" Gavin asked me, not surprisingly laid back and dispassionate at my suggestion. His temperature never seemed to move above or below medium broil.

"Not *see* other people, per se," I replied. "I want to continue our relationship, but I also want the freedom to have sex with someone else here and there."

"That's what you said when we started hiring hookers for three-ways," he countered. "That wasn't enough for you?"

"The threesomes were fun, but I need to feel what it's like to have sex with another person, one-on-one."

"So, basically," Gavin shot back, "you want to have your cake and eat it, too?"

I couldn't help but laugh. He rarely applied American idioms to the appropriate situations, and, in his mind, he was likening himself euphemistically to baked goods. By my logic, anyone who used that cliché simply wasn't smart enough to buy two cakes, but there was only one person in that room who was up for a Mensa membership.

"You know that you were the first and only person I ever had sex with," I reminded him. "I have to know what that connection feels like with someone else. It's just a physical thing."

I actually believed my own words. At the time, I thought they represented a delayed sexual awakening; something inside me, though, knew that I was searching for more. I didn't feel emotionally linked to Gavin. Sure, he was someone to sleep next to, but he wasn't the diamond-dipped romantic hero I had dreamed of.

"Whatever you want," Gavin said half-heartedly. "We can try it and see how it's working out in a couple of months." It was one of the only times in my life that I kept my mouth shut. I got the answer I wanted, and I didn't cloud my head more by counting the cost on Gavin's behalf. I also didn't count on how quickly a life changing sexual opportunity would cross my mattress.

My friend Ricki Lake would often host Broadway sing-along nights at her Brentwood home, evenings that I looked forward to every month. Gavin was never interested in musical theater, but he would tag along for the food, drinks and company. On one particular occasion, the gathering included our friend Alan Cumming, one of his pals from New

York (whom I will call Daniel) and some showbiz folks such as Rachael Leigh Cook and Kathy Najimy, an aging actress.

By his second Stoli, Gavin was able to tolerate tunes from *Hedwig and the Angry Inch* and *Little Shop of Horrors* but had little appreciation for the magnitude of talent in Ricki's living room.

"Can we leave now?" Gavin said in almost a whine. "I have to be at work early tomorrow; I can't roll in on my own schedule like you do."

"It's only 11:30PM," I said, "but you can head home whenever you'd like. I am going to stay awhile." Fortunately, we had arrived in separate cars.

"That's fine," he replied, "you have fun." He kissed me on the forehead, the way he would a friend, and said his goodbyes to the others.

"OK, the party pooper has left the building," I announced the minute I heard Gavin's car pull out of the driveway. "Now we can get down and dirty. Who knows some Sondheim?"

We covered *Follies, Assassins* and *Sweeney Todd* until nearly 4:00AM, when guests began to fall asleep in their chairs. I grabbed my car keys and started to walk towards the door when Alan cornered me in the front foyer.

"Are you going home?" he asked.

I'd had a crush on Alan since I first saw him on Broadway in 1998; his impish grin and Scottish brogue gave him a uniquely offbeat sex appeal. And, admittedly, I pleasured myself more than a few times while looking at the nude ads for his vanity cologne, "Cumming." In fact, when I would hear my married friends talk about their celebrity "free passes" – the movie or rock stars whom they would be allowed to sleep with if the chance ever presented itself, regardless of their marital commitments – I always said that Alan would be at the front of my line.

"It seems like everyone is tired out," I said, "so I figured I'd be on my way."

"It's morning already; you might as well bunk here." Alan gave me a coy wink that was as naughty as it was adorable.

"You and Daniel are in the guesthouse, right?" I asked, even though I knew the answer.

"Yes. You can just hop into bed with us." Part of me was jumping out of my skin; my celebrity crush was interested in having sex with *me*. I had ignored interest from men for so many years, and it was excitingly heady to get it from Alan. Another part of me was thinking about Gavin.

"Let me grab a bottle of water, and I will meet you and Daniel upstairs in a few minutes," I said.

"Don't take too long," Alan answered, making his way up the stairs to Ricki's guest suite.

As I walked into the kitchen to get some hydration, I said goodnight to Ricki who was sitting cross-legged in pajamas on a stool at her counter.

"You're staying over, huh?" she said with a tone of judgment.

"Well, it's now 4:15AM. What's the point of driving home?"

"I don't think this has anything to do with driving in the dark," she smirked. "I think this is about Alan." She had noticed that he was paying attention to me during the evening.

"Maybe he's just being friendly," I said, even though I knew better. "Plus, he has Daniel with him upstairs, and aren't they both in committed relationships with men in New York?"

"Um, Alan wants to be more than friendly with you, trust me. Plus, they both have open arrangements."

"Do you think I am wrong to sleep with them?" I asked. It was less of a question for Ricki and more of an out-loud thought process for me. In retrospect, asking Ricki Lake to be the arbiter of good romantic judgment was like asking Charles Manson if he thought someone was a good person. Her fling with a married musician who had children didn't strike her conscience as questionable. She showed up at his LA gigs like a stage door groupie, even after he made it clear that it was just a one-time – OK, maybe two-time – thing.

"What would Gavin say?" she asked, stirring the pot, as always.

"We talked about opening our relationship, actually. So I think he'd be fine."

"Then I say you should go for it," she said, mixing her messages. What a surprise from the devil on everyone's shoulder.

With my bottle of Arrowhead, I walked slowly up the outdoor stairway to Ricki's guesthouse and knocked lightly on the distressed wooden frame. I saw the movement of two naked bodies just behind the slotted shades that covered a glass-paneled door, and I paused for a moment before accepting their call to, "Come on in." I was thrilled by the idea of turning my Alan Cumming dream into a reality – how many people can say they have actually had sex with their celebrity crushes? – but I was grounded by two nagging concerns. First, Daniel was partnered with an HIV-positive man, and, even with protection, the risk scared me. Second, while Gavin and I had briefly discussed the open relationship scenario, we had not ironed out the terms by which we would explore other sex partners. For example, were we to stay away from people we knew in common – such as Alan – or were they fair game? I had no interest in compromising my honor even if it meant fulfilling a sexual fantasy.

Everything was moving through my head on fast forward until I opened the guest suite door. I decided in an instant that I had spent too many years playing by the rules, and I needed to live a little. As I stepped into the room, time seemed to slow down, and I heard voices in a gargled, drawn out lilt.

"Why don't you hop into bed," Alan said, already stark naked and tucking himself under the covers.

"Will you be comfortable? I'm not sure there is enough room for three people," I replied. Naturally, I knew we could all fit, but my nerves were making me tentative.

"Sure there is," Daniel said, "if you snuggle closely between the two of us." He was standing next to the left side of the bed in a pair of black bikini briefs.

Self-conscious about my body, I removed my shoes and socks first followed by my dark blue jeans.

"You still have your shirt on," Alan said, "and your pants." It took me a moment to realize that Europeans sometimes refer to underwear as "pants."

I removed my orange t-shirt and climbed onto the bed between Alan and Daniel, quickly covering myself with the bedspread before the bright lights of the bedside lamp could highlight my surgically contoured torso. My mind was racing as I felt Alan's bare ass against my crotch and Daniel's semi-erect penis at the base of my spine. I was the filling in a man sandwich, the idea of which would have blown my mind before it actually happened. My nerves had the better of me, though, and I wasn't confident enough in my looks or my sexual experience to do anything but lay quietly between them.

"Goodnight," Alan whispered, pulling my hand onto his chest so that my palm was pressed firmly against his right nipple.

"Sleep well," I said, in what turned out to be a high-pitched squeak. My two heads were confusing each other: the lower was pumped for action, but the upper was considering safety, how I might feel afterwards, how Gavin would feel when he heard the news and how a lackluster sexual performance might drive an awkward stake through the casual friendship I had developed with Alan. The internal discussion ended when Daniel's arm reached across my shoulders, squeezing my entire body against his furry stomach. We were pressed so tightly against each other that, if a woman had been in the mix, she would have undoubtedly gotten pregnant without ever moving.

"This feels good, doesn't it?" Daniel asked, his warm breath grazing my ear lobe.

"Mmmhmm," was all I could get out of my mouth. Feeling Daniel's now stiff cock pressed against my lower cheeks – albeit through the thin veil of cotton that was the only barrier between us – and Alan's small, round ass was sensory overload. I was glued to the sheets, not knowing when a hand, mouth or dick might brush across my body. I wanted to have sex with them, but I was paralyzed by thought. They were waiting for me to give them a touch of permission that would get the show started, but I wasn't that bold. Yet.

Alan and Daniel eventually fell asleep while I stared endlessly at the ceiling in an attempt to manage my raging hard-on. Their alternating snores didn't help to calm me, nor did their wandering fingers. Each time I could feel myself starting to doze, someone's hand would move south, stirring me into full awareness.

Two hours passed until daylight crept through the windows, and I jumped out of bed at daybreak. Alan and Daniel were fast asleep – to have been expected considering the late hour that they passed out and the amount of alcohol they had consumed – and I wanted to get back to my house in Sherman Oaks before Gavin woke up. As I dressed and walked to the door, Alan's eyes opened.

"That was fun," he said. "I'll see you soon, I hope."

"I had a great time," I replied. "You go back to sleep."

I made it to my house before traffic started to congest the 405 Freeway, and I was upstairs in my bedroom before Gavin's alarm clock heralded another workday. I removed my clothes and climbed into bed, hoping to catch at least a few hours of sleep. Gavin was on his side with his back to me.

"I take it you enjoyed yourself last night," he said, startling me with his croaky voice.

"Sorry, I didn't mean to wake you," I said.

"Who did you sleep with?" he asked. He didn't waste time, or use the word "whom."

"I slept with Alan and Daniel."

"Was it everything you hoped?" He was angry.

"I didn't have sex with them," I said. "I wanted to, but I didn't."

"Why didn't you just go ahead and fuck around with them? Isn't that what you have been wanting?"

"Yes," I said, a little bit surprised by his upset. Typically, he didn't get riled up about anything, even when he was slighted or treated poorly. "But, you and I didn't finish discussing the whole open relationship thing, so I wasn't going to experiment until we talked it through a little more." I didn't mention that it was also because of Daniel's partner's HIV status and my own lack of confidence.

"So you literally slept in bed with them – not even blowjobs?"

"Nothing," I said. "And, I didn't sleep very well at that." Gavin rolled over and looked at me blankly, waiting for me to say more. "It sounds like you would have been upset if I had sex with them."

"I guess not," he said. "I basically agreed to an open relationship, so I suppose I have to get my mind past it." His anger appeared to fade into resignation.

"Well, you sounded angry with me, and I didn't even do anything. Would you rather that we just not tell each other when we have slept with someone else?"

"I think I'd rather know," he answered. "You do whatever you have to, and I'll work through it." He was sensing that he would lose me altogether if we didn't make an open relationship work, and I was too much of a support system for him to let go of at that time.

"So, if I see Alan again while he's in town, are you OK with that?"

"I suppose so," he said. "He's better than some random guy."

The minute Gavin hit the shower, I reached for my phone to e-mail Alan. I told him how much I enjoyed being close to him during the night and asked if he might have another evening to get together while he was in LA working.

"I would love to see you again," he replied. "I have a dinner with an old friend tomorrow night, but what if we met afterwards at my hotel for a wee drinky in my room?" That was how Alan talked – "wee drinky" – and it charmed the shit out of me.

Alan was staying at the Chateau Marmont in Hollywood, and I arrived at his room with a bottle of Veuve Clicquot at 9:30PM. He'd had a long day shooting *Burlesque* –the disastrous musical drama starring Cher and Christina Aguilera – and was ready to pop open the bubbly. Although not a drinker, I indulged in a couple of glasses myself, thinking they would make me bolder about my intentions – and they did. Over the champagne, I chatted with Alan about the agreement that Gavin and I had come to, making it clear that I was ready for a sexual encounter. It didn't take long before we were in his bed, and he was helping me out of my red Diesel boxer-briefs.

His soft lips touched mine, and we began kissing in a way I'd never experienced. It felt animal, in a sense, as though we wanted to breathe each other in. With Gavin, kissing was a responsibility; with Alan, it felt like an act of passion – as did Alan's hand on my rock-hard erection. He gently stroked my shaft without removing his mouth from mine; it felt so good that I thought I might cum on the spot.

Within moments, I felt the shiny head of Alan's uncircumcised penis – the first uncut member I'd ever seen in person – rub against my leg. As I reached down to take it into my hand, its extraordinary size became evident. I hadn't noticed his length and girth two nights before; he was under the covers and not facing me. In the heavenly bed at the Chateau, however, I experienced his monster cock in all of its glory. Before I could get both of my hands around it, Alan pushed me from my side to my back and sucked my penis with the pace and grip of an expert. The only thing that kept me from exploding all over the sheets was the voice in my head that told me to pay careful attention to the moment. Alan was the first man I had sex with during which Gavin was not present, and the significance of that rite of passage kept me from squirting too quickly – well, that and the Kate Bush covers of Elton John's "Rocket Man" and "Candle in the Wind" that Alan had playing in the background on a loop.

"You're such a sexy boy, Josh," Alan said, positioning himself on his back with his salt-and-pepper hair flat against a pillow. I smiled crookedly, uncomfortable taking that kind of compliment. Even at the beginning of our relationship, Gavin rarely complimented my attractiveness or my sex appeal; feeling physically desired was, until that moment, foreign to me.

"I want to be sure that we remain friends after this," I said. "The sex won't come between us, will it?"

"I don't think we have to worry about that," Alan replied. "But I do want you to sit on my face." His dirty grin was hard to refuse, even though it was all new territory for me. Gavin was never interested in being anywhere near my ass, and Alan wanted to run his tongue over every part of my body.

As I lowered myself onto Alan's mouth, a shiver ran through my chest. His warm tongue on my most sensitive area drove me out of my mind.

"You taste so good," he mumbled, incorporating a finger or two into the tongue bath. "I really want to fuck you." The pleasure was so intense I thought I was going to collapse.

"Could we try that another night?" I asked, not wanting to disappoint him but also concerned about accommodating his disproportionately large dick.

"Of course," he said sensitively, running his hand softly

up my back while his tongue continued to probe. "I want this to be comfortable for you."

"I feel very comfortable," I panted, grinding myself into his nose and mouth. To show him just how comfortable I was, I leaned forward into a 69 position and gave his entire lower half the same treatment I was enjoying.

"Oh my God," he screamed. "You are amazing." Maybe I had nothing to worry about all along; it appeared that my customer was satisfied. Gavin may not have been a Don Juan, but I had clearly gotten a good education from those adult DVDs in my library.

With a couple of loud moans, Alan shot his load onto my chest at almost the same time that he milked a similar quantity from me. I moved around so that we were on top of each other, face to face, continuing to kiss in spite of all the places our tongues had been. It was hard to catch my breath.

"That was crazy good," Alan said.

"You are the only person I have been intimate with aside from Gavin, not including some three-way experimentation that he and I did together," I admitted.

"Is that true?" Alan asked, surprised by the information. "You seem like such a sexual person."

"I came out pretty late, and I met Gavin right away," I revealed. "Our sex life doesn't exactly have us swinging from chandeliers. That's partially why I wasn't terribly forward with you and Daniel the other night."

"I completely get it," he said. "I hope this was good for you."

"It was fantastic, but I don't want you to be disappointed

that I wasn't quite ready to bottom for you." I looked directly into his eyes as I said it.

"Don't be silly. I was so caught up in you, it didn't matter." He smoothed the back of my hair in comforting strokes and pushed my head lightly onto his chest. "Will you stay the night?"

I never rested better than I did that evening at the famous hotel in the hills of Hollywood. With our arms around each other, Alan and I slept peacefully, never loosening our grips. I felt attractive, cared for and content, and, for eight hours, I enjoyed being in the present without a worry on my mind.

We both woke the following morning to the ringing of the hotel landline. Alan was scheduled to do an interview with *Entertainment Weekly* to promote his work in *Burlesque*, and the journalist had called on schedule. As I lay in the bed, listening to the conversation, I felt an emotional stab through my abdomen. I realized quickly that I was just the boy in the movie star's bed, at the Chateau Marmont of all places. It seemed like a scene in a movie, common and tawdry. What hours before felt meaningful was now piercing my head with doubt. I began to realize, in that moment, that the idea of having an open relationship was less about experimentation and more about yearning for a connection with another man; a connection that I did not have with Gavin. Alan was romantically unavailable, so I ultimately couldn't have it with him either.

When Alan finished the interview, I dragged him back under the covers and we both got off again; I figured I might as well make the most of the moment rather than drown in my concerns.

"Thank you for a great night," I said, as I dressed and

walked towards the hotel room door. "It was really special for me."

"I'm glad to hear that," Alan responded. He kissed me quickly on the mouth as I began to leave.

"Will I see you again while you're in town?" His quirkiness and his brazen sexuality were intoxicating. I realized by that point that I was in danger of getting attached to someone who wasn't interested in anything but a good time; in fact, I knew he had a reputation for playing around. I was drunk on the part that felt good, however, and it outweighed the fear of an emotional bruising that particular morning.

"Do you want to come by the set early next week? It might be fun to hang out while we're shooting the final number," he said. "Maybe Gavin and Ricki will want to come, too." It was clear that Alan didn't feel the need to see me by myself, which put a tiny arrow through my gut.

I walked around in a daze for the next 72 hours, like I was seeing everything through gauze. I'd finally had a mind-blowing sexual encounter – at 36 years-old – and I wanted more. I had become excited about the possibility of having a connection with someone who was interesting and passionate and sparkly. I couldn't talk about it with Gavin, who now felt more like a friend than a lover, so I wound up relying heavily on my good friends for support and empathy. I called Camryn Manheim to tell her what had happened, as she had co-starred with Alan in *Romy and Michele's High School Reunion* and understood his magnetism.

"Honey, I think it's great that you experienced this," she said, "but you have to manage your feelings. You have a life here with Gavin, and Alan is married."

"My head knows that," I said, "but I feel like I need more."

"I think you should move on from this and continue a friendship with Alan over time. You're going to prolong your recovery period if you dip your toe back in the water," Camryn warned. She had never been wrong in my experience, but I put her sound advice aside, like a *Price Is Right* contestant who doesn't listen to the audience's screams and passes up the first "showcase."

The following week, Gavin, Ricki and I took a couple of hours to have lunch with Alan and observe a small part of the shoot. En route to the studio, I had told Gavin and Ricki all of the details about my night at the Chateau. Even after I spilled the beans, I was the only one who seemed to feel anxious about the group field trip – probably because I didn't admit that I continued to have a crush on Alan. Using my PR savvy, I positioned the story as a fun roll in the hay rather than as a milestone moment with emotional gravity.

Burlesque, on paper, was a gay wet dream (before I saw the finished product; after, it became more of a gay nightmare), and it was fun to watch the finale come together. Just after lunch, I was sitting next to Alan, watching the director give notes to the principal actors. I was quiet for a couple of minutes while I gathered the courage to offer a proposition.

"How would you feel," I whispered, leaning into Alan's chair, "about revisiting the fun we had the other night in your hotel room?" It was as if I had spilled my insides onto the floor for everyone to see, and I was terrified that I would be rejected. I had sampled good sex, though, and, like a druggie, I put myself in the pathway of hurt for another fix.

Alan looked at me and smiled, then looked away for a moment.

"Was that just a onetime thing?" I asked nervously. "It's

OK if that's the case." I gave him an out to protect my feelings. If he rebuffed me, I had already told him it was alright.

"I think it would be nice to have another round," he said. "Can we stay in Ricki's guesthouse on Thursday night?" I knew she wouldn't mind; in fact, she would take pleasure in the drama of it all.

"I am sure that's fine," I said. "I feel like we left some unfinished business last week." I wanted him to know that I wasn't planning on stopping short of intercourse.

"The *Burlesque* wrap party is that night, so why don't we make an appearance there and then wind up at Ricki's?" Alan suggested. "Oh, and I am going to have a wee gathering in my hotel room tomorrow night, if you and Gavin want to come by."

"That works for me," I said. "I'll see you tomorrow and Thursday." I wasn't going to miss any time with Alan.

When Gavin and I arrived at the Chateau Marmont, about 20 people were milling around the bed that Alan and I had christened the week prior. I tried to stay focused on the other guests, including late horror queen Karen Black and indie writer/actor John Cameron Mitchell. We ran into film-maker Bryan Singer, who was accompanied by a posse of five very youthful looking men. I had met him six months earlier through a mutual friend. Before even shaking my hand that night, he asked my age; he clearly wanted to know if I was legal.

Just before Gavin and I left, Alan pulled me aside.

"About Thursday night," he slurred drunkenly. My heart sank; I thought he might have reconsidered our scheduled tryst. "Should we include Gavin and make it a threesome?"

"I think I'd like to keep it between us," I said tersely. First, I knew that Gavin didn't find Alan physically attractive, and, second, I wanted this to be my own special experience. I didn't want to share it.

"OK, whatever you want," Alan said, "I just didn't want to leave Gavin out."

Of course, Alan had no idea what I was feeling. He didn't realize that I was wildly attracted to his confidence, his talent and the sexuality that oozed from every one of his pores. He was being his flirty, adventurous self, but I couldn't help being a little saddened. It was clear that he was simply about getting off while I was naïvely investing myself.

On Thursday evening, Alan and I had a drink at the *Burlesque* wrap party and ate dinner at a divey, Korean barbecue. He wanted one last drink before hopping into bed and convinced me to make a stop at FuBar in West Hollywood before driving to Ricki's house. They were hosting a gay themed evening called "Big, Fat Dick," during which they handed out free alcohol shots to anyone who flashed his penis at the bartender. Alan marched right up to the bar, unbuttoned his pants and whipped out his massive cock. I assumed it was more the thrill of exposing himself in public than saving $8 on a Kamakazi that appealed to him, but the environment was dirty and uncomfortable for me.

By the time we got to Ricki's guesthouse, the sexual energy was palpable. We both knew what the evening was leading up to, so we were more than primed for action by the time the clock struck midnight. Our dicks were hard before we removed our pants; we could feel our erections pressing against each other as we stood kissing next to the bed.

"What would you like to do?" I asked as we removed all of our clothing.

"I like everything," Alan said. "Shall we fuck each other?"

Without another word, I rolled a condom onto my penis while Alan lay on his back towards the top of the bed. He bent his knees up to his ears, and I slid inside him using a small amount of lubricant from my overnight bag and some saliva. We looked into each other's eyes, and I rocked back and forth, Alan groaning with each thrust. Thankfully, the Xanax I swallowed before getting into bed calmed my senses because the fun would have ended prematurely otherwise.

After fifteen minutes of kissing and fucking, Alan flipped me over. I was lying on my back, diagonally across the bed. He pulled a Magnum rubber from his suitcase and handed it to me. While I massaged his hairy balls with one hand, I put the condom onto his huge penis with the other.

"Take it slowly," I said, as I felt the tip of his penis touch the cheeks of my ass. "I haven't done this much, so I am a little nervous." Gavin had tried topping me a few times, but his more modest endowment and lack of practice didn't set off any fireworks. My proportioned penis seemed to fit better into his ass than the other way around.

Gently, Alan pushed forward. The initial pain was excruciating, and the fear of bleeding all over Ricki's sheets temporarily softened my hard-on.

"Are you OK?" Alan asked. He was thoughtful and considerate in the moment.

"I will be fine...I hope," I said, squinting and breathing through the fiery discomfort.

With a few more back and forth motions, my stomach began to settle and the rhythm of Alan's pounding became intensely pleasurable. My erection returned, and I began to stroke it as Alan's pace increased. As he leaned in to kiss my mouth, I couldn't control my orgasm. I came across my chest, shooting so far that my hair was plastered to my head with semen.

"Wow! That was far," Alan said. "Impressive." He flipped onto his back, removed the condom and began jerking his own dick. He wanted me to kiss him while he touched himself, but, as his strokes hastened, he pulled his face from mine and stared into my eyes. His breathing got louder, and without breaking eye contact, he shot a considerable load of cum onto his lower stomach.

Exhausted, we moved into a spooning position, practically stuck together by the fluids dripping from our bodies. Alan and I fell right to sleep, waking up early the next morning to prepare for Oscar weekend. Fortunately, I had so much planned that I didn't have time to tumble into the same melancholy free-fall that I had experienced after first being intimate with Alan at the Chateau. His husband was on his way from New York to meet him at the hotel they'd be staying at, and Ricki and I were scheduled to attend the Independent Spirit Awards that same night.

ACE IN THE HOLE

The Sundance Channel was interested in producing an unscripted show about the unique friendship that they perceived Ricki and me to have. They invited the two of us to sit at their table at the Independent Spirit Awards, next to Elton John and David Furnish. The power couple produced a show called *Iconoclast* for the network, and the head of development knew that Ricki already had a casual friendship with Elton.

When we arrived, Ricki worked the red carpet, talking with the media about the potential for our show (which never came to be; she did her now defunct talk show reboot instead). Following the press line, we hustled to our table, where Elton and David were already seated. I had met them previously when I attended a birthday party for David with Ricki, and it was a pleasure to see them again. They both were genuine, generous and down-to-earth people, and they were very easy to talk to. David and I compared notes on our favorite porn stars, pulling up pictures on our cell phones and laughing away the evening.

As the awards ceremony drew to a close, Olympic ice skater Johnny Weir – who also had a show on The Sundance Channel, *Be Good, Johnny Weir* – made his way over to our table. He wanted to meet Elton and David, and pulled a chair between us. After a couple of moments of small talk, he turned his attention to me.

"That's a great jacket," he said. It was a John Varvatos, limited edition lambskin motorcycle jacket that I loved – and I was flattered that he recognized my taste.

"Thank you so much," I said, "I had to own it the minute I saw it."

"Sort of the way I had to come say hello the minute I saw *you*," he answered.

I was definitely walking taller and feeling good that Friday, still in the bubble of my earth-moving night with Alan. Apparently, I was also exuding some sort of sexual energy that reeled Johnny to Table 4.

"That's very sweet," I replied. "It's really nice to meet you."

"Do you two want a moment alone," Ricki chimed in, making sure that the entire table was privy to what was going on. Over-sharing personal information was one of her trademarks, and she was rarely discreet on my behalf either.

"That's OK," Johnny said, "Josh and I will talk later."

He seemed annoyed by Ricki's brash style and stood up from the table. Johnny politely took my phone from my right hand and entered his name, number and e-mail address into my contacts.

"We *will* talk later, yes?" he asked.

"Absolutely," I said. "I will text you tonight when I get home."

We said goodnight to Elton, David and our Sundance Channel hosts and walked into the after-party to visit with our mutual friend John Waters. Ricki and I knew John independently because I worked on the PR campaigns for a number of his films at New Line Cinema, and, as the oversized star of his first mainstream hit, *Hairspray*, Ricki had been his Hollywood Goddaughter since 1987. We chatted for ten minutes, but I couldn't get my mind off of Johnny Weir.

"Are you ready to go?" I asked Ricki once John Waters had excused himself to talk with other friends.

"I take it that you want to have some time on your own to text Mr. Weir?" she replied. "Don't you think it's enough to have banged Alan last night?" This from a woman whose bedroom could have doubled for Grand Central Station since her divorce.

As soon as Ricki dropped me at my house, I began texting Johnny. Gavin was enjoying a night on the town with friends, and I had a rare moment of privacy in my own bed. We exchanged the standard conversational pleasantries until Johnny turned up the heat.

"Do you think we will get along well in bed?" he asked. "I have a feeling we will both want to be the 'woman.'" He wanted an answer to the "top or bottom" question that almost every gay man attempts to discern when he first meets you.

"Your feeling is wrong," I said, "as long as you beg me to fuck you." What? Had that just come from me? I almost couldn't believe what my thumbs were typing.

"Now you're talking," Johnny said. "I want you to come over to my hotel tomorrow night, and give it to me."

Gavin walked through the door a half-hour later, just as I put my phone on the nightstand. My underwear was tented around my hard penis and topped off by a few sticky drops of pre-cum; it would have been difficult for Gavin not to notice.

"It looks like someone is feeling frisky," he said, drunk from his night of bar hopping.

"I am pretty turned on at the moment," I replied. "What are you going to do about it?"

Gavin stripped down to his underwear and straddled me. With his back to my face – reverse cowboy, for those in the know – he pulled down the back of his white briefs just enough for me to slide myself into him. My blood was flowing quickly because of Johnny's expert dirty talk, and, within five minutes, I pulled out and exploded on Gavin's back and cheeks. It was a soulless fuck; we didn't look at each other nor did we speak during the ride. Gavin dismounted my pelvis, went into the shower and fell asleep next to me without a word about my night or his.

That following evening was "The Night Before" party at The Beverly Hills Hotel, a huge bash attended by all of the Oscar nominees and everyone of import in Hollywood. Its appeal was that it was causal and that no press was allowed inside, so everyone could enjoy without being hounded, bothered, snapped or tattled on. Just prior, at the same hotel, Elton and David were hosting a small cocktail party for people who were particularly generous in donating to the Elton John AIDS Foundation. They had invited Ricki and me to attend. As we walked into the small room, we talked with David, who asked me how things went with my admirer.

"My admirer?" I questioned, unsure at first who he was talking about.

"Our favorite little ice skater, Johnny," David reminded. I forgot that Ricki had announced the mutual attraction between Johnny and me to the entire dinner table the previous evening.

"We had a good time texting last night," I winked. "I should probably check in with him tonight." There was no "probably" about it. I had planned to be in touch with Johnny after the two parties, but now he was front and center in my mind.

Elton and David's gathering assembled a strange mix of guests – not to mention one of Elton's bodyguards whom Ricki had slept with in the past. She wanted to avoid the corner of the room he was watching and migrated to a huddle that included celebrity photographer Greg Gorman and notorious publishing heiress Patty Hearst. I had always been intrigued by Patty and the whole SLA kidnapping, and I mentioned to Ricki that I was excited to meet her.

"She's a boring housewife," Ricki said. "You're going to be disappointed."

"It's impossible that someone with her story could be boring," I replied.

"Why? Do you expect her to have a gun and a beret in her bag?" Ricki asked.

"I'd hoped she would," I said jokingly. As it turns out, Ricki was right. No shots were fired, and Patty was a simple and mild conversationalist. She certainly wasn't interesting enough to get my mind off of Johnny Weir.

I knew Gavin was occupied that night – he had planned another bar crawl with friends, since there were no "plus ones" offered for "The Night Before" – so I had some freedom from him and Ricki. I pulled my phone from my pocket and began texting Johnny. He was eating dinner with friends and then going to The Abbey, a popular gay bar in West Hollywood.

"What kind of underwear do you have on?" he asked.

"Black briefs," I answered. "What about you?"

"Right now, I am wearing white underwear, but I plan to change into something special for you later," he said.

Variety magazine was the premier media sponsor of "The Night Before" party; the associate publisher had invited me as her date. Fortunately, aside from being a key media contact, she had also become a friend over the years. Otherwise, I would never have been able to carry on with Johnny via text and attend the party at the same time. I was distracted the entire evening, practically ignoring introductions to Oprah Winfrey and Halle Berry, among others. (If you had read what Johnny wanted to let me do to him, you wouldn't have been paying attention to the Queen of All Media either – you would have had a very different kind of "Big O" on your mind. Trust me.)

Johnny was staying at The London Hotel, and we decided to meet as soon as we were both finished with our respective evenings. The minute my friend dropped me off at home in the Valley, I showered and changed into jeans and a t-shirt. I raced back across town and walked into the lobby of the hotel. As I moved towards the elevator bank, I stopped to think for a moment. Was I there just for sex? Was I hoping Johnny and I would click and that he would take me away from Gavin? Or, was it a good celebrity story to dine out on in the coming months? The answer to all of the questions racing through my mind was "yes," but when the first elevator car door opened, I stepped inside and stopped thinking. I gave myself permission to have fun; I deserved it after 36 years.

When Johnny opened the door to his room, I noticed that he was much more attractive than I thought initially. I was counting on his athletic flexibility as more of his selling point – not his boyish face. Without make-up and a bedazzled wardrobe, he was actually quite handsome. He looked like a young Hugh Hefner in a white hotel robe and slippers.

"Come on in," he said, locking the door behind us and then sitting on a couch in the suite's sitting area. I sat in the desk chair, facing him.

"How was your party?" he asked.

"It was fun," I replied, "but I was a little distracted."

"By this?" he said, spreading his legs wide enough for me to see the bulge in his underwear beneath the robe. The grey, polka-dot briefs were definitely a turn on.

Before I could answer, he stood up and walked over to my chair. He lowered himself onto my lap and began to kiss me while grinding his crotch into my lap.

"Should we move over to the bed?" I suggested.

Without hesitating, Johnny removed his robe and threw himself onto the white linens. He helped me take off my clothes, and I pulled his underwear off with my mouth.

"You're the star top," he said. "Show me what you've got."

His penis was above average in size, and he was manscaped so expertly that I felt I should be admiring as opposed to touching. I got over that quickly when he pushed my mouth onto his dick. We exchanged blowjobs until he grabbed a condom from the night table and rolled it onto my penis. He flipped onto his stomach.

"Give it to me," he said in an aggressive tone that I hadn't heard during sex before. Holding onto his shoulders, I pushed into him, fucking him harder with each scream. We moved into just about every position over the next hour – doggie style, sideways, cowboy and, finally, missionary – and both came on his chest at the same time. Let it suffice to say that his talents weren't limited to toe loops and triple Axels.

We made small talk as we showered together, but our age difference and life paths left little but physical chemistry between us. Although we agreed to keep in contact, I knew that my relationship with Johnny would live its entire life span in that one night. As I drove back to Sherman Oaks, I realized that I had experienced a "hook-up," an intimate encounter that had a foundation built only on testosterone. There was nothing nurturing or tender about my one-night stand with Johnny Weir, as there had been with Alan, but I felt a power and confidence simply because he found me attractive. There were many men at the Independent Spirit Awards who would have gone home with Johnny, but he picked me. Someone famous, someone in the "in crowd" wanted me at his side.

Gavin wasn't yet home when I walked through the front door of my house. I ran into the shower and grabbed a loofa, scrubbing my skin until it was red and raw. I had already washed with Johnny, but I felt dirty again after leaving his hotel. His interest in me was uplifting initially, but the nature of the sex and the fast goodbye seemed to soil my skin. Once I was convinced that every dead cell was exfoliated and resting in the shower drain, I went right to sleep. The next day was the Oscars, and I wanted to get some solid rest.

Ricki had invited Gavin to the big Elton John AIDS Foundation party at the Pacific Design Center that Sunday. She was offered only one guest ticket and, even though I was her primary friend, she thought it was fair to invite Gavin since my weekend had been, well, full of "festivities." When Elton's assistant noticed that my name was not on the guest list, he provided a third ticket so that we could all attend together.

As we walked into the room and located our table, I froze momentarily. Alan Cumming and his husband were seated next to us. And, as if that wasn't awkward enough, Johnny Weir was two tables away. Holy fucking shit. How did that happen?

Once I processed the scene and my brain caught up with my hollow gut – yes, I'd had sex with Alan on Thursday, sex with Gavin on Friday and sex with Johnny on Saturday, and we were all within 20 feet of each other on Sunday – I put one foot in front of the other and made it to my chair. I sat for most of the evening, smiling here and there and chatting casually. I never thought I'd say this, but I was grateful when Grace Jones took the stage to perform; it lifted the responsibility to make further conversation.

When my eyes opened on Monday morning, every joint in my body ached. I lay on my back for a half-hour before attempting to get out of bed, as though a boulder was holding me under its weighty concrete. Gavin had already left for work, and I was floating in the middle of our large bed without anyone to pull me up – not that he was good at getting me through difficult moments anyway. I eventually shuffled to the bathroom and was startled to see my dark, puffy eyes in the mirror. I looked like I had been the loser in a boxing match. I reached for some soap and began to wash my face, wiping the tears that had started to stream down my cheeks. My stomach was empty, but my appetite was gone.

I put off work for that entire week, declaring myself "sick." The hours floated into each other, and I slept for long stretches of time. I would dream about being in a relationship with Alan or running off with other men, only to wake up to the reality of my depression. My sleep cycles became irregular in between starving myself and alternately stuffing my face. I could feel myself spiraling downward, and I stopped calling friends and family for support. The excitement of the previous week had crumbled into emotional misery, as though a grand, traveling show had come to town and then pulled up stakes, leaving me standing alone where the tent had been. (Melissa Manchester's hit song "Don't Cry Out Loud" translated it perfectly into gay.)

Not only was the letdown after Oscar week mentally debilitating, it shined a spotlight on my indifference towards Gavin. The whimsical life that had me falling into bed with people like Alan and Johnny was borrowed for a short period; the stale relationship I had with Gavin was mine to keep. I had to find a way to let go of both.

Enter *Playgirl* centerfold Brent Lachlan, a tattooed fetishist whom I called initially because my depression hadn't squashed my sex drive – and because of his provocative online ad. 5'9" with a hearty beard and a solid, filled-out body that hadn't seen a trimmer in years, Brent had deliciously full lips and eyes large and round enough to dive into. What started as a $225.00 "dick-for-hire" arrangement became a course in the joys of gay sex and, ultimately, a friendship that continued for years.

Sexual exploration was the one thing I actually looked forward to during the weeks that I was feeling so low. I wanted to know more about what satisfied me – Alan and

Johnny had given me a taste – and to try all of the sexual activities I had read about and watched in porn films. Brent had no limits (water sports, bondage, you name it) and was willing to show me everything in his bag of tricks. I came to trust him, and I was comfortable being vulnerable with this pierced and inked sex surrogate. Thank goodness for lunch breaks.

The first time he came to my house, I escorted him to the guest room. I was tentative that day, as he was a stranger, and I didn't really think I would see him again. By that logic, I didn't want him in the bed that I shared with Gavin; it felt dirty. He was understanding, as I think he had a sense that, even at 36, I was still figuring things out.

He took his time, touching me gently, letting his hands explore my body – while I did the same to his. His well-manicured fingertips grazed my skin sensually, and he responded with approving moans when I returned the favor. He was teaching me the art of foreplay, and I was definitely a fast learner. As the afternoon progressed, Brent led me through one of the most fulfilling sexual experiences, giving his body to me completely. He recognized that I needed to feel comfortable, safe and wanted, and he was selfless in giving me a lesson in lovemaking. I knew after only 20 minutes that Brent was not a street-trade hooker but rather a sensitive man who took pleasure in giving me pleasure. In my mind, I was already planning our next afternoon together before he could even get his thick, 8.5-inch penis back into his jeans.

My initial plan was to have Brent for a return engagement a few weeks later, but my crotch had other ideas. Now that I had a frame of reference for how thrilling intimate encounters could actually be, I wasn't really interested in sex with Gavin –

and he wasn't complaining because his sex drive wasn't exactly in turbo. I wanted Brent in my bed in the worst way, and, likewise, called him only four days after our first encounter on the guest room couch.

Happy to oblige, Brent showed up at my door in a tank top, tight gym shorts and a trucker cap. I greeted him in my private garage while finishing a business call on my cordless phone and showed him upstairs into the kitchen. No sooner did we get to the dining room table, he had my pants around my ankles and his mouth around my penis. I squirmed to finish the phone meeting without any noise – probably one of the first times in my life that I was fighting to stay silent – and raced right up to my bedroom as soon as the phone was turned off. Brent was much more aggressive, grabbing and groping in every direction. The sex was passionate and rough and required that I be more submissive than I had been with anyone. I let myself go and enjoyed the moment, cumming three times in an hour.

"How did that feel?" Brent asked, as we collapsed into each other in a sweaty mess. (Naturally, I put towels over the duvet cover to prevent fluids from staining my immaculate bedding.)

"Fantastic," I said, out of breath. "I didn't think I would ever really enjoy bottoming so much. Some of my experiences with that were not the most comfortable."

"It's all about having the right connection," Brent replied.

"That explains it," I muttered. "I don't think Gavin and I have that spark."

"It's certainly exists between you and me," he said, "because that was fucking amazing."

For the rest of that year, Brent and I had a standing, biweekly appointment – until he took a traditional 9-to-5 job and began going to school at night to complete a master's degree in psychology and human sexuality. I was disappointed by the dissolve of our relationship because he had been a mentor of sorts. I never developed feelings for him beyond the physical, but I was grateful to have had such a giving and uninhibited man open my eyes to the fantastic sex I had dreamed of for years. Brent's "retirement" also forced me to face a hard truth: my tea-and-toast life with Gavin just wasn't going to be sufficient. I needed similar heat and excitement on a regular basis, but I had to figure out how to dismantle my relationship with as little collateral damage as possible.

As fate would have it, I didn't have anything to figure out. Gavin pulled the trigger first, just as I gave him an expensive bracelet for our fifth anniversary.

"It's really beautiful," he said, "but I think I will need to have a few links removed. It dangles on my wrist."

"I can take it to the jeweler this week," I said. "I'll have it sized to fit you better."

"Don't worry about it," he replied, putting the silver band back into its box and placing it in a drawer next to his things in the kitchen.

"Are you sure you like it?" I asked. "It wasn't inexpensive, so, if you don't love it, I'd rather get you something else."

"No, it's great," he said. "Thank you."

The bracelet had sat in that same drawer for more than a month when I finally asked him why he hadn't bothered to have it re-sized.

"I think we need to take a break," Gavin announced.

"You mean a vacation?" I asked.

"From each other," he replied. "I think we need time apart."

It was a punch to my ego because I had ignored my unhappiness for nearly four years so that Gavin could have a Green Card and a roof over his head, and *he* thought we needed time apart.

"You know what? Just consider it a permanent time-out," I spat. "If you need to think about whether or not I am the person you want to spend your life with, let me make up your mind for you." I was outwardly angry and hurt but inwardly relieved. I could get out of the relationship without being the ogre who put Gavin on the street.

"I don't think that's what I want," he said, his large eyes dripping with tears. "I love you, and I want to figure it out. I just think we might need time apart to do it."

I was leaving the next day on a business trip, and I didn't want this uncertainty hanging over my head. For my own peace of mind, I thought it better to put a Band-Aid on the situation until I was back on our home turf.

"Let's keep things as they are for now. I'm going to be in and out of town for the next few weeks, so you'll have time to yourself, and we can talk about patching things up when I am back," I said.

My troubles with Gavin wound up becoming a national tour. I was traveling with Paula Abdul on *The X Factor's* first season audition cycle, breezing through cities including Miami, New York, Chicago and Seattle. Thankfully, Paula was a pillar of support and helped keep the mood as light as possible. We were always laughing about one thing or another, which was a pleasant distraction during a confusing time. One afternoon, in Seattle, Paula and I decided to

go shopping at Saks Fifth Avenue before catching our flight
back to Los Angeles; she figured it would take my mind off
of my romantic problems. Neither of us paid attention to our
watches, and panic set in when we realized that we were in
danger of missing our plane. In six-inch heels, Paula stood on
the curb and waved down a soccer mom who drove us back
to our hotel.

"Do you actually want to patch things up?" Paula asked
me during our ride to the airport.

"I have been in this relationship for five years, so there's
a comfort in being part of an 'us' instead of a 'me,'" I said.
"Does that make sense?"

"It makes sense, but being comfortable doesn't always
mean being happy. Remember that." Paula was, indeed,
forever my girl.

When I landed in Los Angeles that evening, Gavin and
I had a pleasant dinner at a neighborhood Italian restaurant.
We discussed my trip and his job but nothing about the status
of our relationship. We had sex that night – mechanical, "I
just returned from a trip" obligatory sex – and fell asleep with
no mention of the rift between us. Over breakfast the following day, though, the line was drawn.

"I think maybe I was meant to walk alone," Gavin said.
Was he the lead singer of Whitesnake?

"So, you're telling me you want to split up?" I asked,
making sure that I was understanding the meaning of the
hair band lyrics.

"I haven't been happy for a while," he continued. "You
nag me all the time, and I constantly feel like I am under
your thumb." According to Gavin, I was very controlling and
treated him like a child. Our earning disparity also helped

to create an imbalance of power that was uncomfortable for him. Many decisions were made based on the fact that I was the significant breadwinner, and Gavin felt emasculated by his lower wages.

There didn't seem to be a good reason to discuss my point of view; I wasn't interested in saving the relationship. In fact, I felt as though the sky overhead had cleared and that I could start living my life as an out, single gay man, essentially for the first time.

"I trust that you're prepared to move out today," I said. He didn't have much in the way of possessions.

"Not really. I didn't think you'd want it to happen so quickly." I had been out of the state for a few weeks, I thought; he had plenty of time to get his ducks in a row.

"You can come back and forth as much as you'd like to collect your things," I said, "but I think it's better if you find another place to sleep." Our guest rooms had been turned into an office and a TV lounge, and sleeping next to me didn't seem appropriate.

"I will leave today," he said with tears in his eyes. "And I do love you."

"I love you, too," I replied, "and I hope we can be in each other's lives eventually."

You don't always know when you have seen somebody or have had sex with him for the last time, until after the fact, of course. Whether because of a death or a break-up – and parallels can be drawn between both – you can be left wishing that you had paid closer attention to what was happening in a particular moment. You might have taken better mental notes of the sights, sounds, smells and feelings that accompanied the end, burning a permanent file onto your brain's internal hard drive. Gavin was such an important part of my becoming. Rather than relying on my memory, I feel fortunate to be able to count on our continued friendship, which has remained steadfast since the day we parted romantically.

ALL YOU CAN EAT

After twenty minutes, the "oinking" was working my last nerve.

"Spank this bad, little pig," Dylan shouted, wiggling his fuzzy tush in the air while he crawled back and forth on my bedroom carpet. "Oink. Oink." He'd had me insert a large butt plug with a protruding pigtail into his ass to add some authenticity to the game. Apparently, he *and* George Orwell believed that some animals were more equal than others.

"Um, you're a dirty pig?" I replied tentatively as a question, smacking his butt cheeks with a long, wooden paddle.

"Piggy needs to be hit harder," he yelled. "Oink. Oink."

"I will teach you not to get dirty again," I scolded, trying to keep from laughing. It was hard to spank a 50 year-old who was pacing my floor on his hands and knees with a red, rubber tail sticking out of his asshole; I wanted to just pet him and tell him that everything would be OK.

"I think this piece of pork needs to be fucked; that's the only way he'll learn his lesson," Dylan said. He pushed his head and shoulders to the floor, exposing his pigtailed posterior to the ceiling.

I couldn't get a hard-on to save my life. No matter what porn scene I tried to imagine, my dick was limp at the idea of having sex with a farm animal – even if his name was Dylan and he held an esteemed position at a prominent university. I am sure his sociology students could relate to my dilemma; they probably didn't want to bang Wilbur from *Charlotte's Web* either. There was an upside to the whole barnyard experience, though: it made the guy who wanted a beer bottle inserted into his body – and not through his mouth – seem reasonable.

I knew three years before the curtain finally fell on my relationship with Gavin that I was ready to move on. I had grieved the loss before the break-up happened, so it was only a matter of days until I had a profile on a handful of dating sites. Something about the anonymity of sitting behind a computer screen and not on a barstool made the process appealing, regardless of the number of Dylans out there. I worked with a professional love coach to create a sexy web persona as well as a renowned portrait photographer to capture some eye-catching images. Together, we pushed my "ad" onto Match.com, OK Cupid and JDate, and I sat in front of my brightly lit laptop waiting for Mr. Right to be in touch.

Online dating proved to be a fascinating phenomenon. The life of a relationship could run its entire course before a first in-person date actually occurred. It often began with some form of mobile communication, transitioned into the exchange of personal details, escalated to graphic sex talk and ended because one of us felt it wasn't working. "Textual chemistry," as I called it, was meaningless. Also, many men seemed to be the Hercule Poirots of the Internet, researching everything about me through Google and social media. I tried hard to keep my last name private so that people wouldn't be able to learn about my history and my Hollywood connections prior to knowing me better, but my efforts were thwarted time and time again. Where were the classic gentlemen who wanted to try things the old-fashioned way? I couldn't find them.

There wasn't much marriage potential along the information superhighway, but there were at least some interesting experiences. Anton, whom I met on Match.com, was a 49 year-old Frenchman with an accent so thick that I had an easier time understanding Jodie Foster in *Nell*. A very handsome, in-shape musician – he had been a fashion model in his 20s – he taught cello at a Los Angeles-based university. After a few e-mail exchanges, we had a two hour phone chat, two nights before I was to leave town on a business trip.

"Is there any way we can see each other tomorrow, before you fly out the following morning?" he begged. "I really want to meet you." I'd already had dinner plans, but I agreed to see him in West Hollywood for dessert so we could at least talk in person before I jetted to the east coast.

"How about some chocolate cake at The Palm, after my dinner?" I asked.

"That sounds perfect," he said. "I don't want to seem over-eager, but I think it's better to meet someone right away rather than texting and talking too much." Based on my experiences, his approach sounded well thought out and mature.

Anton was very taken with me during our dessert, staring endlessly into my eyes. He found me to be extremely attractive, which was flattering considering how insecure I was about my looks and my body. I walked him to his car, and he encouraged me to sit in the passenger seat so we could make out for a few minutes before saying goodnight. There was definitely a physical chemistry between us, and we talked for an hour about whether or not we should go back to my house or wait until I returned from my travels. Our hormones got the better of us, and we wound up naked in my bed only forty minutes later.

The proceedings were relatively tame; Anton explained that he had been violently raped as a teenager by a family acquaintance. At 49, he was still tentative about physical intimacy, but he assured me that he would work through it. A "late bloomer" myself –albeit for altogether different reasons – I could certainly relate. What I couldn't relate to, however, was some additional background information about Anton that was less than appealing.

After our brief bit of hanky-panky, we were lying in bed next to each other, talking in general about our lives and our interests. Anton revealed that he had been in two long-term relationships, one that lasted 10 years and one that lasted 20. He was living in a house that he co-owned with Mr. 10. And his roommates? Well, they were Mr. 20 and his new boyfriend. To mix things up further, Mr. 10 and Mr. 20, at one time, had their own romantic relationship. Huh? I wasn't sure I could follow the storyline; even my internship on a national soap opera didn't make this medicine go down any easier.

Anton explained that he had always been madly in love with Mr. 20, but three years into their love affair, Mr. 20 lost interest. Anton was so enamored and love-struck that he stayed with Mr. 20 for 17 additional years, forgiving sexual dalliances in hopes that Mr. 20 would come around. Eventually, Mr. 20 fell in love with someone else, opening Anton's eyes to the reality of moving on. There was no question that, if Mr. 20 ever developed a renewed interest in Anton, they would rekindle their relationship – and it would be relatively easy since they shared a home.

I did my best to process all of the facts, thinking it over and over in my head during my plane ride the next morning. I continued to talk to Anton on the phone and by text during my trip, but his situation was just too strange for my tastes. He was really sweet and smitten with me, so I held on as long as I could. It felt really good to have met someone who thought I was so fantastic, and I wanted to make it work for that reason alone. But, a few days into my travels, I sabotaged things by relaying my concerns about his living arrangements and his hesitance to engage in more intimate sexual activity. His broken English and limited understanding of American phrases and sentiments didn't help matters, and he got frustrated, as well. I had been hopeful about him as a potential boyfriend prior to learning all of his backstory, but I was relieved that it all unfolded the way it did. Had I waited until my return to meet him in the flesh, I probably would have continued to fall for his charming phone manner – which would have made everything even more disappointing when it eventually combusted.

It has been posited that there's a sucker born every minute; likewise, it wasn't counter to the mid-1800s circus statistic when Leo came into my life via OK Cupid's iPhone dating app.

"You know what really gets me hard?" he asked over Italian food and a glass of wine.

"I couldn't even venture a guess," I said, surprised that our first date conversation had taken such a sharp, provocative turn.

"Sucking toes," he smiled. "Nothing gets me off more than a foot in my mouth." He was a handsome, slender 40 year-old research executive from Silverlake.

"Interesting," I replied. I had seen porn films in which one partner munches on another's southern digits, but the eroticism attached to the fetish of "shrimping" – as it's called on the street – was lost on me. None of my previous dates had shown interest in it, which was fine because it seemed like such a waste of screen time in the movies.

"Do you care if the toes are polished?" Now and then, I have my nails painted black or navy, a personal secret that I enjoy hiding in my tube socks.

"I prefer more masculine feet," Leo said. "Why? Do you have polish on?"

"Yes," I answered. "Would it turn you on to take it off with a bottle of acetone and some cotton balls?" I was joking, but he was getting a boner.

"That would drive me crazy; you have no idea," he said. I couldn't help myself; I had to see if my Size 8 feet could really stiffen his cock. I was also curious to know if it would do anything for mine.

"Would you like to come back to my house and ruin my pedicure?" I laughed. Within a half hour, we were sitting on my couch with a bottle of nail polish remover.

"This is so hot," Leo said. He worked diligently on my right foot, pressing Cutex soaked cotton against each nail for a couple of minutes before gently removing all of the OPI Black Onyx with salon precision. By the time he finished the left foot, there wasn't a trace of color; if I had the authority, I would've granted him a nail technician's license on the spot. Unfortunately, I wasn't any more sexually aroused by the process than I was when "Monica" Chen did the same work at Bella Nail Garden – other than the fact that he had saved me $10.00 for a polish change that week.

For the next hour, Leo gave me an expert foot massage. It was so relaxing and luxurious that I fell asleep midway.

"You're loving this," he said, as he woke me by stroking my thighs.

"It feels really good," I replied. I wasn't lying, but it wasn't doing anything for my dick. His, however, was at full mast. He cradled my left foot in one hand and began to give my big toe a blowjob while he used his other hand to press my right foot against his crotch. I could feel his erection through his pants.

"You're definitely at attention," I grinned, as he continued sucking my toes. The slurping noises, which sounded like Maggie Simpson with her trademark pacifier, didn't have the same dulcet appeal that they did when applied to my penis by other gentleman callers. Leo was ready to cum in his chinos, and I was so bored that I was trying to will myself back to sleep just to pass the time.

"I think we should stop here," I said, ready to end the evening.

"Good thinking; it'll give us something to look forward to." Leo was initially optimistic that there would be a second date. As bright and engaging as he was, though, I didn't want to cultivate a relationship with someone who was more sexually excited by my hooves than the rest of my body. Instead of using my feet to get Leo off, I used them to walk him to the door, sending him on his way with a quick kiss goodnight. He got the message.

Next came Raymond, a gynecologist with a daughter from a previous "straight marriage." It made me laugh that I was planning a date with a man who "wasn't in the vagina business" but was, in fact, literally in the vagina business. He was Jewish and gorgeous, but my boner went soft the minute he went "green" on me. He was vegan, drove an electric car and lived in a house that was solar powered – all of which he told within the first ten minutes of our date. How could he even find himself behind everything he stood for? It was almost as if there wasn't a real person inside the body on the soapbox. I will keep my plastic bottles and Styrofoam cups, thank you very much. At some point, I will be able to dive headfirst into my own carbon footprint, but I am strangely OK with that.

I was not OK, however, with Christopher, the next online caller who wanted a dinner date with RedDiamondFlame (yours truly). His profile indicated that he was interested in only "HOT" guys – yep, you heard me; in all caps – so I suppose I should have been flattered by his solicitation. In his initial e-mail, he noted that, if I would provide him with my phone number, he would text me clear photos of himself. He led me to believe that he was a public figure who couldn't post his pictures for general consumption. Curiosity killed the cat – but it had to get out of the bag first. So, I sent along my cellular digits.

Christopher replied immediately with two professional photos, each bare-chested, his shirt around his waist and his pants unbuttoned; the top of his pubic hairline was startlingly visible. His face was reasonably attractive, but not one that I recognized.

"What do you do for a living?" I asked casually.

"I will have to tell you when we speak," he replied. I explained that I was on my way out the door and that I would have to call him later that evening. He seemed slightly annoyed that I could wait to hear who he was. I should have waited indefinitely.

Christopher turned out to be a dentist who had appeared on a handful of talk shows. Yes. A dentist. Not the long lost Kardashian brother he would have had me believe with his mysteriously cagey behavior on OK Cupid. He had been married to a woman, was a father to two children and had just started exploring sex with men. He told me right away that he would never be comfortable holding hands with a man in public and certainly wouldn't want tabloids finding out that he was bisexual. I think he could tell that I was trying to stifle a laugh.

"No, you wouldn't want *The National Enquirer* to find out, would you?!" I said, sounding as serious as I possibly could. "So, are you looking for just sex, or an actual relationship with a man?"

Christopher claimed to be searching for a long-lasting love affair, but I explained that his photos and profile told a different story. Who sends a semi-nude photo when he's looking for something more than a few hours in bed? Apparently, Christopher. As gently as I could, I told him why even casual dates would be insufficient: I would never be comfortable being a "secret" or taking steps back into the very closet that it took me so many years to escape. Plus, the pressure of being linked to such a high-profile celebrity (sorry, I mean *dentist*) would have been too much.

People like Christopher opened my eyes to a particularly interesting trend. During my time in the entertainment business, I had often met men who were not "out" but whom I presumed to be gay. They'd surprise me sometimes and suggest that I meet their wives. Inevitably, the little ladies turned out to be either fat or Asian. I always joke that "Beef" and "Bamboo" are the last two stops on the train before "Gay." My theory is that heavyset women often have low self-esteem and undervalue their bodies. Likewise, they don't expect much sex from their closeted gay husbands. They feel lucky to have men on their arms, and they don't question the lack of physical interest. Similarly, some Asian women are deferential to their spouses because of their cultural upbringing and related sexual repression.

Not much could be more unnerving than my brief stay at the Bates Motel. Evan, a 47 year-old insurance broker in Calabasas, told me that "his mother lived with him" up until she passed away, a year before we met. He was very deliberate in how he structured the delivery of that information; he even hesitated after starting to say that he had "lived with his mother." It was funny how the former painted a picture of a devoted son caring for his aging mom, and the latter suggested a video gamer who lived in his mother's basement or spare room. Regardless, he definitely had a relationship with his mom that seemed, shall we say, uniquely close – evidenced by how careful he was to make it sound less than creepy.

The final straw was when I heard his phone ring and then noticed a portrait of the old bat flash across his iPhone screen. She was either trying to break through from the other side, or he had programmed her image into his device – and I realized quickly that Patricia Arquette was nowhere around to provide some *Medium* insight. People handle life's passages in different ways, but I was not sure I would want to get a call from a lover, friend or bill collector, for that matter, and see my dead parent splash across my display panel. "Listen to your mother, Norman!" I thought, half laughing to myself. I have to admit, I was scared to get inside the shower each time Evan left my house. It was about time for a sequel to *Psycho*, and I didn't want to audition for the lead.

Evan, by the way, never even put out sexually. Perhaps he thought "Mother" was watching – which, frankly, I would have been OK with – but there was definitely some sort of deep-seeded repression that needed professional attention. At the end of the day, I made it out alive – even though my balls had turned a dark shade of blue. Better to leave with achy testicles, I suppose, than wrapped in a tarp.

Another online gem, Shane, was almost 10 years older than I was and had dated women for years before discovering his overwhelming attraction to men. He had the personality of a ragdoll – almost an insult to Raggedy Ann – but I was turned on for some reason by his limited sexual experience. I felt like I was opening his eyes to all kinds of new activities, including full-blown intercourse with a man. Funny that I turned into the teacher in this scenario; it felt really satisfying. (One quick aside: Raggedy Ann was such a product of its time, no? What little girl – in the age of the Disney princess culture and couture-clad role models – would want a doll described as "raggedy?" It must be a difficult toy to market in these times.)

Shane always wanted the room to be nearly pitch dark, which was boring to me. I liked to see what I was getting into, as it were, and he was a cold, wet towel when it came to visuals. After five or six "playdates," when I complained of feeling like Stevie Wonder in a porn shop, he lit some candles, which told me everything I needed to know. First, he had some areas of discoloration on his penis; his spotted dick looked a little bit like something Cruella De Ville would kidnap and make a coat out of. Second, there was a partial foreskin that covered half of the head of his member. I couldn't tell if he was actually circumcised or not – so I asked candidly.

"I was circumcised when I was born," he told me, "but I decided, as I got older, that I wanted the foreskin back."

Interesting, I thought. I had to know more

"So, how exactly did you wind up with a halfie?" I asked.

As it turned out, Shane was a true "do-it-yourself" kind of guy; he attached small weights to the skin around his penis for long periods of time, causing it to stretch to the point of covering a portion of the tip. I had to give him credit for going after what he wanted; bonus marks for creativity and perseverance. Unfortunately, I had to subtract points from the finished product, which was a funny looking, one-eyed monster that did, in fact, look much better with the cover of a very dark room. The candles were the only things that wound up getting blown in the boudoir that night. Lights out.

I branched out from online dating sites to GPS-based phone applications such as Grindr, designed to help gay men find nearby buddies for hook-ups. The apps didn't yield any dating material, but there were plenty of fulfilling sexual encounters. Damon, a 22 year-old cutie with a huge penis, kept me busy for a few nights, as did Kevin, a sweet nymphomaniac who had some psychological problems but a rabid willingness to explore his sexuality. Ronan, an Irishman who was a professional flute player, and I met multiple times when our paths would cross in the same cities, and his musical talents translated well to my penis. In fact, I considered making "flute player" a dating perquisite for potential partners.

Who knew that signing on to a sex hook-up site would also bring Divine Intervention? Harris, a 45 year-old priest, was attracted to my boyish looks – surprise, surprise – and invited me to his tiny studio apartment during one of my trips to New York. Stocky and balding, I ordinarily wouldn't have given his photo a second look if he wasn't a man of the cloth. The idea was so naughty to me, and I was hard thinking about the forbidden nature of the circumstance. I couldn't get to his place on 70th and Broadway fast enough.

"Wow," I said, "how are we going to fit two erections in this shoebox of a room?" I was half joking, until he pulled his pants down. Harris had a micro penis: a dick so small that it was difficult to find in the thatch of short-and-curlies that surrounded it. Had *my* cock been so tiny, I probably would have converted to Christianity and joined the Church myself.

"It's what I have to work with," he acknowledged, "but, since I am not a top, it does the trick." (Or doesn't do the "trick," Harris. I don't think he realized that his phrasing was so ironic.)

"Does that mean you want to bottom for me?" I asked, turned on by the idea of putting my kosher Hebrew National inside a priest.

"I don't like to bottom," he said. "It gives me the piles." Ew. The shits. The squirts. The runs. But, the piles? Who says that in the 21ˢᵗ Century? Especially in front of ten crucifixes and three portraits of the Virgin Mary?

"What would you like to do then?" I asked.

"I want to be a football coach who's giving a young athlete his physical," he answered. "You don't stop me when I cross the line, and you wind up cumming all over me."

I had not engaged in role-play previously, but Harris's teeny weeny called for creativity. He took his time, removing my clothes piece by piece, inspecting every part of my body as thoroughly as an MD. I felt a little dirty, surrounded by hanging clergy robes and Catholic imagery, but when Harris fingered me in all the right places, I hosed his bearded chin with enough pearly fluid to make the angels sing.

With no long-term success through technology, I began to lean on friends to set me up with men. I had initially avoided that method of dating because I feared that it could potentially impact the primary friendships, but, after a wild year of online exploits, I was willing to take a chance. Ricki Lake attempted to match me with a psychiatrist named Duncan whom she met through a friend, but he turned out to be more interested in my industry connections than my heart.

Duncan, whom I nicknamed "Shrink Wrap," was a Yale-educated doctor who had moved from Maine to Los Angeles hoping for a career as a television personality or talk show host. In the meantime, he was working in a seedy section of Los Angeles, seeing patients who were unable to pay for traditional mental healthcare. Tall and slim with angular facial features that were strikingly strong and sexy, Duncan knew he was handsome. He also knew that I was close to Ricki.

We had a terrific first date, and we talked for hours. He seemed very engaged in the conversation and appeared to be genuinely excited about our chemistry. After dinner, while waiting at the valet for our cars, Duncan asked me to have a meal again the following week, suggesting that I ask Ricki to join us. A red light flashed in my head. Ask Ricki? On our second date?

After our next evening together, it would have been obvious to even Forest Gump that "Shrink Wrap" was using me to get to the people I knew. He wanted a meeting with Twentieth Television about a possible expert appearance on Ricki's new talk show, and I almost went along with it. When we would talk on the phone, the conversations inevitably headed in a professional direction, and being used felt horribly uncomfortable.

We had a third and final date during which I changed my friend Todd's name to "Angelina Jolie" in my phone. I instructed Todd to call three times throughout dinner, during which I would ignore the ringing. I left the phone at my side so Duncan could see the "calls" I was missing – and there was no question that he was getting a hard-on for the whole celebrity thing. It felt good to at least fuck with his head a little since it was clear that I would never be fucking around with him in any other way.

When I called Duncan to explain why I wouldn't be seeing him again, I realized what a mistake it was to attempt to unmask someone who was operating duplicitously. They become so steadfast in their assertion that their intentions are pure, fighting to the death to preserve their "integrity." "Shrink Wrap" was playing head games, trying to make me doubt my assessment of his motives. Thankfully, my mind was unwavering. Every few months after, Duncan would text me to say hello, often throwing in a little joke or pop culture reference that would make me smile – followed each time by a line that would explain how I could help him reach his TV dreams.

With "Shrink Wrap" out of the way, another friend introduced me to Connor, a Bradley Cooper look-alike who was seven years my junior. I was away for the weekend, so we relied on texting, phone calls and the exchange of photos to maintain the excitement until I returned to Los Angeles that Sunday night.

"I think I am in love with you," Connor texted the Saturday evening before we actually met in person.

"That's not possible," I replied. "You haven't even met me. We've been texting for only two days."

"I know, but I can just feel it. I want to marry you."

What the fuck? It appeared that we had similar interests and temperaments – and, naturally, I loved the idea of someone being gaga over me – but it was all very fast. It could have simply been "textual chemistry" at play again.

"Well, if you want to marry me," I said, "you'd better have a ring when you see me tomorrow night." I didn't think he would take me seriously, but, when he showed up at my door with a red rose and an engagement band, I realized that he meant business.

"I know this is crazy," he said, "but it's what I feel in my heart."

"Don't you want to get to know me better? There's quite a bit more to me than what you have learned and seen by text."

"Of course," he answered. "I want to know everything

about you. But, I know right now that I want you to be mine."

As ridiculous as it all was, I loved that he was so enamored with me. I wanted to believe that someone could be head-over-heels. No one – not even Gavin, whom I'd spent five years with – was ever so adoring. I had been marginalized since childhood and felt horribly insecure about my appeal, and Connor claimed to see my value before ever laying eyes on me.

"Let's do it," I replied, without letting my rational brain urinate all over my emotions. It was absolutely crazy to accept his proposal, but the magic beans he was selling looked and felt real.

"You won't be sorry," Connor said. "I am going to treat you like a king."

For three weeks, he did. He sent flowers for our first week anniversary and had my favorite cake delivered for our second. Our third week together was marked by a beautiful dinner at a pricey restaurant in Downtown LA. He opened doors for me, he made the bed in the morning – he was beyond chivalrous and did everything he could to make my life easier. To Connor, it appeared, I walked on water, and he doted on me accordingly. I got used to it quickly.

What was missing, however, was intellectual stimulation. The only thing Connor and I talked about was how much he loved me. Don't get me wrong, it was wonderful to hear that I was "everything" to him, but I also wanted to talk about life and art and books.

"That's not who Connor is," our mutual, matchmaking friend said. "He is a great, fun-loving guy, but he's not your equal in that way."

"I need that connection," I said to her. "Gavin and I didn't have the same level of cultural literacy, and it was always an issue for me."

My engagement to Connor was likely one of the shortest lived in the history books. Fortunately, I had told only a couple of people – it all seemed too good to be true from the beginning – so undoing our union wasn't difficult. It was as simple as taking the ring off of my finger.

"I think I dove in too deep, too," Connor said in a note that he wrote on the back of brown paper bag and left on my kitchen counter the day we parted. "I'm scared and running, and I'm sorry." Obviously, he recognized that he leaped before he looked, and, thankfully, we both realized how foolish we had been before we were further enmeshed. Like the situation with Anton, I was initially inclined to force the relationship, making myself fit into a design that didn't match my style. Fortunately, I rang the alarm before actually allowing myself to settle for less than I wanted; I sensed that I had become a stronger person. I didn't dodge the hurt altogether (it stung more than I would have expected), but I wasn't fatally wounded. And, for the record: his Size 13 shoe meant only one thing. He had big feet.

I next decided to engage Choices, a dating service based in Los Angeles. A friend of my sister's had been a member, and he met his life partner on the first set up. He wasn't exactly Rob Lowe circa 1986 (you remember *About Last Night*, right? Yum.); if he could find love quickly, so could I. Let it suffice to say that they never presented a viable man. One gentleman they sent my way had legally changed his name to Flytime Faithful following a drug induced lapse in judgment and another took me to a seafood restaurant at which he ate a plate of jumbo shrimp using only a spoon.

Even my friend Patti Stanger, Bravo's *Millionaire Matchmaker* herself, attempted to set me up. She maintained that I was a tough case because I didn't have a "type." I always found different people attractive for various reasons, which made homing in on any one kind of person difficult, she said.

Craig, who was not Patti's client but rather a personal contact, was, in fact, a middle-aged millionaire. So-so in the looks department, he had two children who, from what I could glean, were being raised by around-the-clock nannies. After a brief e-mail introduction from Patti, Craig invited me to dinner at the Chateau Marmont, which is never high on my list of dining options. They have a lovely patio, but it's such a Hollywood scene, and the service has always been lacking in my experience. Sure, it's sometimes fun to watch Zac Efron zoom in on his skateboard or to spy on Ashton Kutcher tucked in a corner, but it's more fun to enjoy your food and get a little attention from your waiter.

Nonetheless, I pulled into the Chateau's valet, and headed upstairs to the restaurant. Craig was already seated, wearing sloppy clothes and a baseball cap. So glad I had decided to shower and put on a jacket. After some light conversation, he excused himself and didn't return to the table for 10 minutes.

"Don't you find what people talk about when they're outside smoking amusing?" Craig asked when he returned. "It's just small, ridiculous conversation."

"Um, no," was all I could get out of my mouth. I did not usually huddle with smokers, nor did I understand why he would leave me sitting by myself so he could have a cigarette. He couldn't control himself for an hour?

"Maybe he was nervous," Patti reasoned, after I had an opportunity to give her the date download. "You can't be that rigid," she said. I almost couldn't believe she was making an excuse for him.

"Well," I replied, "if he was that nervous, he should have popped a Xanax before dinner like I did." Nothing like a small dose of Alprazolam to take the edge off.

"Very funny," she said, "but you should probably just come on my show."

"If you have a viable client, I will do it," I answered. "I have tried online dating, phone apps, set-ups by friends and a traditional matchmaking service. I might as well try cable television."

Within months, the casting agency for *The Millionaire Matchmaker* booked me for an episode. They wanted me to meet Micah, a Jewish, 32 year-old trust fund baby who was round, bald and had a lisp that would put Russell Simmons to shame.

"He's obnoxious," Patti said, "and totally not for you."

"So, why am I doing the show?" I asked.

"Because there will be 10 other cute guys at the mixer, and one of them might be your dream man." She had a point; what did I have to lose?

As it turns out, I lost two days of my life. The millionaire was a dud, and I was old enough to be the father of just about every other person who had been recruited as a potential date for him. As I left the mixer, I made a pact with myself to give dating a rest for a period. I felt like I was being proactive to the point of standing in my own way. I had become the terminally single friend who complained to everyone about being on his own. I needed to breathe and let something happen organically.

To my surprise, that "something" would come in the shape of a porn star.

WORKING STIFF

I don't think it was the "Fuck you, cunt!" kind of Tourette's; Kyle's case was characterized more by repetitive tics and sniffles than wild expletives.

"Sometimes, people think I'm just breathing heavy," he said. "It sort of goes with my line of work."

I wasn't sure whether to laugh or nod in understanding, so I passed a nervous chuckle.

"I have learned to control it," he continued. "If I hadn't said anything, you might not have even realized that I have an issue." Probably not, especially considering that his being a porn star and a hooker dwarfed the whole neuropsychiatric disorder thing.

Kyle Rexx was one of the sexiest adult film actors in the porn business. His mature good looks – he was 38, older than many of his contemporary sex workers – were topped with dreamy, strawberry blond waves that receded adorably at his temples. 5'8" and 150 pounds, Kyle had a muscular build and a solid frame; his body was memorably marked by a tattoo of a tiger that began at his navel and wrapped around much of his lower back. I recognized him from one of my favorite films, *Crack Down 2* – you don't need to see the original to enjoy the sequel – the minute I logged on to Rentboy.com.

One of the leading websites to provide same-sex, male companionship, Rentboy.com became my monthly go-to source for hands-on, adult entertainment. I was exhausted by all of the dating avenues I'd been traveling, and I was working around the clock on the production of a daytime talk show; pounding the pavement to find someone to pound just wasn't efficient. I needed to accommodate my sex drive without the drama and personal baggage associated with traditional dating, and $300 per hour eliminated the headaches.

PORN STAR KYLE REXX IS AVAILABLE IN LA;
BOOK NOW FOR THE BONDAGE MASSAGE OF YOUR LIFE!

I had no idea what a bondage massage was, let alone that some were much better than others. Leave it to my fantasy slut Kyle Rexx to be at the top of his field.

"What exactly *is* a bondage massage?" I asked Kyle when he answered my call one Tuesday morning.

"I tie your hands and feet to the sides of the bed," he said. "After that, how and where I touch you is out of your control."

"When you say, 'touch,'" I continued, "does that mean intercourse?" I wanted to be the aggressor with Kyle more than the other way around, but he was so cute that I was willing to take what I could get.

"If we both decide to go there, it could lead to that, yes," he said. "But I am a top only – just so you know up front. And I don't kiss." Another Julia Roberts.

"Are you available tonight?" I was horny and didn't want to waste time. Not to mention, the adult entertainers I had encountered previously were fairly transient. Today's online profile in LA is tomorrow's "personal ad" in Michigan. I learned to act fast when my favorite porn stars became available locally.

It was 9:55PM when Kyle showed up at my door, five minutes before his 10:00PM call time. His punctuality didn't go unnoticed; it was hard to find a considerate hooker.

"Should we head to the bedroom?" he asked, going right down – er, getting right down – to business.

"Would you like something to drink first?" I responded. "I don't keep much alcohol in the house, but I have water, juice and soda." I liked the idea of chatting for five minutes before peeling my clothes off, and since Kyle was going to be tying me up, I felt that I had the right know him a little better. That has to be in a hooker handbook somewhere.

Kyle looked incredibly hot that evening. In a pair of skin-tight blue jeans that showcased his package to perfect effect, he wore a neatly starched, white button down shirt and a brown leather belt. His outfit bordered on collegiate, and when he turned sideways to take a bottle of water, I could envision myself mounting the campus jock's shapely ass.

"I'm a fan of your work," I said, not sure how exactly to break the ice.

"You've seen *Crack Down*?" he asked. I nodded; I didn't want to hurt him by admitting that I liked the second one better. "It's some of my best material."

"Definitely something to be proud of," I answered. The conversation was going nowhere.

"So, is your bedroom upstairs?" He felt the lull, too. "Let's have some fun."

As I lay across my duvet cover, still clothed, Kyle unzipped the grey canvas duffle bag he'd carried in from his car. He removed pieces of black rope and placed them onto the bed, looking at me with a grin. It was the first time I saw humanity in his eyes.

"You're really cute," he said. "I didn't expect that when you called." The cool air he'd brought in from the outside was warming up.

"Why do you say that?" I asked, trying to keep him engaged.

"Your voice sounded a little nasal and feminine on the phone," he said. "Don't take it personally."

"Then should I take it professionally?" I asked, launching a joke to dull the nerve he'd just hit. People always thought I was a woman on the phone, which made me self-conscious about my communication style. "We should probably get to the rope and massage now," I said.

"Did I hurt your feelings?" Kyle asked as he put the rope down and climbed onto the bed. "I really didn't mean to. I actually meant it as a compliment." He stroked the top of my head, staring at my face with genuine concern.

"It's fine," I said, excusing the entire exchange. "I am just not the most confident person."

"You have every reason in the world to be confident," he said. "You're cute as hell, you have a beautiful house and you're clearly successful."

"But my voice is unattractive?" I smiled.

Before I could say another word, Kyle's mouth touched mine. Plump like two pink pillows, his lips were soft and tender. I could feel his breath in my mouth, the warmth of his kiss working its way from my face, through my chest and down to my penis.

"I thought you don't like to kiss," I said, surprised by what had just happened.

"I didn't say that I don't like to," he answered. "I said that I don't when I'm on the job."

"So are you just trying to make up for the insult?" I asked.

"Absolutely not," he responded emphatically, almost as though *I* had now insulted *him*. "I did it because I felt like I wanted to in the moment."

I looked up at Kyle, who was now lying next to me on his side. I could see small lines around his forehead and eyes that revealed a hard lived past. The imperfections seemed right at home on his pale skin, as though their purpose was to tell me that a damaged soul lived beneath the beautiful brown eyes I was staring into.

"Can I kiss you again?" Kyle asked, without waiting for an answer. Our tongues swirled around, our lips parting only to look at each other's faces. "You really are adorable," he said, breathing in and out with quick sniffles.

"Do you need a tissue?" I interrupted.

"No, it's just one of the symptoms," he said, giving me the background on his Tourette's syndrome. "But let's get back to kissing."

We undressed and continued to lock lips, our bodies pressed against each other. The same height and similarly endowed, I could feel our hard dicks touch.

"Do you want to be inside me?" Kyle asked.

"Are you serious?" He was clear that he was a top only, and I had already resigned myself to putting out.

"I know what I said on the phone, but I feel differently now." Kyle ran his hands down my hairy chest and kissed me again. "Please make love to me."

As I put a pre-lubricated condom on my cock, Kyle stood over me, lowering himself slowly onto my rigid shaft. I watched his eyes roll to the back of his head while he took its entire length, writhing his hips back and forth in a bull riding motion. It was definitely not his first time at the rodeo, but, for me, the sensation was unparalleled. He leaned forward, without pausing his hips, to kiss me, keeping his mouth against mine.

"I'm going to cum," I said within only 10 minutes, giving him the option to dismount before I exploded. He didn't.

"My name is Adam," he said, just as I ejaculated into the latex sheath.

"Adam," I said. I attempted to catch my breath and recover from the intensity of the orgasm. "Adam."

"Not as sexy as 'Kyle Rexx,' huh?" he laughed. "I'm just Adam Stone from New Jersey." He kissed me.

"'Adam Stone' is more appealing," I said. "He sounds like a real person."

As Adam rinsed off and dressed, I handed him a neatly folded stash of $20 bills.

"You may want to make sure I counted correctly," I said. He took the cash without looking and sheepishly tucked it into his front pocket. We both felt awkward about the exchange of money for his "services," as neither of us antici-pated a connection.

"Do you think you'll be calling again?" he asked. "My

schedule usually fills up, and I want to make sure I can be here if you want me." I was pretty sure that was the hooker version of "asking me out" again.

"I think I'll be calling next week," I replied with a wink. "Which night is good?"

Adam and I made another 10:00PM appointment for the following Tuesday, but I wasn't sure how I was going to get through the week without being in touch. He wasn't a date. He wasn't even a close friend. He was an "ass-for-rent" with whom I had outrageous sexual chemistry. Regardless, I couldn't stop thinking about him.

"I had sex with a really hot guy last night," I told my mother by phone the morning after Adam and I met.

"Is he Jewish, and were you careful?" she asked, typically the first two questions out of her mouth when I broached the subject of romance.

"I don't know his religion, and yes, we were safe," I answered. "He's a porn star whom I hired, but there was definitely something between us."

"If it's just for fun, that's fine, but I don't think you should get too involved," my mother said.

My uniquely close relationship with my parents has been a point of intrigue among friends. The frank nature of our conversations – which happen multiple times per day by phone – includes everything from work to romance to sex. My well-being is their top concern, but they are understanding of and sensitive to my personal decisions – even when those choices include callboys.

The Sunday prior to my second "date" with Adam, I texted him to make sure that I was still on his schedule for Tuesday. He seemed conscientious about his work and his calendar, but I wanted an excuse to interact. He answered within seconds.

"Hey, happy to hear from you. I'm looking forward to Tuesday," he wrote. "I'm bringing something special for us to play with."

So sweet, I thought; he was thinking ahead. His surprise, however, left me shocked. Literally.

Right on schedule, Adam arrived at my house. This time in black slacks and a grey shirt, he was dressed to impress. His pumped chest and meaty ass filled out his clothes nicely, and his arms were around me in a bear hug as soon as he walked through the front door. He dropped his duffle bag to the floor.

"It's so good to see you," he said, kissing me gently without unlocking his arms from behind my back.

"I bet you say that to all of your customers," I answered. I wanted to feel like I was special to him, but I knew he was in the business of making all of his clients feel that way. I reminded myself that it was simply a transaction and that I had hired someone who was expert at delivering the goods.

"As you get to know me better, you'll see that I am the real deal," he said. "I like you, Josh."

"Tell me about this surprise you have for us." I changed the subject quickly. I didn't want to be disappointed when he got to the inevitable part about *liking me but not being in a headspace or career that would allow for anything more.*

Adam opened his bag and removed what looked like a portable audio board or control panel. Attached by long wires were leather rings that could fasten with snaps around a finger or an arm. Or a penis.

"You're going to love this," Adam told me as we walked

upstairs to my bed. He pushed me onto my back and unzipped my jeans. Pulling my underwear down to my thighs, he wrapped a wired cock ring around the base of my dick.

"What does this contraption do?" I asked. I can't say I wasn't a little nervous; it looked like a science experiment.

"Just relax," Adam said as he pressed one of the buttons on the base panel in his hands. An electric current ran through my balls and up through the head of my penis. It was an odd feeling, alternatingly painful and euphoric. "Can you feel that?"

"It's really strange," I said. "I can't decide if I like it or not."

"Your cock really likes it," Adam smiled. I was hard as a rock, and he began to massage my crotch in tandem with the pulsating waves of the electric device. When he finally put his mouth around the head of my erection, I thought I was going to jump out of my skin. The sensation was mind-numbingly blissful. I closed my eyes; I couldn't process one more piece of stimulation.

"Someone is in heaven," I heard Adam say as he moved his face up to mine. Somehow, the current traveled through my body, and when Adam kissed me, I could taste the energy and sparks on his lips. I was worked up like never before, but I wasn't ready to cum.

"Get on your back," I said to Adam, removing my clothes and the electric ring from my groin. He complied immediately, taking his pants and underwear off. He spread his legs and bent them at the knees.

"I've been waiting all week to do this again," Adam moaned. I put on a condom as fast as possible and slid into his ass. For twenty minutes, our bodies moved in perfect harmony. We kissed and held each other, rocking back and forth with the sensual motion of my thrusts. It was the first time that sex didn't feel selfish; my only thought was to give Adam as much pleasure as possible. I used his breathing and sighs as signals to adjust my speed to his liking.

"You're going to make me cum," Adam yelled, pulling my face to his. His entire head was beaded with sweat. We pushed our lips together while he jerked himself to orgasm; I came inside him at the same time.

"What are you thinking about?" Adam asked as I rolled off of him and onto my back. I'd never felt so spent.

"Just how fantastic that was," I said. There was more going on in my brain, though. I felt a bond with Adam that made the sex altogether different than anything I had experienced before. It was entirely reciprocal; I had never been as focused on giving satisfaction to another person as I was on receiving pleasure. Getting off was Priority One, until Adam. Strange, considering that I was paying *him* to take care of *me*. It fucked with my head.

"You look like you're getting sleepy," he said. "I'm going to let you wash up and get to bed." I gave him his $300, feeling a twinge of disappointment when he put the bills in his wallet. Naturally, he'd earned his money – and a deal was a deal – but a flash fantasy in my mind wanted him to decline the fee and stay the night.

"Josh, honey, I don't think a porn star is a dating option," my mother said the next morning, after I told her about Round 2. "And, we better ask Dad if that 'electric shock' device is safe. I never heard of anything like it."

"You don't think I should call him again?" I asked. "There's definitely something between us."

"Why don't you hire him one more time next week, and see what happens," my mother suggested. "If the chemistry is still strong, talk to him about it. But you can't keep spending $300 every time you want to have sex." My mom was a voice of reason when it came to navigating the whole hooker/client relationship. Props to her.

As fate would have it, I had hit the "Jewish Jackpot." Adam Stone was another member of the Hebrew tribe, single, had an MBA and wasn't hurting for money. It all came out the following Tuesday at 10:00PM.

"How does someone with your background fall into the sex industry?" I asked.

"I was on vacation in San Francisco, and I was spotted by a porn talent scout," Adam said. Obviously, he was the Lana Turner of adult films. "I was bored with my marketing gig in LA, and I thought it would be fun to earn a living having sex with hot guys."

"And that led to hooking?" I continued.

"When the porn work dried up, I needed money and started seeing private clients. It's not a glamorous story, but it's the truth." We were lying on the bed side by side, holding hands and looking at the ceiling.

"Do you plan to stop doing this?" I asked.

"I'm trying so hard to quit, but it's like turning a ship," Adam said. "I can't make a sharp change until I have enough money saved up to support myself while I look for legitimate work. I have to get motivated."

"What do you think would motivate you?" I felt like Diane Sawyer.

"Maybe if I had someone in my corner," he said. "Someone to think about other than myself. But, it's not easy to meet a partner when you're sleeping with men for money."

The conversation was undoubtedly a downer. Adam was lost, having given up stability for the quick thrills and fast life of the porn business. I could tell he wanted something else, but a sense of helplessness and despair shadowed whatever drive was left inside him.

"I'm not taking any money from you tonight," Adam said. "It doesn't feel like you're a client anymore."

"Plus, we didn't have sex; we just talked," I joked. "I certainly wasn't planning to pay for a chat."

"Totally fair," he said with a laugh.

"How would you feel about dinner and a movie on Saturday night?" I asked. "I'm not planning to pay you for your time; it would be a real date." Adam's eyes started to well.

"You have no idea how much I was hoping you would ask me out," he said. "I was afraid to cross the line, but you did it for me."

Saturday couldn't come fast enough, even though I was half expecting Adam to cancel for a paying gig. When my phone message indicator beeped that morning, I braced myself for disappointment.

"Hey, Josh, it's Adam. Just wanted to confirm the time for tonight. I had some car trouble, and I had to leave it at the shop, but I rented a car, so we're all set." I almost couldn't believe it. He was keeping his word without a monetary incentive.

He showed up looking hotter than I'd ever seen him. A perfectly fitted, pink shirt and beautifully filled out jeans. I almost couldn't look at him without staring. We hopped into my car and headed to Spark, my favorite neighborhood restaurant in the Valley. We had a fantastic meal with terrific conversation. He told me all about his family, how his mother put herself through college and graduate school and how proud he was that she had become a successful corporate communications executive on her own money and perseverance. He was charming and present, and I couldn't wait to get to the movies so I could hold his hand.

We went to see a Woody Allen movie – Adam's interests ran more indie than blockbuster – and we sat arm-in-arm for the entire feature. My heart and mind were racing. Was it possible that I could have been falling in love with this man? He was kind and reliable – more than I could say for the dates I had met through traditional channels.

After a lengthy goodnight kiss, we made plans to have dinner during the week, during which Adam told me that he'd be going out of town for a short time.

"I am going to visit my mom in Queens," he said, "and I have a client in Manhattan who is paying for my trip."

He saw me flinch at the mention of a client.

"I know it's weird to tell you that, but you're aware of what I'm doing to earn money at the moment," he said. "I want to be honest with you about everything."

Our bond was undeniable, and I was falling for Adam. I had no idea how I would make peace with his professional life or whether he would wind up being another Gavin, an adult in need of rescue. But, I had developed such a deep feeling for him that I couldn't turn back.

"Will you be in touch during the two weeks you're gone?" I asked.

"I will text or call every single day." And he did.

Adam, without fail, greeted me each morning and wished

me sweet dreams before bedtime. He was attentive without being clingy, making sure to demonstrate his continued interest while he was away. He did everything right.

"How's your mom?" I texted, two nights before Adam was to return to Los Angeles.

"She's OK. A little sad to see me leave," he said. "But, I have to get back so I can have dinner with you on Thursday." It felt good to hear that he was so anxious to see me.

"I can't wait to have you back," I said.

"I really need to get my shit together as soon as I'm home," Adam continued. "I will kill myself if I don't have a reputable source of income by the time I'm 40."

"Please don't say that," I begged. "I have been the person left behind before, and it still haunts me."

"I shouldn't have phrased it that way. Don't worry; I'm not leaving the planet anytime soon," he said. "Having a single Jewish mother is about as much assurance as you need. I could never leave her alone in the world." It was 2:30AM eastern time.

"Shouldn't you be asleep?" I asked. "It's the middle of the night in New York."

"I'm really scared right now," he replied. "Really scared."

"What are you talking about?" His texts were beginning to startle me.

"Things just aren't right, and my mind is spinning."

"What's not right?" I pushed for a coherent answer. "Explain what you mean."

Adam's responses read like a stream of consciousness mess. I had no experience with illegal substances, but I imagined his alarming and erratic messages to be the product of a drug binge or a paranoid personality.

"Can we talk on the phone?" I didn't want to go to sleep without knowing that Adam was OK.

"I can't talk right now," he said. "Everything is going to be better in the morning."

"Can we keep texting?" I asked. I was disquieted by his wild tangent and wanted to be there for him.

"We both have to go to sleep; I'm going to call you in the morning," he said. His communication stopped with that last message.

I was up all night, worrying about Adam and what exactly had caused his strange outburst. In my head, I replayed the entire month that we had known each other, trying to pinpoint conversations and behaviors that might identify problems I didn't want to notice. I began to think about the Tourette's syndrome and the sniffles. Perhaps they were signs of drug use rather than a neurological issue? A million thoughts raced through my brain until Adam called at 9:00AM the next day to apologize for his upsetting texts.

"I'm so sorry," he said. "I was exhausted. But, I want to be clear about something: I really want to explore things with you." Relieved to hear his voice and his interest in a relationship, I didn't share the concerns that had plagued me during the night.

"Does that mean you are going to try to get your life on course and leave the sex work behind?" I asked.

"It might take a little time, but, yes," Adam said.

"You made my day," I answered. "I have to run into a meeting, but I can't wait to see you tomorrow. Will you text before you fly in the morning?"

"You know I will," he replied.

That evening, I sent a message and was saddened to go

to sleep with no reply. I woke up three times to check my phone, but nothing had come in during the night. Floating in and out of sleep, I tossed and turned restlessly, unsettled by the silence from New York. I woke up at 6:00AM and grabbed my phone immediately, hoping there would be a morning note or a plan for dinner that evening. Nothing. I tried calling and texting but got no answer. I reasoned that Adam was in flight with no WiFi.

Thursday came and went, and I didn't hear from him. Everything I feared flashed before me; had I invested in a person who sold emotional and sexual fantasies for a living? Had it, in fact, been business to him all along? I shared my embarrassment with only one person, a compassionate friend who tried to jolt me into reality.

"You can't be surprised that he disappeared," my friend said. "He's a porn star and a hooker. What kind of standard were you holding him to? What were you even thinking?"

"You're right," I said, as not to look any more the fool. "I suppose I wanted to be the person who was worth turning his life around for." I became angry at Adam's thoughtlessness. Had he not considered how I would feel, discarded and unworthy?

"People who live on the fringes are not capable of being who we want them to be," my friend said. "It's just the shape of things."

The next morning was difficult to get through. My parents were arriving from Florida that night for a week-long visit, and I was in a daze. I couldn't shake Adam's disregard for my feelings, and I was mortified to tell my mom and dad that this person I started to care for was nothing more than a fantasy who should have stayed inside the DVD player.

While stopped at a traffic light on my way to collect my parents from the airport, I realized that Adam and I were Facebook friends. I quickly opened the mobile app, curious to see what kind of photos and updates he had been posting during the time he was supposed to be with me. I waited a few seconds for the application to load onto my phone, and I typed his name into the interface using only one thumb. A-D-A-M S-T-O-N-E. I swerved to the side of the road, slamming on my breaks to avoid colliding with a roadside median. My chest became tight, as though fishing twine had been threaded through my heart and pulled in both directions.

Adam had passed away the Wednesday afternoon that I stopped hearing from him. A stream of RIP and condolence messages flooded through his page. In shock, I didn't move for five minutes. I stared out my windshield into the freeway traffic, thinking about the conversation I'd had with my friend the night before. I had talked through every reason why Adam wasn't good enough for me. I tore him apart in an attempt to process what I perceived to be rejection; it was the ultimate lesson in "It's Not Always About You."

The following week, from a friend who attended an Alcoholics Anonymous meeting, I learned that Adam had died of a heart attack caused by a drug relapse in New York. The lines I noticed when I first looked closely at his face did, in fact, tell the story of a broken person, a story of fear and depression that were managed with heroin and cocaine.

"The guy you were seeing was Adam Stone, right?" my friend asked. I had told him the whole story shortly after Adam died.

"Yes," I said. "Why do you ask?"

"They made an announcement about his death at AA this morning. He had been clean for a long time and was going to meetings regularly. Everyone was shocked that he fell backwards."

"Did they say anything else about Adam?" I wanted every detail I could get.

"A bunch of guys were talking after the meeting, and they all said what a good person he was," my friend answered. "It sounded like he was a really kind, special man."

I found Adam's mother's home address in Long Island and scribbled it across a yellow Post-it that sat on my desk. For weeks, I looked at her name – Beth Stone – and thought about writing a note. Maybe she'd be glad to read that her son had met a nice, Jewish boy. Perhaps she would feel a tiny bit better knowing that, throughout his struggle, someone brought a small amount of happiness into his life. But then, I realized it was also possible that I would be putting her face to face with difficult truths about her son's past. I decided that I was motivated more by my own need for closure than by enlightenment for Beth. I never wrote the letter.

To soldier through the loss, I convinced myself that the Universe had at once removed the pain from Adam's life and an eventual heartache from mine. It was as though an old Band-Aid had been ripped off quickly, resulting in a fast sting as opposed to prolonged agony. The hurt in the moment, I believed, was easier to deal with than attempting to save Adam. In hindsight, it was callous and selfish logic, but it gave me peace in the darkness.

CIRCLE JERK

The heat was at a record high on the early-August afternoon that I ran into a celebrity pal at Neiman Marcus in Beverly Hills.

"We really need to catch up; I have so many important things to tell you," my friend said. "How about November 5th?"

"Wow, that's three months away," I answered. "We would need a double appointment just to catch up from the catch up." She laughed, but I was passive aggressively making a point.

"You're hilarious," she replied. "I can't wait!" Obviously, she could. 90 days.

The last time I'd seen this comely actress was during a visit to the set of her popular television drama. She had invited me to have lunch and spend the day, as she knew there would be hours of down time during that week's shoot.

"You can take a day off from work, can't you?" she said, whining into the phone.

"I have a lot going on," I answered, "but I could probably sneak away for an hour." I wouldn't have played hookie for anyone else; in fact, had my sister asked me, I'd probably have said no. This was a television star, though, which made me feel glamorous.

"I need you to be there for me," she continued. "It has been a tough month, and I could use some support. One day won't kill you." Her "tough month" consisted of a wardrobe problem, a quarrel with an ex-boyfriend and arriving 20 minutes late to a benefit gala at which she was scheduled to present an award. The little girl I sponsored in Africa would have given her eye-teeth for such a difficult four weeks, but who was I to argue with the toast of television?

"I'll spend Friday with you," I said, "but I may have to take some calls and answer some e-mails." My calendar was like a Jenga puzzle, and it took some maneuvering to clear my schedule for an entire day. Nevertheless, I came through.

"You're the best," she said excitedly.

When I arrived at the set that morning, Ms. Drama was beside herself. I could hear her raised voice as I approached.

"How are we behind schedule already?" she shouted to a production assistant. "The day is just starting." Fortunately for the PA, she got distracted when I entered her Star Wagon trailer.

"Josh! I'm so glad you're here. The day is a disaster already," she said. It's a good thing the Hurricane Katrina survivors – for whom she helped raise money – couldn't hear her.

"It sounds like they're only one scene behind," I said. "Hardly a disaster."

"You know it's going to keep me on set at least an extra hour tonight," she answered. "Thank goodness you're here to keep me company." I was expected to stay late, as well. Maybe it *was* a disaster.

The day turned out to be pleasant; we chatted in between scenes, lounging in director's chairs on the perimeter of the studio sound stage.

"How are things with you? Are you dating anyone interesting?" she asked. I was surprised that the subject of me even came up; it wasn't often that she gave away the spotlight.

"Well, there is a guy who has potential," I began.

"Every guy who 'has potential' doesn't wind up working out," she said. "I had an argument with my ex two weeks ago; you won't believe what he said. Don't get me started."

She continued her story until lunchtime when we returned to her trailer for the lobster Cobb salads she had ordered. Hers was served by a production assistant on a white plate; mine was handed to me in a plastic container.

"Why is my food on a plate?" she shrieked. She sounded like a beeping smoke detector with a drained battery.

"I didn't think you'd want to eat out of plastic," the PA explained, embarrassed to be chided in front of her guest. "I noticed that you'd been using dishes and silverware earlier in the week."

"I want mine to be just like Josh's," she ranted.

"No problem. I can get the original container." He was flustered, but Ms. Drama seemed assuaged by the remedy he proposed.

"Wait!" she screamed, as he began to walk out of her trailer. "Josh's salad has more lobster on it. Did you take some off of mine and put it into Josh's container?" She clearly existed in an alternate universe where lobster bandits redistributed meat across salads just to fuck with people.

"Of course not," the PA answered. "All I did was empty one of the plastic containers onto a plate." He looked at the floor without making eye contact with Ms. Drama or me.

"Forget it," she said. "I am just going to eat it the way it is. This whole thing has already cut into my lunch break." She leaned over and used her fork to spear a piece of juicy claw meat from my salad.

It was early in my career when I met Ms. Drama, working as a publicist on a small ensemble film. She had a tiny part but, given her television pedigree, figured prominently into the marketing campaign. I was young enough to be dazzled by her celebrity; in fact, I had been a fan of hers growing up.

"You're very smart and efficient," she said to me during the weekend press junket for the movie. "You'll probably wind up running the studio. What's your name?"

"Thank you; I'm Josh," I replied, thrilled that she acknowledged me, let alone my brain and work ethic.

"Give me your number before you leave today; we should stay in touch," she said. "I like you."

I couldn't wait to call my family and let them know that Ms. Drama had singled me out. She was a household name, a special person, who saw something special in me. Never mind that Andy Webber didn't want to be seen with me in high school; Ms. Drama, who had fame, money and power, wanted to be my friend. Fuck Camp Shalom. Fuck high school. Fuck Andy Webber. (By the way, I totally would have fucked Andy Webber, given the opportunity.)

It took a few years until I realized how drained I was by Ms. Drama. She monopolized my free time, holding me hostage in her Bel Air mansion while she talked endlessly about tumultuous romances, producers who screwed her over and colleagues who didn't recognize how talented she was. We rarely talked about anything happening in my life; it was a one-way street, and she relied on my ears and my counsel.

Her dependence on me was exciting to my "regular" friends. They loved my social media updates and the photos of my adventures with Ms. Drama. I, in turn, kept her in my life because she cast a glow that made me shine to everyone else. She siphoned all of my energy, and I wasn't enjoying the friendship. Had she not been famous, I wouldn't have allowed our relationship to continue, but I needed Ms. Drama to feel worthy of the love and attention of others. It was a lopsided equation to be sure: what was making me feel valuable on the outside was eating away at what little sense of self I had.

I forged a similar bond with another television personality whom I'd also met through work. Not long after we became friends, she invited me to join her in Las Vegas for the birthday party of one of her rock star (literally) friends. The night of the event, we went to watch Mr. Rockstar perform, but Ms. TV Personality was three sheets to the wind before the curtain lifted. Mid-show, she got up to use the bathroom and returned with wet hands. She was holding a bundle of toilet paper, reaching her palms out to each seated guest as she clumsily walked across our row to her seat.

"Hey! Look what I found in the toilet. A $100 bill," she yelled, loud enough for the entire audience to hear. "I fished it out. I'd have done it even if it was only $5!" I knew the night was heading downhill fast.

After the performance, we filed onto a party bus, complete with a full bar and half naked male and female dancers grinding against metal poles. A neon blue concoction was being passed around, along with some hash brownies that a B-list movie actress – coincidentally known for her role in a Vegas stripper film – had in her bag. Ms. TV Personality continued to drink, downing the blue liquid like water. As she started to feel more of a buzz, she began to scream inappropriate things to the entire bus. If I could have gotten the driver to slow down, I'd have jumped out of a window onto Las Vegas Boulevard to avoid further embarrassment.

Not soon enough, we arrived at Ago, an upscale restaurant in the Hard Rock Hotel. We were seated at a table with Mr. Rockstar and eight other well-known celebrities. Instead of being able to concentrate on conversations with the various luminaries, I wound up having to keep my eye on Ms. TV Personality. She was continuing to drink the wine that was on the table, and I could see her eyes getting glassier by the minute. At one point, she stared directly at me and gave a "come hither" motion with her finger. No sooner did I get to her chair, she grabbed my arm and asked me to walk with her to the bathroom.

"I feel completely fine," she said, as she stumbled down the pathway to the women's lounge, anchored to my arm. "I just wanted you to keep me company."

"You're very drunk," I replied, "maybe we should go back to our room."

"You're a buzz kill," she snapped. "You just don't know what a good time is." Apparently, I hadn't experienced the pleasure of passing out on a public toilet.

I waited for her to come out of the ladies' room so we could return to the dinner. After 20 minutes, I began to worry and asked the restroom attendant to check on my friend.

"Is she wearing a Herve Leger sleeveless and black Louboutins?" the attendant asked.

"That's her," I said. "Is she OK?"

"She's asleep on the toilet. The door to the stall is open, and her dress is hiked up." Homegirl knew what was happening on her turf *and* she knew her designer labels.

"Would you mind trying to wake her?" I asked. "I will walk her back into the dining room."

As we re-entered the party, guests were starting to notice Ms. TV Personality's drunk cadence. Only five minutes back at the table, poor Mr. Rockstar was subjected to the rambling, booze fueled words that were dripping from her mouth.

"Guess who has to go potty again," she announced. "That red sauce is going through me like a train." Too bad the dropped jaws at our table didn't swallow me whole.

"Come with me," I commanded. I grabbed her sagging upper arm and pulled her out of the restaurant. This time, we didn't make it as far as the restroom. She draped herself over some stone steps and began to moan in discomfort just as Mr. Rockstar's assistant came running over to see what was happening. There to protect her, I made excuses.

"She hadn't eaten anything until too late, I think, so the alcohol got to her head quickly," I said. The assistant just smiled knowingly, and we hatched a plan to get her back to our room at Mandalay Bay. So much for a fun all-nighter.

The assistant sent a chauffeured SUV to the restaurant, equipped with a wheelchair. Because Ms. TV Personality was passed out, she was dead weight – and wasn't light as a feather to begin with. The assistant helped me shift her into the wheelchair, but I was concerned that tourists might recognize her and take photos.

"You know what, I'll throw her coat over her," I said. "Hopefully, no one will notice."

Ms. TV Personality came to consciousness just long enough to scream, "No one is putting a coat over me," then belched and zoned out again. We finally got her to the car 30 minutes later.

During the ride back to our hotel, she was burping non-stop. The driver was using all of his willpower to keep a straight face, but I started to laugh because of my nerves and embarrassment. When we arrived at our hotel, he helped me put Ms. TV Personality back into the wheelchair and cover her again with a coat. He accompanied me through the lobby.

"Wow, rough night!" people would say, pointing at our covered wagon as we coasted through the casino. When we got to the room, the driver carried her to the bed. During the process, her legs fell open, revealing some unwaxed skin around a sideways smile. I didn't have any cash with me or presence of mind, so I considered that to be his tip.

I removed Ms. TV Personality's jewelry so she wouldn't scratch herself during the night and positioned her comfortably under the covers. I woke up periodically to check her breathing, just to make sure there were no alcohol related emergencies. By the next morning, she had no recollection of what occurred the night before, and I was more than ready to head back to Los Angeles.

When the fairy dust wore off and the craziness of the weekend settled into a few days of downtime at home, I started to reflect on what had happened. I very much wanted to be the person who stayed out all night and partied like a rock star with, well, rock stars. I relayed the story of the Las Vegas debacle to many people, telling my family and friends how much fun I'd had and how edgy, cool and "inside" Ms. TV Personality's behavior had been. They all wished they could be *me*. Who wouldn't want my life? Actresses, television personalities, music superstars – they were all on my speed dial.

Every fiber of my being knew, however, that I was making excuses for and embracing a way of life that didn't look good on Ms. TV Personality. And, at the end of the day, it surely wasn't going to fit me. I ignored my instincts because I still thought that, by following her rocky trail – nearly off a cliff, mind you – I might find the exciting person who was buried inside of me for all those years. Unfortunately, the only place I followed her was to Utah for another wake-up call.

"I am going to take a private jet to Salt Lake City for Ms. Character's birthday party," she said. "Will you come with me?"

"Are you allowed to bring a guest?" I asked. I didn't like the 80s character actress who was celebrating a milestone year, and I was fairly certain that she wasn't a fan of mine either.

"No, not exactly. But, maybe you can get a spa treatment at the hotel while I am at the dinner. I'll pay for it." I was an accessory to Ms. TV Personality, not an evolved person who would feel like he hadn't been asked to sit at the cool kids' table. "It'll be fun; we will have a few days in Utah to play around."

"Maybe it's not such a good idea," I said. "I don't like tagging along where I know I am not wanted."

"*I* want you there," she said. "Isn't that enough?" What she wanted was a playmate who would give her undivided attention for three days. The private plane sounded exciting, though, and I knew my other friends would marvel at the jetsetter I'd become. I agreed to join her at the expense of my own dignity.

Ms. TV Personality had invited the birthday girl, her husband and a couple of their friends to travel with us, which made the two-hour flight particularly uncomfortable. They all knew I was a tag-along and not included in that night's festivities, and they were conspicuous in referring to the party with whispers and veiled language. It was as though they were passing notes about me, right in front of my face.

Eventually, even Ms. Character – who, in my experience, was always an exclusionary bitch – realized that she had to mop up the shit piles dumped by the elephant in the room (or, in this case, airplane). She walked to the front of the eight-passenger jet, where I was reading a magazine.

"Josh, someone just canceled for tonight, so I have a spare seat at the dinner," she said. "Would you like to join us?" Was it really necessary for her to reveal that my invite was contingent on a no-show?

"Yes, he'll definitely come," Ms. TV Personality interjected, before I could consider the situation.

Ms. Character's 20 guests filed into the restaurant dining room that evening and took their chairs in front of printed place cards. Mine was at the farthest extremity of the long, rectangular table.

"Josh, I am so happy to be sitting next to you," a former television host, whom I'd known peripherally, said. She hadn't worked in a number of years, and I think she realized that I was the "Guest Most Likely to Give Her the Time of Day."

As I scanned the table and noted the seating arrangements, it was clear that each person was positioned based on his or her status in the entertainment industry. Even among the "in crowd," there was a hierarchy, and Ms. Character – whose own stature was questionable considering that her last starring role had been on the Hallmark Channel – was doling out a heavy dose of reality to a table of insecure notables. The former sitcom star turned Oscar-winning actress was placed at the center, just next to one of America's romantic comedy sweethearts – who was gabbing with her seatmate, a comedic actress/singer whose glory days passed with the 90s. Toward the ends of the table were the cable television hosts, the washed up actors and the obligatory family members who, without question, dragged down the star quality of the party. Sadly for Ms. TV Personality, she was seated on one side of me; obviously, her Hollywood career forecast was bleak.

My photographs from the party painted an altogether different picture. There I was, smiling and sipping drinks with a *People* magazine come-to-life. Everyone looked happy to be celebrating Ms. Character, and my friends across the country were texting comments and questions about the glittery showbiz party that I was documenting on Facebook. What they couldn't see – behind the camera flashes and the blindingly white veneers on every tooth – were the battered egos and broken spirits of the dinner guests. Sure, it appeared to be fun in photos, but I knew in my heart that I was a hanger-on who, by Ms. Character's standards, should have been seated in Toledo.

Friendships have always been extremely important in my life, and I have relied on them the same way that many people lean on their families. For a large part of my adulthood, I've lived on the opposite side of the country from my parents and my sister, and I attempted to surround myself with quality people who were honest, upstanding and invested in my personal growth. In the give-and-take that represents almost all friendships – either close or casual – I have traditionally been in what I call "80/20s." As in, I would do 80% of the heavy lifting and my friend was responsible for only 20% – which made me the perfect celebrity pal.

For years, I attempted to make peace with the inequities of the friendly relationships I cultivated. I knew that my parents raised me with an unparalleled sense of fairness and respect, and I wrote the shortcomings of others off to poor childrearing on the part of their folks. Or, I would explain things away by outwardly recognizing the various burdens and life events that were weighing down those friends who were not present or considerate in circumstances that required their participation. Eventually, it became evident that excusing the bad behavior of others was simply a way of not facing the truth – basically, an effort to keep hurt at bay. Sometimes, however, I couldn't stop the pain.

I'd become close to a famous pop singer whom I met through mutual acquaintances. Over ten years, we developed such a close friendship that a nightly phone chat became our bedtime ritual.

"I want to do something big for my birthday," she said, just as I was about to fall asleep late one evening. "Do you think I should throw a party in Los Angeles, or should I make it a destination event?"

"Most of your friends are in LA, so you might as well make it easy on everyone." By "everyone," I meant me. Celebrities often forget that a handful of their friends have neither the time off from work nor the funds to be traipsing across the globe for a shrimp cocktail and slice of cake.

"You're probably right," she said. "I think I'll do a dinner and an entertaining program, sort of a roast."

"Do you think it's strange to throw your own roast?" I asked. "It might be a little self-indulgent." Over the years, I got much bolder about calling it like I saw it.

"Maybe, but I'm OK with that. I think it'll be fun." For the most part, "fun" to a star is a movie, series, book, magazine, product line or event that revolves around him or her.

"Then go for it," I said. "Who are you going to ask to roast you?"

"I am going to ask people who are funny, who have something special to offer. People who really know me," she replied. When I found out that I wasn't a member of that group, it impaled my chest like a sharp stake. She had been an extremely thoughtful friend for almost a decade – never once disappointing me with a social misstep, surprisingly – until she made it clear that I wasn't in the line-up of her "show."

The dinner was held at a nightclub in Downtown LA that Ms. Pop had rented for the evening. The room boasted wall-to-wall film and television actors, a few comedians, a handful of notable musicians and a smattering of non-famous friends.

"This is a great party, isn't it?" she asked, just before the lights dimmed for the presentation. Celebrities often ask leading questions, guiding friends to the answers they want to hear. She didn't ask what I thought of the event; rather, she suggested I agree that it was "great."

"I am excited to see the show," I replied, skirting her initial question and changing the subject.

"I think you'll get a kick out of it. The presenters wrote

some really meaningful things," she said. Presenters? Was this The Golden Globes or a birthday party?

One celebrity after another took the stage, many of whom she hadn't been in touch with for months. An Oscar-winning actress, an acclaimed indie actor, a bawdy comedienne; they all delivered beautiful speeches and hilarious punch lines, one right after the other. It was a "Who's Who" of marquee stars rather than a representative sample of the people who truly populated her inner circle. She had produced a show, and the part of "Close Friend" was recast with a bigger name.

After the standing ovation, I stepped outside to breathe in some fresh air and take stock of how I was feeling about my personal relationships. I had given so much of myself to Ms. Drama, Ms. TV Personality and Ms. Pop. I was forever treading behind them, picking up the pieces of their fractured love affairs and their self-centered existences. I gave them everything I had, running on a wheel to stay in their lives so that I could appear important to the people who really counted.

Five days after Ms. Pop's birthday extravaganza, I received a call from my friend Jacqui.

"I need to get something off my chest," she said, "and I hope you won't take this the wrong way."

"Give it to me straight," I answered, always adhering to my "honesty is the best policy" philosophy.

"Your fancy friends have sort of kidnapped you," she said. "I don't see you anymore, except on Twitter. It's really disappointing."

She was right; I had ignored the people who truly cared about me in order to make them think I was an exciting person to know. I filled myself up with the empty calories of celebrity instead of the nourishing heartiness of real friends, and Jacqui called me out on it.

Social media was another hill to get over in the friendship landscape. Platforms such as Facebook, Twitter and Instagram gave birth to cyber cliques, exclusive clubs that many still use as yardsticks of acceptance. Often times, I have heard celebrity friends and executives comment on associates who have not "followed" them or who haven't "accepted a friend request." I see flashes of my high school and its social structure when I hear privileged adults talk about these perceived slights from their "worldwide wenemies." I can't say that I wasn't guilty of falling into the trap myself on occasion, having been pushed headfirst into the online social sphere as a studio mandate when working as an entertainment marketer. At the beginning, when it was all new, I paid very close attention to those friends who didn't follow me back, maintaining their status as "special." They tended to keep their networks exclusive: famous followed famous. I was good enough to keep their deepest secrets but not dazzling enough to matter when it wasn't all about them.

One famous actor – with whom I'd been intimate on more than one occasion – never joined my social media following. Many times, I did him the favor of Tweeting to support his various projects, but, rather than returning the gestures, he channeled his social media energy to other celebrities and porn stars. It was an eye opener to see him posting photos of himself in the adult actor's clothing line to help shill the hustler's duds, especially when he showed no interest in being linked to me. I didn't have the cache one earns from fucking on camera, I suppose. When another celebrity friend and I grew apart, she made what she thought was a bold statement;

she removed me from her Facebook account and blocked all Twitter interactions. On a human level, I felt the sharp bite of being cut from someone's life, someone to whom I had been so important. Yet, in reality, her childish lash-out was a much needed reminder of how low and small her level of thinking was and how she no longer met *my* criteria for friendship.

I am definitely able to see the value of social media in terms of marketing; it creates awareness and support for so many valuable projects. In addition, it gives a voice to some interesting people with important things to say. But, there's always a dark side, and these outlets have also given a high-rise podium to bullies and mean-bees who look to buzz around open targets. I learned to take it all with a grain of salt and not allow my own self-worth to be dictated by someone's ill Internet intentions.

Hollywood is a particularly treacherous place to make friends. Bad manners are not merely accepted but encouraged and rewarded, and many apply this lower standard of operating to both professional and personal situations. Everyone has had those movie star fantasies: "I bet Jennifer Lopez and I would be great friends!" or "Madonna and I would have the best time together." No slight to Jenny from the Block and Madge – I am sure they're both lovely – but public people are traditionally not able to see beyond themselves. Their lives and careers center around their own images and personas, and they typically know exactly how *you* should be there for *them*. Very rarely are they capable of the concern and empathy necessary to make things even close to reciprocal. Their catered lives are not designed to accommodate traditional friendships, and they expect you to both understand and accept that. Many innocent bystanders go along for the ride – I was one of them – because they are seduced by the bright lights and the access that go hand-in-hand with being a celebrity buddy. It is the loneliest kind of dance, especially if you think you're the one who will make them care enough to look outside of their mirrors.

There are the rare celebrities who don't fit into the Hollywood mold. One statuesque brunette – lauded as much for being a sci-fi action hero as a comedic and dramatic actress – has continued to be upstanding and true in our casual friendship, as has a fiery, blond television lawyer who remains one of my dearest confidants.

Prior to my move to Los Angeles in 1999, I had been living in Manhattan, working in a satellite office for a major movie studio. I shared a two-bedroom apartment with my sister, across the hall from which lived a petite, blond southerner whose genuine charm radiated through every "Honey Bunny" and "Darling" she tossed my way. I walked my Jack Russell terrier, Remington, at the same time each evening, just as Ms. Bombshell would be arriving home from her cable news job.

"What's the good word, Sugar?" she'd say as we walked into our apartment building together, after which we'd chat about my prized puppy dog for a few moments during the elevator ride to the 9th floor. Remington, whose rare heart disease claimed his life after only 14 months, was the bridge to a years-long friendship with the brightest, most honorable and loyal person I know.

Truth be told, she was among the few friends whom I was nervous to tell about my sexuality; I feared that her southern sensibility would frown upon my "lifestyle."

"So, is there anyone special in your life?" she asked over

lunch while I was visiting Manhattan during a particularly cold winter. It had been seven years since I'd moved to Los Angeles.

"Yes," I said, "and I don't know..." I hesitated.

"Don't know what?" Patience was never one of her virtues. "Spit it out."

"I don't know if it will surprise you to know that the 'someone special' is a man," I said. Ms. Bombshell rolled her eyes in relief.

"What's his name?" she asked with a grin.

"Can you believe his name is Norm? That's the name of an 80 year-old who lives in Century Village," I joked.

For the next hour, we talked like girlfriends, giggling about how handsome Norm was and how I hoped it would turn into something long-term.

"How many dates have there been?" Ms. Bombshell asked.

"Five," I said. It was turning into a ping-pong match of questions and answers.

"What's his house like?" she replied.

"I don't know; I haven't seen it yet."

"He hasn't invited you over? After five dates? He's guilty of something," she said in her signature tried-convicted-hanged style.

"Guilty of what?" I asked.

"Just trust me," she exclaimed, "all of the evidence is at his house. If he doesn't invite you over the minute you get back to LA, I can promise you that the relationship isn't going anywhere."

Obviously, she was right. I learned to trust her instincts more than my own. To this day, I don't make a move without at least talking it through with her – but I also don't let her meet any potential beaus in person before I search their living spaces.

Ms. Bombshell has stuck by me through every landmark life event. She cheered me through my first job, blessed my move to Los Angeles, coached me through career ups and downs, accepted my coming out and advised me wisely on all things dating. There's nothing we don't know about each other, and neither of us would have it any other way. She is that rare "50/50."

BLACKBALLED

Does a talk show host shit in the woods? Ricki Lake has been known to drop a deuce while hiking the Southern California canyons, and she has the photo to prove it.

"I had to take a picture," she said as she held up her iPhone so her assistant and hair stylist could see clearly. "It was huge; it looked like it was from an animal."

"That's so funny," her assistant remarked, sitting in a far corner of the dressing room. "I love that you took a snapshot of it." With forced cheer and pep, Maggie was always quick to laugh along or agree with Ricki, even though she'd admit to being disgusted once her boss was out of earshot. For about $80,000.00 a year, her obsequious pleasantries came easily.

"That's a big crap," her hairdresser added. "How did you wipe?"

I tuned out before I heard Ricki's answer. I had always

known her to go overboard on providing personal details, but what little filter she once had seemed to vaporize with her rabid appetite for pot.

"You need to try some weed, Josh." She turned her attention from the photograph of her excrement – a very brown selfie – to me. "Christian says it would make you a lot calmer and less negative." Her new husband had said the same thing to my face on more than one occasion.

"I have never smoked pot or any illegal drug, and I am not planning to start," I replied.

"You don't have to smoke it. You can eat it." It was obvious that she had been taking her own advice. She enjoyed marijuana in baked goods, chocolate bars and hard candies; her waistline ratted her out. Ricki and Christian often laughed about a party during which he claimed to have slipped a mood altering substance into an acquaintance's drink, so I avoided having refreshments at their house. It wasn't out of character for either of them to attempt to get me high without my knowledge. She had become someone other than the best friend I'd made nearly six years earlier, or, rather, I became painfully aware that I shouldn't have invested in her from the outset.

I had been a fan of Ricki's since her star turn in the original *Hairspray* and was excited to have the opportunity to work together on the DVD release of her home birth project. The subject matter and heavy-handed messaging of the documentary feature – not to mention the graphic footage of a baby coming out of her vagina – was of no appeal to me, but her seemingly grounded and whimsical personality won me over.

Following our first marketing strategy meeting, I took Ricki to lunch at a Hollywood hot spot at which she ordered a pitcher of margaritas. It was mid-day, and I don't drink often – I have never been drunk, in fact – but she needled me along until I caved. One glass led to a second, and quickly we were sharing very personal stories. I learned later that Ricki's MO was to discuss intimate information, creating the illusion for people she encounters that they're special, trustworthy and in her "circle."

"You have to come over to my house. Plus, you're going to love my kids," she said when we finished our first meal together. I was beside myself; the TV host I idolized through-out high school had invited me to her inner sanctum. In only three hours, she recognized that I was someone worth knowing.

"Do you want to have dinner tomorrow and then hang out on my couch?" she asked. "You can pick me up at 7:00PM." She already had the evening planned for us, and I was too excited about her interest in me to make any alterna-tive suggestions.

"We need to make a stop on our way to the restaurant," she said as she climbed into my car that next evening. "Can you pull into the pharmacy? I need to pick up something important." She gave me a smirk that demanded I ask the obvious.

"What do you need to buy?" I enquired. Ricki sighed, as though it took me too long to get the question out.

"The 'morning after' pill," she said. "Last night was hot, but I already raised two kids. I don't need a third." She had met me only one day earlier and was already comfortable enough to trust me with such a private matter. I sat a little taller as we laughed over dinner and returned to her house to lie on the living room sofa and gab.

"My kids are with their father tonight, but you'll meet them next week," she said, already considering our next visit.

"How long have you been divorced?" I asked.

"Not long enough," she answered, "but the whole thing was fascinating. It turned into a court battle."

"That sounds awful," I said. "It's hard enough to dismantle a family, but then to have to fight in court must be horrendous."

"It was actually pretty entertaining," she said, as though it had been a stage show she enjoyed watching. "I still have the transcripts of the court hearings. Let me get them from my room; I'll do a dramatic reading for you." Her edgy sense of humor had me falling for her.

For the next two hours, Ricki dissected her entire divorce. Nothing was sacred: not her ex-husband's personal problems, her inappropriate rapport with the courtroom bailiff or the exact financial terms of her child support arrangement. I was charmed and flattered by her unfettered honesty, as though I had been carefully chosen to be her new best friend. I had become a "cool kid" at her discretion.

I couldn't remember the last time I had such an engaging evening; Ricki and I laughed until 3:00AM. I admired the joyful outlook she maintained in spite of the messy divorce, and I loved how forthcoming she was about the ups and downs of her life and career. Her world, as she saw it, was a fairytale, and her positivity was infectious. She was passionate about every topic that came up, like a force of nature strong and resolute enough to disband whatever clouds tried to block her sunshine.

Our friendship zoomed from zero to a hundred, and Ricki's frequent phone calls cemented an enmeshed relationship that had us in touch all day long. We spoke about everything from our bathroom regularity to our sleep patterns; she was reliable and caring, checking in on me routinely. Her consistency made me feel strong, as though I could get through anything with her energy by my side. She was the first friend I'd made since coming out of the closet; everyone else in my life knew me before I took steps towards my authentic self. She loved the real me, and I loved her for that. Our emotional connection made the New York publicity tour for her DVD release more of a vacation than a grueling, four-day media blitz.

"Let's have fun in Manhattan," she said. "Maybe we can see a couple of Broadway shows?" She appreciated live theater and show tunes as much as I did, just a couple of the many interests we shared.

"Since it's a business trip, the studio will pay for whatever the talent wants," I hinted.

"Well, 'the talent' wants to see *Rent* one last time before it closes," she answered.

"And so it shall be," I said. "Let's have a nice dinner and then watch some 40 year-olds pretend to be 20-something bohemians."

"I have to make some time to see this guy I like, though," she warned. "So, we have to build that into the schedule."

"Who is he?" She hadn't mentioned him previously.

"Some Brazilian man whom a friend introduced me to," she said.

"How do you know you like him yet?" I asked.

"I don't, but he's hot." That was her criteria for "like," and "building him into the schedule" meant leaving *Rent* at intermission for a booty call. I didn't hear from her until my phone rang the next morning.

"Rise and shine," she said at 7:00AM.

"You're up early." My voice was still weighed down with sleep.

"I never slept," she said, excited to tell me about her evening. "We fucked all night. He put it everywhere; even up my ass."

"Wow; you're a triple-entry girl," I laughed. "Too bad you don't have a glass eye; you could remove it and have a fourth point of insertion."

"Very funny," Ricki said. "But guess what?"

"I am afraid to ask," I said.

"We didn't use rubbers. He's really into me." He had, in fact, been into her. Unprotectedly.

I wrote her irresponsible behavior off to the edgy, exciting things that celebrities do – similar to Ms. TV Personality, whose inebriated indiscretions seemed glamorous to me in Las Vegas. These women appeared to be invincible; if I were in a plane crash with either one of them, I'd likely survive just because of my association with her greatness.

Ricki continued to be an extremely generous and giving friend. The huckleberry lemonade was deliciously sweet at the Amangani Resort in Wyoming; our "family vacation" with the kids was replete with spa packages and poolside treats. Even more fun? Our trip – on a private jet – to the Sundance Film Festival in Utah. The five-star experience, not to mention screening access and meals with A-list celebrities, was easy to get used to. I started to believe that it was *my* life; Ricki and I were so securely attached that it was hard to tell the difference.

My other friends in Los Angeles had more pedestrian existences, and my new life with Ricki found me floating inside a glittery snow globe that was as excitingly exclusive as it was isolating. We were almost like twins who spent all of their time together and had developed their own language. We were difficult for outsiders to understand, but they envied our bond when they peered into our bubble.

"You spend an awful lot of time with Ricki," my mother said during a phone call one afternoon. "I am not sure how healthy it is."

"What's unhealthy about it?" I asked. "I would think you'd be happy that I have someone in LA who's looking out for me."

"It's not that I'm unhappy about it," my mom continued. "It just seems like you have shifted your entire life to fit into hers, almost like you're married."

"She has her own family," I said. "So, she has a lot going on outside of me."

"Just be careful," my mom replied. "I worry about this friendship a little bit."

Oddly, I continued not to worry when Ricki brought up the subject of her living will.

"If you're OK with it," she said, "I want to stipulate that you become the guardian of my kids should something happen to both me and their father."

"That's a big responsibility," I said, "but I love your boys and would gladly step in if I needed to."

"That's how I want it. No one in my stupid family should have them, and my girlfriend Naomi raised an awful little cunt – so I don't need her involved with my kids." Already a few years into our friendship, I was used to the two-faced talk about her family and others close to her; Ricki was an over-grown "mean girl." I'd seen her tire of solid relationships for no apparent reason, making fun of and cutting those people from her life as easily as clipping a hangnail. Her decision to make me part of her will in such an important way misguided me into thinking that I was immune to the detached disregard with which she treated the many sycophants around her. I had convinced myself that I was different.

■ ■ ■

Against the push of 55 units of fresh Botox, my eyebrows raised at the arrival of Aaron, a charming European who was skilled at creating an eye-catching, online dating profile. He was a handsome, mid-thirties British "artist" whose confidence and self-esteem were unparalleled. A self-proclaimed multi-hyphenate – filmmaker, writer, actor, singer and songwriter – Ricki couldn't help but reach out to him on Match. com. In a way, she was experiencing her own "coming out;" after she divorced the father of her children, she moved right into a torrid romance with a personal trainer. When they finally ended their relationship a few years later, she wanted to jump on top of anything that had a hard penis (yet another interest we shared). The Worldwide Web provided a catalog of men, and Ricki was an obsessive shopper.

Ricki and Aaron began a "just-add-water" romance that saw him moving into her home only one week after meeting. A starving creative-type, he didn't have so much as a bed in his downtown, one-room apartment. Ricki took him shopping and began buying his continued interest. In return, he washed her brain.

"Are you sure you want to have someone move into your house so fast?" I asked.

"Are you jealous?" she replied.

"No, but I think you have a responsibility to the two young boys who already live there," I said, hoping she'd recognize that she needed to consider the impact that this life change would have on her impressionable, young sons, Milo and Owen. "You don't know that you can trust this guy," I continued, "and what are the kids supposed to think when they see a man they don't even know move in?"

"You're going to have to get used to the fact that there's another guy in my life," she said, dismissing my concerns about how the familial upheaval might affect her children.

One of the most appealing things about Ricki was that the worldview from her window was something Walt Disney would have dreamed up. Rainbows hovered over the clear, blue sky and small animals – crafty chipmunks and birds that were handy with thread – sewed her into her tunics and muumuus each morning. She lived in an uplifting, animated movie and so did everyone she welcomed into her life. No one faced difficult realities or confronted problems in her film; they simply rode on her unicorn – her kids included.

"Milo and Owen will be fine," she continued. "They're going to love Aaron as much as I do."

"How much *do* you love him after eight days?" I asked.

"Can't you be happy for me? You worry too much, and you're bringing me down," she said. Uh oh. I was about to be banished from her magic kingdom.

Aaron was a conspiracy theorist, and, just after moving into Ricki's house, began to convince her that the Swine Flu vaccine (H1N1) was the government's attempt to weed out the population. He believed that the American people would be forced to have the injection and were more likely to die from the intervention than the illness itself. Accordingly, she

considered moving to Venezuela to escape the US government – as anyone would – and starred in an anti-vaccine
music video that Aaron wrote, produced and directed. In the
meantime, Ricki was withdrawing from her close circle, and
Aaron insisted that she push me, in particular, out of her life.
Just like in any horror film: the funny best friend usually bites
it first.

"Is there a reason I haven't heard from you?" I questioned
when I finally got her on the phone. It had been two weeks
since the debut of the music video.

"I just need time to nest with Aaron and my boys," she
said. "We have to bond, and that process doesn't include outsiders."

"Outsiders? I'm closer to you than anyone," I answered. "I
get the kids in your will. There's something you're not telling
me." Ricki was not a consistently great actress – just take a
look at *Babycakes* and *Mrs. Winterbourne* – so it was easy to
tell when she was lying.

"OK, you want the truth? Aaron doesn't feel like you're
good for our relationship," she said. "We can speak from time
to time, but that's about it."

As though she'd flipped a switch, I was shut out of her life.
She swept me into her tornado and tossed me to the ground
just as quickly for a man she'd met online less than two weeks
before. I felt like I had been hit with such blunt force that
I couldn't speak. I stopped communicating with my family
and lived in pajamas for what felt like endless cycles of time.
I had made her the center of my life – at the expense of many
pre-existing friendships – against warnings from my parents
and my sister. Thankfully, when I reconnected with them a
few days later, the words "we told you so" didn't surface. I was

battered, and they were kind enough to keep from kicking me while I was down.

Behind the scenes, Ricki's assistant and the housekeeper, Cecilia, would secretly call me to report Aaron's sinister behavior in hopes that, as a team, we would be able to save her from what was sure to be a disaster. Each time the phone rang with a "Ricki and Aaron Report," I felt like a fresh wound in my stomach had been stabbed with a jagged hunting knife. My head pounded with migraine-like thumps that rang through my ears, resulting in crippling nausea. In a fetal position on my bed, I'd hold the phone to my ear, hoping that my broken breaths and tears wouldn't reveal how much emotional pain Ricki had caused. I felt stupid for not seeing it coming.

Cecilia saw Aaron eavesdropping on some of Ricki's phone calls, and Maggie observed both stormy fights and Aaron's misplaced sense of entitlement. In addition, her other good friends began to call me with their concern about her distant behavior. What they didn't realize was that, for the first time in our friendship, Ricki wouldn't listen to me. In fact, she was so sure that I was jealous of her romantic relationship that I couldn't possibly be operating in her best interests. She was blinded to the truths of this dark relationship, losing herself to the idea of a "boyfriend." Believing that Aaron could be "the one" – and wanting nothing more than Mr. Right for her 41st birthday – she completely lost her senses for the affection of someone she'd just met.

"She needs you now more than ever," one of Ricki's friends in New York said during a late night, SOS phone call. "Something's wrong with this guy, and someone has to be there for her kids."

"She doesn't talk to me anymore," I replied. "I'm not sure what to do." I was worried about the damage – psychological or otherwise – that Aaron might do to the people I loved, but I was also stewing in the anger and hurt of being disregarded by someone whom I'd given such a special place in my life. She had broken up with me, and my head hurt with the idea that maybe I wasn't good enough to have her. Was there something I could have done differently to maintain her affection? Was being fiercely loyal to her and her family not enough? What could I do for her that would make everything OK? She was part of my whole, and, likewise, I thought I needed her. I was willing to give up any part of myself to have her back and to prevent the embarrassment of admitting that I fell for an illusion.

"She's not in her right mind; I can tell," the friend said. "If you really care about Ricki and those boys, you have to hang in there."

"I am taking a short trip to New Orleans," I answered, "when I am back, I will try to reinsert myself." A good friend of mine had a starring role in a movie that was shooting in Louisiana, and I took the opportunity to escape with her for a week. I hadn't had a restful sleep in days, and I thought that getting away might help me to decompress. As soon as my flight landed, however, I received an urgent message from Ricki.

"It's over," she cried into the phone. "Aaron is gone." Weeks before, I had been excommunicated from the Church of Ricki, but, in a sudden twist, I was embraced again. No mention was made of the gap in time.

"He left you?" I asked.

"No, I found out the truth," she sobbed. Aaron had been

dating another woman all along, biding his time to see who would marry him for a Green Card first. He'd start fights with Ricki so he could run out and sleep with his other potential bride.

"I should have known," she continued, "because he would fuck me doggie style all the time. He would never look at my face." Asking her to dump her best friend wasn't a red flag, but banging her only from behind was a dead giveaway? "You know what, though? I'd probably do it all again."

"I'm going to say goodnight; it's late here, and I need to get to sleep. Let's talk when I am back in LA," I said. I wasn't ready for a conversation about how she had treated me, and attempting to soothe her didn't feel comfortable considering the circumstances. It was particularly difficult to have empathy for someone who couldn't see the cautionary lesson in her own story.

"When you're back in LA? Isn't that in a week from now?" she asked.

"Yep, seven days," I answered.

"OK, you sleep well. I will call you tomorrow morning." It was as if nothing had happened.

I moved around my hotel room restlessly that night, not catching more than 30 minutes of sleep in any one stretch. An unshakable sadness enveloped me like a heavy, suffocating blanket. I realized that Ricki looked for affection and approval from a man she hardly knew to feel valuable and loved as a human being. Even more upsetting was that my own self-worth was similarly tethered to my relationship with her. Unlike with Ms. Drama, Ms. TV Personality and Ms. Pop, I believed that I had an unconditional love affair with Ricki that was mutually nurturing and secure. Instead, she was "fool's gold," a sparkling piece of rock that was worth nothing more than mineral pyrite. She gave me a false sense of love and support that I believed made me important to the friends who saw flashes of my life in the fast lane.

When I returned to California, Ricki felt that peace had been restored and that our relationship would resume, business as usual. She invited me to her house for dinner, and I imagined that she would take the opportunity to apologize and to talk through the six weeks of drama that had just played out in three acts.

"I'm so glad you're back," she said. "I feel like I haven't seen you in forever." Was she kidding?

"You *haven't* seen me in awhile, no," I answered. "You pushed me out, remember?" I started to become angry at her attempt to gloss over what had happened.

"I don't really want to talk about it," she said. "I made it through a hard time, and I just can't relive it." She wasn't at all concerned that my feelings might have been hurt during her toxic romance and my subsequent exile. And, if she was, she swept the worry under her expensive Oriental rug.

"Then I will leave it at this," I said. "If you ever do something like that to me again, don't expect me to be there on the other side. You can lose my number." I remembered how upset I'd been during that first night in New Orleans, and a previously untapped strength rose to my head. In my hurt, I'd passed a point of no return. I saw the fault lines in our foundation, and I transitioned into self-protection mode.

"Oh, come on, you know we'll always be friends," she said, ignoring my tone. "With you for me and me for you, we'll muddle through, whatever we do . . . together!" She smiled and flashed her best jazz hands as she sang "Together (Wherever

We Go)." I forced the corners of my mouth to turn upward. "There's my Josh," she said. "I missed you so much."

Over the next couple of weeks, Ricki and I fell back into a pattern. We weren't in touch quite as often as we had been before Aaron entered the picture; I was wary of a repeat performance. But, I didn't want to entirely lose the parts of Ricki – or her kids – that I had fallen in love with when we first met. She appeared to bounce back from the Aaron debacle easily; in fact, her bedroom was like a theme park turnstile, with sexual suitors visiting by the double digits. She was enjoying herself, and, for the first time in years, had a renewed interest in her career. She signed a deal with a major television syndicator and started to develop a brand new talk show.

"You have to be involved with my show," she said. "I know you want to try your hand at producing, and this is your chance." I had already been handling her PR through the firm I'd launched after leaving the corporate world, and this would entangle us even more professionally.

"Do you think our friendship can survive working together so much?" I asked.

"It'll be fine," she said, giving it no further consideration.

What we couldn't survive, however, was Christian, a tall, highlighted blonde who was introduced to Ricki by her friend Naomi. He was a stoner with little to say, and Ricki initially showed no romantic interest in the unkempt beach dweller. Odd, considering that her only standard until that point seemed to be simply a man with a penis that worked.

Within days, Ricki was "in love" with yet another downtrodden "artist" who liked the couture clothes she was buying for him and all of the pain management appointments she financed. His upkeep turned out to be very costly: yoga, hair coloring and cuts, eyelash tinting, Invisiline braces, among other spoils.

What bothered me most, though, was that he had a five year-old boy from a previous girlfriend whom he rarely saw or paid for. He claimed that the child's mother tricked him into getting her pregnant – was she Erica Kane in Pine Valley? – which was how Ricki explained away his limited interest in his own son.

"You don't see that to be an alarming character issue?" I asked when Ricki inquired about my thoughts on Christian.

"No, I don't," she said. "Besides, I don't want the kid around anyway."

"That's not the point," I continued. "He has a son who is not a priority to him. That's concerning to me."

"Here we go again," she said in a raised voice. "You don't want me in a relationship with anyone other than you."

"If that's what you believe, so be it," I snapped back. "Let's just keep things professional going forward." Interestingly, I didn't feel a punch to my gut or the sick turns of my stomach that plagued me when Aaron came between us. I was prepared for the fact that history would eventually repeat itself, and *I* was drawing the line this time around. Ricki didn't have as much power.

Never one to hold confidences, she shared our argument with Christian, who began a campaign against me as soon as he and Ricki were married. There was no point in ruminating or attempting to forge some sort of relationship with him. I believe that, like Aaron, Christian was threatened by my strong tie to Ricki and made it his business to wedge an irreparable divide between us. She began to pull away, which

I had expected. What I didn't anticipate was the degree to which she had turned on me.

I was the host of *After Ricki*, a one-hour, online program that streamed live after each day's episode of *The New Ricki Lake Show* aired on television. The project was conceived by Travis, a show staffer, with the idea that viewers could interact and further discuss the topics that had been covered on that day's episode.

"You should host the after show," Travis said to me a month before Ricki's program went into production. "You're Ricki's best friend, so viewers will feel like it's a close link to her." Travis and I had become extremely close during pre-production. It was rare that I responded to men, but when he opened up to me about having been molested repeatedly by a very close family member along with his previous drug and alcohol problems, I couldn't help but develop a soft spot for him. And, admittedly, I was attracted to his tall, hunky frame.

"That sounds like fun," I said, "but is the studio willing to pay for my time?"

"Yes, there's a budget for it," he answered. "The whole idea could be groundbreaking if we do it right."

Relative to Ricki's television ratings, the online show pulled in a decent viewership in spite of the fact that Travis and I began to butt heads. It turns out, he was a modern-day Eve Harrington who had his own designs on the online hosting job. One month after the project took off, I was called into a meeting with the head of development.

"I don't know how to tell you this," he said, "but we are going to have to let you go from the after show."

"Why?" was the only word I could get out of my mouth. I had never been fired before.

"We think you're a little too edgy," he said. "The online program is going to head in a different direction."

"This isn't something we can fix?" I asked. "I haven't received any negative feedback until now, so I assumed that I was performing as you'd hoped."

"Sorry it didn't work out," he finished. "I have to run into another meeting."

I went into my office and closed the door. As I lied on the couch, I pushed my face into a pillow to stifle the tears that had turned my face into a sweaty, red mess. The shock turned into anger; Ricki hated the development executives, and her instinct was clearly right. I dialed her cell phone.

"What's wrong, baby?" she said as she heard me cry into the phone.

"They fired me from the after show," I said. "Apparently, I'm too edgy."

"I am really pissed," she said. "They didn't even discuss it with me, and my name is in the title of this show. I hate those motherfuckers." I was calmed by her outward dislike for the person who had just fired me and by the fact that it was a Friday. I had the weekend to lick my wounds before showing up the following week to continue producing the show.

By Tuesday, I was still feeling down, and I walked into Ricki's office hoping for sympathy and comfort. I stretched across her oversized couch in a cozy blanket and dozed off until lunchtime.

"You're bumming me out," Ricki said as soon as my eyes opened. "Your depression over this whole after show thing is killing the mood here. I am unhappy coming to work as it is;

I don't need you moping through the halls." I couldn't believe what I was hearing. On Friday, she seemed outraged over my dismissal.

"Do you hear yourself?" I asked. "You don't sound like a friend." She stood up and walked to the hair and make-up area of her dressing room.

"Come to think of it, you don't have to come to the set every day," Ricki said.

"Actually, I do; the production company is paying me to be here and help produce this show," I replied. I felt a sting in my chest; it was awful to hear that someone I cared so much about didn't want me around.

"Well, I am the star of the show, and I am telling you that you can stay home some days," she said. I almost couldn't take her seriously when she was only half made-up and sitting in a wig cap. She was very self-conscious about her thinning hair and had taken to wearing obvious wigs. She looked more Fairfax than Farrah, which I don't think was the look she was going for.

"A few weeks ago, you bought me an $800 pair of boots to thank me for being on set all the time," I said. "Perhaps you forgot."

"Oh, I remember. You can wear those to walk to your car," she hissed. Her disdain tore through me, and it took all of my energy to hold back the tears that were pooling in my lower eyelids. The embarrassment of being treated so disposably – especially in front of Maggie and Ricki's beauty team – paralyzed me for a few seconds. Nobody made eye contact with me; it was clear that they knew it was coming.

"Let me help you get your things to your car," Maggie said, walking me to the front lounge and offering to carry some of the odds and ends I had stored in Ricki's dressing room.

"I'll just come back this afternoon," I said, wanting to get out of the room as fast as possible.

"We're actually leaving early and locking up," Maggie said. "Ricki is taking us all to a cooking class. She didn't want me to mention it to you, but, considering what just happened, I guess it doesn't matter." I am sure it was one of many things that Ricki didn't include me in after her marriage to Christian, but it was the first that Maggie was stupid enough to talk about openly.

As I gathered my couple of bags and walked to the parking structure, I bumped into a junior development executive.

"Are you moving out?" she asked jokingly.

"Sort of," I said, forcing a smile. I didn't want to get into a conversation with her.

"That sucks about the after show, by the way," she continued, "but you know that the star always gets her way."

"Excuse me?" I asked her to repeat her comment.

"Did I speak out of turn? I should probably shut up now."

"Can you please repeat what you said?" I asked sharply.

"The star always gets her way," she said. "Ricki wanted you fired from the after show; she asked our team to break the news to you. I personally thought you were great."

"So, the studio had no problem with how I was hosting *After Ricki*?" I questioned.

"Not at all," she replied. "But I think Ricki and Travis decided that he should take over." It was the closest I had ever come to passing out. "Are you OK?" she asked.

I ran to my car and threw my bags into the trunk. As I settled into the driver's seat, I smashed my fists against the steering wheel nearly breaking the controls that were positioned at its center. I felt light headed, as though my rage was burning through every brain cell in my head. I was angry at Travis and furious with Ricki, but I was hardest on myself. She had shown me time and time again how capable she was of bringing me to my knees, and I kept going back for more. I wanted to believe that the fun and amazingly dynamic woman I fell in love with six years earlier cared enough to treat me better than she did everyone else. I screamed as loudly as I could in the privacy of my SUV, peeling out of the studio lot at a dangerous speed.

"What happened?" my mother said, after hearing me sob into the phone. She was panicked by the tone and hoarse rasp of my voice.

"Ricki and Travis," I said. "They had me fired from the after show." I told her the whole story.

"Honey, I think this happened for a reason." She was trying to calm me down.

"Not everything happens for a reason, Mom," I said.

"It was time that Ricki be out of your life," she continued, "and you weren't doing anything to remove her. You were basically throwing yourself at her feet."

"Yeah, well, I guess she won. She got rid of me first, even though I was nothing but a loving friend to her," I cried.

"You can't expect more from someone than she is actually capable of giving," my mom said. "She revealed her limitations a thousand times over. You just wanted to believe in her."

I didn't let on to Ricki and Travis that I was told they were behind my firing. In fact, I had a pleasant attitude the morning I showed up on the set for the final taping of the show. It had been canceled due to poor ratings, and I wanted to be there to wish the production team well as they moved on to new projects.

I held my head up high as I walked into Ricki's dressing room, knowing that I was standing on elevated ground by saying a formal goodbye to everyone. I realized that it was likely the last time I would ever see them.

"See you soon," Ricki said dismissively, as she turned her entire body away from me and continued to chat with Travis. They were talking about her ex-husband.

"I had no idea that your divorce was such a nightmare," I heard Travis say.

"It was actually pretty entertaining," Ricki replied, "I still have the transcripts of the court hearings. I'll do a dramatic reading for you if you want to come over for dinner next week."

FULL RELEASE

I didn't know whether I should shuffle off to Buffalo or to Albuquerque. Having a severely cross-eyed tap dance teacher made it difficult to learn the choreography, even after three months of lessons.

"You have to watch my feet, not my face," Isabel, the owner of TapTronix Dance Studio, instructed. Her challenged extraocular muscles and untamed unibrow upstaged her fancy footwork. "You're not going to learn to tap from the mirror, Josh," she reiterated. "Stop looking in front of you, and look down." It was tough to focus on the ground with Frida Kahlo flashing jazz hands in my face like a Broadway hoofer on Speed.

"I'm not planning to be part of the year-end recital," I said, trying to manage Isabel's expectations. "I'm here purely for fun." As appealing as it seemed to be dancing to "Top

Hat, White Tie and Tails" alongside twenty bored "real house-wives" of the San Fernando Valley, everything I needed from the private classes was in my reflection.

"I understand," Isabel said, "but you're not even keeping time with the music." I began to tune her – and Ella Fitzgerald – out and stared past her frizzy up-do into the mirror on the wall.

"That's OK," I answered, looking straight ahead. "I'm enjoying myself."

"It's your money," she said, "but I'm not sure how many steps you'll have to show for the cash."

"I already got what I wanted," I replied, "everything else is icing on the cake."

"There's a freedom that comes with being able to dance," she continued. "I just wanted to help you experience that." A tear rolled down my right cheek. "Are you alright? Did I upset you?" She became concerned.

"I'm perfect," I said, my gaze still fixed on the 40 year-old man in sweats and split-soled tap shoes whose eyes were locked just as intensely on me. Isabel and the music faded into the background as the truth of my story took center stage: I had been alive for four decades but was just starting to live. In the dance studio, I wasn't judged by anyone or anything other than my "flaps" and "heel drops."

It was obvious, looking at myself in the mirror, that losing 15 pounds wouldn't be so bad for my health. I wasn't terribly concerned, though, about how the weight affected my appearance. The idea of finding a local gym and perhaps a part-time trainer – and maybe even buying pants with a larger waist size – crossed my mind. My midsection jiggled a little bit with particularly active dance steps, but keeping my drawstring pants tightly around my hips had me covered. A surgical remedy was no longer my go-to solution; I wasn't willing to take the risk or suffer any more pain electively.

A professional reinvention was also on the horizon; one that didn't include the dangerously alluring glamour of Hollywood. The guy looking back at me from the glass was OK with that. Maybe it was time to pursue old passions; to become a writer or go back to school for an MBA, two possibilities that now got me more excited than a red carpet premiere. I realized by watching myself – vulnerable and trying something new with Isabel – that my identity wasn't wrapped up in a job or high-level title. And, it certainly wasn't defined by the celebrity affiliations that came as a "gift with purchase."

"Let's take a quick break after this next song," Isabel said, changing the music on her iPod, "Straight Up" from Paula Abdul filtered through the room. "Don't you love Paula? Her songs just don't get old."

"I *do* love Paula," I answered, but I didn't feel the need to tell Isabel that my personal relationship with the pop star went beyond a topical enjoyment of her 80s hits. In the past, I wouldn't have missed such an easy opportunity to generate positive attention for myself by spending an hour dropping names. Nailing my first tap routine seemed like a better use of time, even when I heard my mother's voice rush into my head.

"I don't think that's a great idea; other boys wouldn't understand." In 1982, my interest in tap lessons was met with a disapproval that, while commensurate with the social attitudes of the time, jailed me in a lonely self-hatred that forced me to steal my sense of identity from the outside.

The week after my first dance class, during their biannual

visit to Los Angeles, my parents agreed to run some errands with me after lunch in West Hollywood.

"What's the 'Pleasure Chest?'" my mom asked, as I pulled in the parking lot of the adult superstore.

"It's a sex shop," I answered casually. "I need to buy some funny greeting cards for a few friends' birthdays that are coming up."

"They sell cards?" My father was surprised by the scope of merchandise.

I quickly looked over the racks and put my selections into a hand basket. "I'm going to look at some videos upstairs; are you and Mom OK to browse here for a little while?"

"Sure; take your time," my father said. "Mom and I will meet you in the porn section if we finish before you." The two short, cotton-topped 70 year-olds were fish out of water in a sea of pierced and tattooed hipsters.

It was hard to choose between *Dawson's Crack* and *Scrotal Recall*; both had hot cover models, and the scene shots on their back covers promised kinky, hardcore fun. I took them both from the shelf just as my parents turned the corner.

"What are you buying?" my father asked, grabbing the two boxes out of my hands and examining them front to back. 33 years after my plea for tap dancing classes was over-ruled, my folks were reviewing my choices in pornography – and I wasn't the least bit embarrassed. "Wait, these are $60 a piece?"

"Yes, porn is expensive. They don't sell as many copies as the studios do of mainstream films, so they charge more per DVD." Thankfully, my years in the movie business helped me explain the exorbitant price point.

"Do you really need both? It's the same penis going into

the same hole," my father reasoned, holding up both titles in front of me. It was as if I were a kid at a restaurant all over again, being told that I could choose between ice cream and a cookie; I didn't *need* two desserts.

"The appendages and holes are attached to different people," I said, "so they're not the same video."

"I think one is fine," he continued. "Mom and I are treating, so pick the movie you want more."

"*Dawson's Crack*, I guess," I said, disappointed that the men of *Scrotal Recall* would have to wait until I could sneak back to the store with my own credit card.

"You could buy a week's worth of groceries with that money," my dad harped. During the hour-long car ride back to my house, he talked non-stop about the price of porn these days.

"Howard, I think you've made your point," my mom interjected from the back seat, "but if the videos make Josh happy, let it go."

"It just doesn't make any sense." My dad's voice was getting louder. "Can't you re-watch older videos in your collection? Penises, butts and mouths haven't changed over the years."

"I like *new* penises, *new* butts and *new* mouths," I laughed. "The porn industry doesn't make billions of dollars a year because other men share your point of view."

"How many times do you watch one of these DVDs?" my dad asked.

"I probably see each scene twice, so about 10 times total," I replied.

"If you amortize that out, it's $6 per orgasm," he said. "It's ridiculous, if you ask me."

"I *didn't* ask you," I answered in an attempt to end the circular conversation.

By the time we pulled into my garage, we agreed to disagree; but, I was warmed by the debate more than irritated. There was no disgrace attached to our discussion about my sexuality or my interest in adult movies. The two most important people in my life – from whom I had hidden the real *me* for so many years – were not ashamed to have *me* as their son. In fact, they seemed downright proud.

"Honey, here's $60 in cash." My mother slipped three $20 bills into my hand as soon as we walked into the house and my father disappeared into the bathroom with a newspaper. "Go ahead and buy *Scrotal Recall* the next time you're at the Pleasure Chest." She remembered the title. "No need to tell Dad."

As soon as my parents returned home to Florida, I returned to the sex shop.

"Guess what? There's a sale this week on all of the pornos." I called my mom on the way home to share the good news.

"Was there a discount on the one you wanted?" she asked.

"Yes; so I got the DVD *and* a sex toy for the $60.00 you gave me." With 40% off the movie, the add-on dildo came in on budget.

"That's fantastic." She seemed genuinely thrilled that her money stretched beyond one item. "Enjoy!" (I absolutely planned on enjoying my gifts; they were ideal stand-ins for the elusive boyfriend who still hadn't crossed my path.)

"Thanks, Mom," I said, as I parked my new, no-frills sedan in front of the TapTronix Dance Studio. "I am about to walk into my class. Can I call you tomorrow?"

"It's funny that you're learning to tap at this point in your life," she replied. "You begged me to take you when you were little."

"You never did, so I suppose I'm making up for lost time," I said with a hint of indignation. I no longer needed anyone to *take* me; I could chart my own course.

"We just thought...well...you know," she hesitated.

"No, I don't know." I waited quietly for her to finish. I did, in fact, *know*, but I wanted to hear the words.

"Dad and I were young, and dance seemed like a feminine interest that might impact you a certain way."

"You mean you thought it would make me gay?" I asked directly.

"I suppose so," she answered.

"I guess I showed *you*, didn't I?" I said. After an awkward pause, we began to laugh hysterically.

"We didn't know better, honey," my mom continued, "and we didn't want anyone making fun of you. We wanted you to be happy."

"I am happy. Now."

Smiling confidently, I walked into the building; it was liberating considering that my life would seem disorderly to the uptight, anxiety-ridden depressive I'd been for so long. My career, my friendships and my romantic life were all in transition, but I was finally navigating them on my own. Approval from others still felt good, but it wasn't the necessary fix it had been since I was seven years-old.

■ ■ ■

Isabel hadn't come back from our break yet; I was standing in the middle of the room alone, facing the large mirror. As I re-laced my tap shoes, "What a Feeling" from *Flashdance* streamed through the loud speakers. My first thought was to adjust my t-shirt so that my love handles weren't noticeable, but, instead, I turned sideways and studied myself.

My chest was a little broader than it had been in a while, complementing the small belly that could have benefitted from daily sit-ups. The faint lines on my forehead – matched by light crow's feet around my eyes – showed some wear and worry. I wasn't flawless. But, I could live with that.

I was *me*.

ACKNOWLEDGEMENTS

I am eternally indebted to Benée Knauer, my extraordinary editor, whose talent, savvy and sound judgment are unparalleled. What began as a professional relationship transitioned into a beautiful friendship that I will cherish forever.

Thank you to Nick Khan and Cait Hoyt at CAA for believing in *Porn Again: A Memoir* from its inception and working diligently on its behalf.

The front and back cover photographs are a testament to Kate sZatmari's amazing artistry, dedication and creative vision. Nobody makes me look better.

Marilyn Cheek, Nancy Grace, Terry Greenberg and Renée Iacono, four of my dearest, longtime friends from whom I continue to draw strength, have been my cheerleading team throughout the writing of this book. I couldn't have completed it without their love and encouragement.

On more than one occasion, Gigi Levangie Grazer kept me from jumping off the ledge. A force of nature whose intelligence and sense of humor always lift my spirits, she is a beloved confidant.

A handful of loyal family and friends lent their eyes, ears and counsel to this memoir. I am grateful to Laura Abele, Jesse Bering, Simone Bienne, Lisa Dampier, Christine Fahey, Susan Fleishman, Jessica Horwitch, Jennifer Lake, Betsy Lerner, David Mack, Wil Mata, Barbara Pflughaupt, Jennifer Abrams Rosenberg, Tammy Rubel, Michelle Sobrino-Stearns, Trish Suhr, Michael Ullman and Leila Warren.

My junior high school English teacher, Sylvia Bastaja, had a troubled life that ended prematurely. She is often in my thoughts and would be beaming about this project. I hope I did her memory justice.

Nancy Sabarra and Jason Karlinsky, my sister and brother-in-law, have been in my corner unconditionally and are responsible for Bethany and Ella, two little "chicken nuggets" who provided laughter, smiles and "princess kisses" throughout the writing process. In addition to long lives filled with health and happiness, my wish for my nieces is that they always feel "free to be" themselves, on their own terms.

The incomparable Howard and Deborah Sabarra are the most wonderful parents a son could ask for. Honorable, loving, accepting and without judgment, they sent me into the world with an invaluable sense of security. Their insights and support made my dream of writing a book come true. They combed through every word studiously, finding typos and suggesting changes to the more explicit moments – none of which I made. I love them always.

ABOUT THE AUTHOR

Josh Sabarra is a veteran marketing executive and television producer who has held positions at The Walt Disney Company, Warner Bros. Studios, Miramax Films, New Line Cinema and Lifetime Networks. He resides in Los Angeles, California, where he is the president and CEO of his own public relations firm, Breaking News PR®. This is his first book.

CPSIA information can be obtained at www.ICGtesting.com
Printed in the USA
BVOW08s0854161015

422825BV00004B/77/P